# CRITICAL APPROACHES TO
# ANGLO-IRISH LITERATURE

# THE
# IRISH LITERATURE STUDIES SERIES
## ISSN 0140–895X

1. *Place, Personality & the Irish Writer.* Andrew Carpenter (editor)
2. *Yeats and Magic.* Mary Catherine Flannery
3. *A Study of the Novels of George Moore.* Richard Allen Cave
4. *J. M. Synge & the Western Mind.* Weldon Thornton
5. *Irish Poetry from Moore to Yeats.* Robert Welch
6. *Yeats, Sligo and Ireland.* A. Norman Jeffares (editor)
7. *Sean O'Casey, Centenary Essays.* David Krause & Robert G. Lowery (editors)
8. *Denis Johnston: A Retrospective.* Joseph Ronsley (editor)
9. *Literature & the Changing Ireland.* Peter Connolly (editor)
10. *James Joyce, An International Perspective.* Suheil Badi Bushrui & Bernard Benstock (editors)
11. *Synge, the Medieval and the Grotesque.* Toni O'Brien Johnson
12. *Carleton's Traits & Stories & the 19th Century Anglo-Irish Tradition.* Barbara Hayley
13. *Lady Gregory, Fifty Years After.* Ann Saddlemyer & Colin Smythe (editors)
14. *Woman in Irish Legend, Life and Literature.* S. F. Gallagher (editor)
15. *'Since O'Casey', & Other Essays on Irish Drama.* Robert Hogan
16. *George Moore in Perspective.* Janet Egleson Dunleavy (editor)
17. *W. B. Yeats, Dramatist of Vision.* A. S. Knowland
18. *The Irish Writer and the City.* Maurice Harmon (editor)
19. *O'Casey the Dramatist.* Heinz Kosok
20. *The Double Perspective of Yeats's Aesthetic.* Okifumi Komesu
21. *The Pioneers of Anglo-Irish Fiction 1800–1850.* Barry Sloan
22. *Irish Writers and Society at Large.* Masaru Sekine (editor)
23. *Irish Writers and the Theatre.* Masaru Sekine (editor)
24. *A History of Verse Translation from the Irish, 1789–1897.* Robert Welch
25. *Kate O'Brien: A Literary Portrait.* Lorna Reynolds
26. *Portraying the Self: Sean O'Casey & the Art of Autobiography.* Michael Kenneally
27. *W. B. Yeats and the Tribes of Danu.* Peter Alderson Smith
28. *Theatre of Shadows: from All that Fall to Footfalls. Samuel Beckett's Drama 1956–76.* Rosemary Pountney
29. *Critical Approaches to Anglo-Irish Literature.* Michael Allen & Angela Wilcox (editors)
30. *'Make Sense Who May': Essays on Samuel Beckett's Later Works.* Robin J. Davis & Lance St. J. Butler (editors)
31. *Cultural Contexts and Literary Idioms in Contemporary Irish Literature.* Michael Kenneally (editor)

# CRITICAL APPROACHES
# TO
# ANGLO-IRISH LITERATURE

edited by
Michael Allen and Angela Wilcox

Irish Literary Studies 29

BARNES & NOBLE BOOKS
Totowa, New Jersey

Copyright © 1989 by Catherine Belsey, Patricia Coughlan,
Seamus Deane, Gerald Fitzgibbon, Ruth Fleischmann,
Margaret E. Fogarty, John Wilson Foster, Eamonn Hughes,
Tom Paulin, Michael Kenneally, Walter T. Rix, Nicholas Roe

First published in the United States of America in 1989
by Barnes & Noble Books, 81 Adams Drive, Totowa, NJ 07512

**Library of Congress Cataloging in Publication Data**

Critical approaches to Anglo-Irish literature
edited by Michael Allen and Angela Wilcox.
p. cm.—(Irish literary studies: 29)
Bibliography: p.
Includes index.
ISBN 0–389–20790–x
1. English literature—Irish authors—History and criticism.
2. Ireland—Intellectual life. 3. Ireland in literature.
I. Allen, Michael. II. Wilcox, Angela. III. Series.
PR8714.C75 1989
820′.9′9415—dc19   88–3215

Originated and published in Great Britain
by Colin Smythe Limited, Gerrards Cross, Buckinghamshire

Produced in Great Britain

# CONTENTS

# ILLUSTRATIONS

# FOREWORD

The fifth Triennial Conference of the International Association of Anglo-Irish Literature was held on July 1985 at the Queen's University of Belfast on the subject of 'Critical Approaches to Anglo-Irish Literature'. No umbrella could have been more capacious than that afforded contributors by this title, and the following collection of lectures and papers assumed no more doctrinaire principle than the title suggests.

All of the lectures and most of the papers here do, in their various ways, recognise the pungency of the contemporary critical atmosphere. But in selecting the papers we had no hesitation in choosing what seemed to us the best pieces of criticism, regardless of the contemporaneity or traditionalism of their theoretic assumptions.

It is customary in these Iasail volumes to publish the lectures, and those delivered to the conference by Catherine Belsey, Michael Kenneally, John Wilson Foster and Tom Paulin (who nobly stepped into the breach left by an eleventh-hour cancellation) are included here. A substantial part of the lecture delivered by Seamus Deane was already promised for publication elsewhere, and the paper printed here represents a subsequent development of his original lecture. Unhappily, it seems to have become almost equally customary for the editors to experience difficulty in retrieving all the lecture manuscripts, and John Kelly was unfortunately unable to supply a copy of his lecture in time for this publication.

The writings of W. B. Yeats quoted in these papers are reproduced by kind permission of A. P. Watt Ltd. on behalf of Michael B. Yeats and Macmillan London Ltd. In the United States of America, acknowledgement is made to the Macmillan Publishing Company and Anne Yeats.

We are grateful to all our contributors for their co-operation, and to John Cronin and Edna Longley for assistance on points of scholarly detail. Special thanks are due too to Walter Rix, who arranged for the illustrations which accompany his paper.

Michael Allen
Angela Wilcox
The Queen's University of
Belfast, January, 1988.

# MOBILIZING BYZANTIUM

CATHERINE BELSEY

The opening lyric of Yeats's *Collected Poems* proclaims the appearance of a poet and constitutes a manifesto on behalf of poetry. According to 'The Song of the Happy Shepherd', 'Words alone are certain good' (ll. 10, 43).[1] The context of this incisive claim is an altogether less incisive and very Romantic poem about dreams and poppies as a remedy for a world sickened by 'Grey Truth' (l. 4). What differentiates this text from any number of nineteenth-century poetic rejections of science, from Keats's 'Lamia' onwards, is a particular group of concerns which runs through many of the *Collected Poems*. In this poem these concerns appear as loss, transience, the dead; as song, story, words, poetry; and as heroic violence leading to death.

At the risk of simplification, I want to characterise these three areas as change, art and death. Of the three, change is consistently identified as the problem, while art is one of the proposed solutions, and death is alternatively part of the problem, as the culminating moment of change, or a projected solution, because it puts an end to the process of change. Change in Yeats is registered as difference and (usually) as cause for regret, whether culturally, in the elegies for a vanished past, or personally, for instance in the recurring image of the scarecrow. I want to attempt to trace the relationships between these three terms in some of the poems, not only in the hope of illuminating aspects of the texts themselves, but also in order to identify certain discursive shifts in which the poems participate. These shifts are still in process. The tenacity with which Yeats's poems pursue solutions to the questions they raise enables us to read them as markers of the collapse of traditional ideas concerning the relations between the individual subject and signifying practice.

'The Happy Shepherd' begins by lamenting the contempt for poetry which prevails in the modern world, and goes on:

> Of all the many changing things
> In dreary dancing past us whirled,
> To the cracked tune that Chronos sings,
> Words alone are certain good.          (ll. 7–10)

1

The rhetoric implies that poetry has a quality which enables it to withstand the destruction of time. A much more confident version of this proposition is familiar from English Renaissance verse, which inherited from Latin poetry the claim that art transcends change and death. But in Yeats's poems of the 1880s there is a new element which links this text, however tenuously, to the twentieth century:

> Where are now the warring kings
> Word be-mockers? — By the Rood
> Where are now the warring kings?
> An idle word is now their glory . . .          (ll. 11–14)

The kings, men of action, mocked words: heroic violence and the sign are juxtaposed, antithetical. But in what follows the sign itself lays tentative claim to supremacy: their glory has become a word. 'Glory' incorporates the heroism, inscribes it in legend, in art. But 'idle' in the same line privileges the violence again and subordinates signifying practice, relocating words where Locke had left them. In Locke's analysis words are signs *of* something, of a presence which is always elsewhere, and thus always and inevitably secondary — or indeed tertiary, since for empiricism words, even the words of the poet, are signs of ideas of things, and thus at two removes from things themselves. In these circumstances poetry shares the status of dreams.

And yet the poem, bringing together two antithetical traditions which are its heritage, the Renaissance valorisation of art on the one hand, and the empiricist subordination of the sign on the other, continues to worry at the problem of the relationship between change and signification, and momentarily suggests a remarkably radical solution:

> The wandering earth herself may be
> Only a sudden flaming word,
> In clanging space a moment heard,
> Troubling the endless reverie.          (ll. 18–21)

Although this seems to propose the priority of language over the world, it is not, of course, to be mistaken for post-structuralism. Post-structuralist theory points to the primacy of the signifier, and rejects the metaphysics of presence which privileges the signified. In Yeats's poem the transcendental signified, the *Logos* which anchors the signifying system of differences, is still in place in extra-linguistic, unmediated reverie, and the world/word is no more than a noisy moment troubling this endless self-presence. But the momentary equation of world and word, 'flaming' out among the rather misty imagery of the rest of the poem, refuses the empiricist account of language, and in consequence calls into question for an instant the conventional division, which is an effect of empiricism, between the public, scientific, objective truth of *things*, and the private, subjective truth of *our ideas* of things, dreams, the material of art.

\*

The image of the world as a sudden flame, no more than a moment of combustion, eliminates difference, which is the condition of both change and signification. A world defined in these terms knows no time and no change. In a sense it also knows no meaning: a single, instantaneous word, complete and undifferentiated, identifies all that there is, at once perfection and plenitude.

The image of the sudden flame was to recur thirty years later in the poem 'In Memory of Major Robert Gregory', where a modern Renaissance man, 'our Sidney' (l. 47), whose twentieth-century heroism eliminates the intervening and differentiating three centuries, shares with the warring kings in the 'discourtesy of death' (l. 48). An idle word, this poem, is now *his* glory, and this time it is death which is characterised in terms of an instant of flame:

> Some burn damp faggots, others may consume
> The entire combustible world in one small room
> As though dried straw, and if we turn about
> The bare chimney is gone black out
> Because the work had finished in that flare.      (ll. 81–85)

The paradox defined in this poem is that death itself, the final change, the ultimate difference, is also the dissolution of difference, the transcendence of change and the perpetuation of plenitude:

> Soldier, scholar, horseman, he,
> As 'twere all life's epitome.
> What made us dream that he could comb grey hair?
>                                                   (ll. 86–88)

As becomes clear in the following and companion poem, 'An Irish Airman foresees his Death', the moment of perfect intensity is set against the processes of time and change, and it is death which is preferred:

> The years to come seemed waste of breath,
> A waste of breath the years behind
> In balance with this life, this death.          (ll. 15–17)

It is a condition of such a moment of plenitude that it should be in a sense meaningless: 'Those that I fight I do not hate,/Those that I guard I do not love . . .' (ll. 3–4). Unmotivated by law or duty, politics or public opinion, this death is the effect of 'A lonely impulse of delight' (l. 12).

The project is absolute sovereignty for the subject. The individual subjectivity becomes the sole origin of true meaning, and its only guarantee. Death, which marks the subject as finite, as precisely subject to difference, is the means by which difference is overcome and subjection is repudiated. The flame which consumes the subject also destroys the objects that give the subject meaning by their difference, 'The entire combustible world'. The verbs in the quotation from 'Major Robert Gregory' affirm the subject as the sovereign author of its own death: 'Some burn damp faggots, others may consume/The entire combustible world . . .' The Irish Airman deliberates and chooses: 'I balanced all, brought all to mind . . .' (l. 14). The 'lonely impulse of delight' (where the preposition identifies the impulse as an effect of the joy which is also its purpose) comes from deep within the subjectivity whose triumph it determines.

It is all, of course, intensely Romantic. Keats's 'Ode to a Nightingale' also confronts mutability and mortality, the desire to reconcile subject and object, poet and nightingale, in a single and continuous plenitude, and the concomitant longing for death:

> Now more than ever seems it rich to die,
>     To cease upon the midnight with no pain,
>   While thou art pouring forth thy soul abroad
>         In such an ecstasy.[2]

But 'seems' in the first line of that extract marks a hesitation which the text goes on to confirm: 'still would'st thou sing, and I have ears in vain'. The song continues in the absence of the poet, re-asserting its own otherness. Death, which puts an end to change, also reaffirms the finite character of the subject.

In post-structuralist theory the subject is no more than an effect of language, that which has learnt to say 'I'. The subject inevitably oscillates between identification with the 'I' of utterance on the one hand, and recognition on the other hand of the difference between the self which speaks and the self which takes its place in the utterance, the self it speaks *of*. The sovereign subject speaks and knows. But it cannot say or know what it is, since it cannot be at once both subject and object of its own knowledge. In quest of a self-presence which must always elude it, the subject seeks the elimination of the difference which gives it being, the difference *between* the subject and the objects of its knowledge, and the difference *within* subjectivity, the otherness of the linguistic system of difference which is the condition of the subject's existence. The difference within the subject is the source of desire, eternal and indestructible, which finds a succession of objects. Death, willed, chosen, imaged in a flame lit by the subject in which the subject itself is consumed, offers a place beyond difference and beyond desire — which is no place at all. The Irish Airman can only *foresee* his death, can only speak of it in the future. In the undifferentiated present of death there is no subject to know or to speak. The instantaneous flame leaves no residue: 'and if we turn about/The bare chimney is gone black out'.

*

Without difference there is no meaning, no distinction between 'I' and 'you', and in consequence no subject. But the price of the subject's autonomy, the freedom we prize, is the gulf of difference between the subject and the objects of its knowledge, and this is supremely so when the object in question is identity itself. The subject is in this sense always other than itself, and this alterity within the subject initiates desire, which may be desire for the other, for mastery by possession or incorporation of the other, or desire to surrender to alterity, to lose the self in an otherness which heals division and obliterates difference. Change, meanwhile, threatening the subject's mastery of its objects and of itself as object, acts as a marker of difference and reinstates division.

In 1930 Yeats recorded the following reflections in his diary:

I am always, in all I do, driven to a moment which is the realisation of myself as unique and free, or to a moment which is the surrender to God of all that I am . . . If men are born many times, as I think, that must originate in the antinomy between human and divine freedom. Man incarnating, translating 'the divine ideas' into his language of the eye, to assert his own freedom, dying into the freedom of God and then coming to birth again. So too the assertions and surrender of sexual love . . .[3]

Like the privilege accorded to the sign in 'The Happy Shepherd', this is not post-structuralism. The theoretical framework which has now supplanted the misty Romanticism of the early poem is an equally misty Orientalism. And yet here again Yeats's text troubles common sense, registering in its own terms the difference within subjectivity. It consequently implies an interrogation in the twentieth century of the certainty at the heart of nineteenth-century European liberalism, the sovereign subject, self-knowing and self-determining, self-determining because self-knowing. A generation later, drawing on the theoretical work of Saussure and Freud, both of them Yeats's contemporaries, Jacques Lacan would also call in question the unity and thus the sovereignty of the subject.

According to Yeats's diary, the assertion and surrender of sexual love parallel or re-enact the assertion and surrender of the self to God, each a figure of the other. Meanwhile, the repudiation of death as the dissolution of difference has left the subject in a world of change, where the exuberance of nature can readily be seen as proclaiming precisely the proximity of love and death:

> The young
> In one another's arms, birds in the trees,
> — Those dying generations . . .
>
> Fish, flesh, or fowl, commend all summer long
> Whatever is begotten, born, and dies.
> ('Sailing to Byzantium', ll. 1–3, 5–6)

The 'sensual music' of the first stanza of 'Sailing to Byzantium' (l. 7) thus paradoxically echoes in 1927 'the cracked tune that Chronos sings' in 'The Song of the Happy Shepherd'. For an aged man who scares away the birds, sexual love is no solution to the instability of subjectivity. As an alternative the self seeks a place beyond difference, in the undifferentiated Other, God, both subject and object, the infinite I AM, a place of surrender which is also a guarantee of the subject's own continuous being as part of the immobility of art, the immortality of the aesthetic. 'Only an aching heart/Conceives a changeless work of art' ('My Table', ll. 13–14). Gathered into the artifice of eternity, the aching heart consumed by a holy fire, the subject moves out of nature, beyond time and change, beyond desire, into the plenitude of an immutable golden world.

'Sailing to Byzantium' juxtaposes the aching heart and the changeless realm of art in terms of an opposition between two locations: 'that', which is nature: salmon and mackerel, fish and flesh, the young; and this, 'the holy city of Byzantium' (l. 16), monumental, mosaic, metallic, continuous because unageing. The antitheses are precise: organic birds and golden bird; scarecrow and sages; generation and eternity. The sensual world of nature is one of desire, of lack which is inevitable because birth leads inexorably to death and summer ends too soon. That the object of desire can be gained must mean, in a world of change, that it can also be lost: difference implies that only desire itself is indestructible. The scarecrow, sick with desire amid the sensual music of the birds in the trees, learns an immortal song and becomes changeless metal. No longer subject to history, to the fatal difference by which begetting, giving life, entails death, the bird-poet becomes the subject *of* knowledge, able to sing equally and equably of what is past, or passing, or to come, in possession of history, no longer at its mercy.

'Sailing to Byzantium' inscribes in metre the opposition it proposes between nature and art. In the opening stanza the teeming life of nature seems to exceed the constraints of verse in the abundance of extra unstressed syllables: 'mackerel-crowded', 'Caught in that sensual music'. The fifth line, rendered in the normal rhythm of speech, includes seven stressed syllables in a single pentameter: 'Físh, flésh, or fówl, comménd all súmmer lóng'. The expressive human voice is audible here, asserting itself against the confining patterns of art. By contrast, the second half of the poem, defining Byzantium, displays a surrender of the voice to poetic form in the internal rhymes of 'Come from the holy fire, perne in a gyre' (l. 19), and in the measured, rhyming symmetry of 'hammered gold and gold enamelling' (l. 28).

Byzantium appears to us with the advantage of hindsight the obvious emblem of eternal artifice. The meeting-point of east and west, vanished and yet there to be seen, it seems to contain and transcend difference. Yeats drew for his image of Byzantium on W. G. Holmes's book, *The Age of Justinian and Theodora*, the first section of which conducts the reader in the present tense, in the manner of a guide book, through a rich and inviting city, 'laid out in colonnaded squares and streets, to the adornment of which all that Grecian art could evolve in architecture and in statuary has been applied with a lavishness attainable only by the fiat of a wide-ruling despot'.[4]

No doubt the politics would have appealed to Yeats as the spokesman of a decaying aristocracy. Class relations in Byzantium seem, according to Holmes, to have been quite exceptionally exploitative. Holmes's account of the socio-economic orders bears virtually no relation to the idealisation in *A Vision* of a Byzantium where architect and artist 'spoke to the multitude and the few alike'.[5] If they spoke to both, they spoke with different meanings. But the politics of Byzantium may not be as irrelevant to my argument as appears at first sight, in the sense that the oscillation of the liberal-humanist subject, which both Yeats and post-structuralism identify, between the omnipotence of the self and its negation, may well find its most perfect emblem in a dream of possession of or surrender to the most absolute of empires.

Holmes's Byzantium, luxuriously decorated, inlaid, gilded, eternalizes and immobilizes in art the world of nature. Palaces, for instance, Holmes explains, might contain a central colonnaded courtyard, giving light and air to the whole building. 'Much wealth is often expended in order to give this space the appearance of a landscape in miniature. Trees wave, fountains play, and artificial streams roll over counterfeited cliffs into pools stocked with tame fish.'[6] Art constructs a replica of nature and thus brings it under control, eliminating change and death, and consequently excluding desire.

A term Yeats could have found in *The Age of Justinian and Theodora* is *iconostasis*.[7] In its literal meaning the word designates an image-stand, a carved screen decorated with figures of sacred personages, perhaps depicted on a golden ground, like the sages standing in God's holy fire. But in its more general sense the term perfectly characterises the mythic city itself as the two Byzantium poems depict it: a place of icons, of sacred images, which is itself iconic, itself a sacred image; a place of stasis, fixed, immobile because it excludes the possibility of change, of lack, of death.

And yet there are difficulties here, and not only, as is commonly suggested, because the metallic stasis of Byzantium is in many ways so much less enticing than the kinetic fertility of the natural world. The poem, as an instance of the mimetic art it endorses, is an imitation in miniature of an experience. In its use of the present tense, in the opening demonstrative pronoun, which creates the illusion of a reference to a knowledge shared with the reader, and in the absence of any explicit allusion to such a reader (or to any interlocutor), the text simulates a meditation or a soliloquy, thought or uttered by a subject-speaker. This figure, implied from the beginning, specified as the 'I' of line 15, and thus retrospectively identified as an aged man, is apparently fully present to himself in the process of reflection, the object of his own knowledge. It is only his (aching, desiring) heart which 'knows not what it is' (l. 23) and must in consequence be consumed away.

And yet *where* emblematically is the experiencing subject of the poem? The 'that' of the opening line has the clear effect of distancing the speaker from the world of nature, and indeed the text goes on to confirm that that is not where he is to be found: 'And therefore have I sailed the seas and come/To the holy city of Byzantium' (ll. 15–16). But in so far as Byzantium represents the artifice of eternity, he is not there either, as the imperatives indicate: 'be the singing-masters of my soul' (l. 20); 'Consume my heart away' (l. 21); 'gather me/Into the artifice of eternity' (ll. 23–4). If the country identified in the opening stanza is elsewhere, so too is Byzantium. It is a promise, not yet realised: 'Once out of nature I shall never take/My bodily form from any natural thing' (ll. 25–6). Purely geographically it is perfectly intelligible that a poet might be sailing to Byzantium; but in the emblematic geography of this poem, which proposes a clear antithesis between two conditions, life and art, in nature or out of it, a place in between is in practice nowhere to be found. The 'I' of the utterance, so richly present in the process of reflecting, determining, imploring, is not identical to the subject of the enunciation, the poet-speaker, who in the event has no place in the figurative world he has constructed. Like the Irish Airman, he can only foresee his absorption into a condition beyond difference, because here to surrender, to be passively gathered, to be made (by Grecian goldsmiths), to be set (upon a bough), is to cease precisely to be a subject, the agent of action, the origin of meaning.

Ernest Schanzer has drawn attention to the parallels between 'Sailing to Byzantium' and Hans Christian Andersen's story of the nightingale.[8] The protagonists in each case are a bird or birds in the trees, a mechanical bird and an emperor who lives in a palace of art. The differences too are instructive. In the Andersen story the jewelled bird supplants the organic one in the favour of the emperor only until its clockwork goes wrong, and then, since no one is able to repair it, the superiority of the organic nightingale becomes evident to all. What is at stake is autonomy. The fairy tale has a different ending from the poem. Death comes to remind the emperor that absolute sovereignty is nonetheless finite. Facing Death's great hollow eyes, the emperor commands and then implores the artificial bird to sing to comfort him. But the bird is silent. All of a sudden the living nightingale, of her own free will, begins to sing from a branch outside the window, driving Death away so that the blood begins to flow once more through the emperor's body. He rises strong and well. The nightingale promises to return, but not at the emperor's bidding. She will come when she chooses. Only the living bird, the tale makes clear, is free and self-determining.

The two stories represent alternative versions of the contest for supremacy between art and life which has such a long history. In one account art triumphs because it immortalises what is transitory; in the other art appears cold and lifeless beside the miracle of nature. But the contest takes place within a shared theoretical framework which is mimetic. Mimesis depends on a parallel between art and life — and a corresponding difference between them. Art is like life, but whether it appears as richer, because it orders the chaos of experience, or poorer, as a mere copy, it is always by definition differentiated from life. Where the mimetic theory of art is dominant as it was in Europe from the Renaissance till the end of the nineteenth century, where art is an imitation of life, art is always finally, whichever term is privileged, not-life, lifeless, immobile.

In the twentieth century the mimetic theory of art has been challenged, most obviously by the practices of modernism and post-modernism, but also by critical theory, and especially poststructuralist theory. All these have had in varying ways the effect of deconstructing the parallel and the polarity between art and life. 'Sailing to Byzantium' participates, whether consciously or not, in the deconstruction process. First, as I have suggested, it records the fate of the experiencing subject which seeks to move beyond difference, and consequently disappears, since it exists only as difference, as what is not an object, not 'you', not other. And secondly, it records the reinstatement of change in the *iconostasis* of art. This was always inevitable, because the subject reappears, of course, in Byzantium. How could it be otherwise in a text which is as much a manifesto for the poet as 'The Song of the Happy Shepherd'? The golden bird will sing, giving meaning, like all great poets, to 'what is past, or passing, or to come' (l. 32), and with the reaffirmation of meaning and of the knowing subject-poet comes, in consequence, the reinstatement of difference, history, change. It is history in its blandest form, of course, purged of all reference to begetting, birth and death, as continuous, as undifferentiated, as words can make it. But the metrical and syntactic echo of the first phrase in the second ('Whatever is begotten, born, and dies'; 'what is past, or passing, or to come') introduces more than a trace of difference into the undifferentiated world of Byzantium.

According to the mimetic theory, art is at once like life and not life. 'Sailing to Byzantium' throws the mimetic theory into crisis. The text presents itself as a life-like (experienced) account of a transition to the world of art in its difference from life. But in the course of the poem the experiencing subject disappears — in the interests of maintaining the polarity between art and life, Byzantium and nature. The elimination of experience from the realm of art undermines the mimetic account of art as a replica of life. At the same time, since the project of the poem was the immortality of the subject, and the subject is an effect of difference, difference reappears in Byzantium, undermining the polarity between art and life which the text sets out to establish. The parallel and the polarity cannot be simultaneously sustained.

*

The first recorded deconstruction of 'Sailing to Byzantium' was by T. Sturge Moore, who wrote to Yeats in 1930 pointing out that the opposition between art and nature broke down in the image of the golden bird, since a bird made by a goldsmith was 'as much nature as a man's body'. Yeats replied that he had written 'Byzantium' in response to this comment, which had convinced him that 'the idea needed exposition'.[9]

The exposition takes the form, in the first instance, of an intensification of the polarity between Byzantium and nature, art and life, and an equally intensified assertion of the superiority of art. The dome of line 5, symbol since the Renaissance of the triumph of engineering over nature, and of perfect visual symmetry,

> disdains
> All that man is,
> All mere complexities,
> The fury and the mire of human veins. (ll. 6–8)

The golden bird scorns 'In glory of changeless metal/Common bird or petal' (ll. 22–3). 'Blood-begotten spirits' submit to 'flames begotten of flame' (ll. 27–8). They are broken by the smithies and on the marbles of the dancing floor. Human figures, barely specified as 'drunken soldiery', 'night-walkers' (ll. 2–3) recede at the beginning of the poem, giving way to a floating image, a breathless mouth that speaks, the superhuman.

In another sense, however, the world of art now incorporates the polarities that the earlier poem had struggled to keep apart. 'Before me floats an image, man or shade/Shade more than man, more image than a shade' (ll. 9–10). The image, man or shade, living or dead, not quite either, subsumes, the syntax implies, something of each: 'I call it death-in-life and life-in-death' (l. 16). The beginning of the next stanza echoes the syntax of the previous lines: 'Miracle,

bird or golden handiwork,/More miracle than bird or handiwork'
(ll. 17–18). Again the text offers alternatives that subdivide the first
term into the opposing categories of life and art, before reaffirming
the first term, 'miracle', which thus seems to contain them both.
The project is the recognition of difference, which is then surpassed
in a mysterious synthesis, multiplicity contained in a oneness which
is beyond nature: an image, the superhuman, a miracle. The inevitable trace of otherness within the selfsame is this time
acknowledged — and transcended. The city of art now includes
death by fire, but this time it is a death which has no power to
destroy. Byzantium also includes begetting, but this is a begetting
which eliminates desire. The flames are self-begotten, much like the
imagined fountain of 'Ancestral Houses', which 'rains down life until the basin spills,/And mounts more dizzy high the more it rains'
(ll. 4–5). The fire, unfed, unlit, like the fountain can lack nothing
and therefore desires nothing.

If 'Sailing to Byzantium' dramatises a conflict for supremacy between art and life, in 'Byzantium' the conflict is already resolved —
in favour of art. The later poem is correspondingly less mimetic.
The speaker-as-subject is far less evident here, specified only in the
second stanza, and then merely as the agent of a vision and a
salutation. The real subjects of this text are the mythic city itself,
and the images it contains, which also constitute it. There is no narrative, no record of an experience, only a series of definitions,
of images, displaying the pure *iconostasis* appropriate to an
autonomous and autotelic realm of art. The project is evidently
that the poem should be an instance of the art it celebrates.

The signifying practices of the poem are almost entirely
figurative. Byzantium stands in metonymically for art; the golden
bird, which can crow in triumph or in scorn, is metaphorically the
poet; the syntax of the opening lines permits us to read even the
drunken soldiery as no more than images — as indeed they are.
Figurative language, which conventionally differentiates poetry
from prose, art from exposition, divorces signification explicitly
from the referent, removing signification to a realm of analogy
which is in a sense autonomous. Figurative language is an effect of
the recognition that the sign betrays the thing itself, an
acknowledgement of the 'idleness' of language brought about by
the empiricist subordination of the sign. It offers to recast the
object, to bathe it in a new light which reveals its truth, presents
its essence. But at the same time figurative language is also always
a substitution, further removed from the thing itself, and thus a
reaffirmation of the difference between words and things. 'Byzantium'

implicitly recognises the difference and, compelled to choose, repudiates things, by implication reiterating the Happy Shepherd's proposition that 'Words alone are certain good'. Byzantium thus comes to represent a realm of pure signification, the *Logos*, word as image, more image than a word, unmediated presence, which at the same time draws attention to its own imaginary nature, its existence as a substitute.

And this is in a sense the text's undoing. The *Logos* too has meaning only as difference, only by contrast with what it is not, the complexities of mire and blood. Once again difference inhabits Byzantium, and with it desire. The poem is unable to be an instance of the serenity it celebrates. 'Among School Children' offers a kind of commentary:

> Both nuns and mothers worship images,
> But those the candles light are not as those
> That animate a mother's reveries,
> But keep a marble or a bronze repose.
> And yet they too break hearts — O Presences
> That passion, piety or affection knows,
> And all that heavenly glory symbolise —
> O self-born mockers of man's enterprise.          (ll. 49–56)

Here too the images common to nuns and mothers (sculptured saints or living children indifferently) subsume the opposition between art and life. But the images themselves, as presence, as heavenly glory, constitute a source of longing, break hearts. The *iconostasis* of Byzantium, at once an essence and a substitute, in either case unable to be realised, becomes an object of desire for the mere complexities of mire and blood. The irreducible otherness of *iconostasis* thus invites not serenity but something like the desperation to be found in the improbable gaze of Byzantine art's more illustrious products, mosaic figures who look both at us and beyond — in the hope, Lacan suggests, of arousing the desire of God.[10]

Richard Ellmann found this poem a 'hymn to the human imagination'.[11] It could be argued, on the other hand, that there is nothing human there at all, unless it is a recognition of the lack which is an effect of difference, and the indestructible desire which is its consequence. There are parallels between Byzantium and the full moon, a moment of 'perfected, completed, and immovable/ Images', so perfect, so complete that they disrupt the plenitude of the observer, 'break the solitude/Of lovely, satisfied, indifferent eyes' ('The Phases of the Moon', ll. 81–3). At the fifteenth phase 'All thought becomes an image and the soul/Becomes a body' (ll. 58–9), but the price of the dissolution of difference is death, 'Body and soul cast out and cast away' (l. 62), 'For there's no human life at the full' (l. 35). Byzantium too is a realm of death.

But if there's no human life in Byzantium, there is, on the other hand, a single incidental phrase which occurs in both poems, a marginal allusion which I want nonetheless to take as a momentary focus of attention, on the grounds that it condenses in itself something of the pattern of meanings I have attempted to trace. The 'golden bough' has no obvious source in the books on Byzantium that Yeats is known to have read. He himself laconically mentioned that he had read somewhere of an artificial tree in the emperor's palace,[12] but the texts are more specific than that. J. G. Frazer's monumental work was first published in 1890 as *The Golden Bough*. It subsequently appeared in 12 volumes with separate titles, and the one-volume edition was issued in 1922 under the original title.

In 1937 Yeats wrote of 'a modern man, *The Golden Bough* and *Human Personality* in his head'.[13] Evidently for him Frazer's work was a major influence on contemporary consciousness. There he would have found the sensual music of a universal fertility cult. In *The Golden Bough* the young of widely different cultures sing and dance all summer long, performing ancient rituals to ensure the fruitfulness of the earth. As the text makes clear, that is no country for old men. The royal and priestly lover of the vegetation goddess has to die in his prime, in case his impotence should cause the failure of the crops. Diana's priest at Nemi, the King of the Wood, is required to kill his predecessor after plucking the golden bough. Diana personifies the teeming life of nature. Her lover-priest, relieved of the obligation to till the soil, since he ensures the health of the community in another way, is a sombre, watchful and isolated figure, surrounded by taboos and restrictions. As soon as he grows old or infirm, he becomes a liability and is ritually killed by his successor.

Frazer identified the golden bough as the mistletoe, miraculous and transgressive, since it grows without roots in the earth, and flourishes in winter when its host-tree seems dead. Its meanings are plural and contradictory: it signifies 'death-in-life and life-in-death'. An emanation of the lightning, the celestial fire, the mistletoe is a symbol of life and an object of desire. While Diana's priest keeps it safe, it protects him. But it is simultaneously a signifier of death, the instrument which (either literally or metaphorically) kills him. It is at the same time an emblem of the immortality of the priesthood itself, a vocation of dedication and toil, a life caught and held, it might be suggested, 'in the cold snows of a dream' ('The Road at my Door', l. 15).

In Book VI of *The Aeneid* the golden bough is Aeneas's guarantee of life. When he visits the underworld he dedicates it to Proserpina, who in return unlocks the gates of death for a living man. In the underworld Aeneas meets his old comrades and his father, who tell him of what is past, or passing, or to come. The condition of these narratives is that those who recount them are dead. The living Aeneas cannot embrace Anchises, who is a wraith. Proserpina requires the golden bough as an offering, and Aeneas, on the Sibyl's instructions, leaves it at her door in the world of the dead. The miraculous emblem of life thus becomes the property of death.

The golden bough, perhaps more than any of the images in the Byzantium poems, collects and condenses the meaning of art as these texts define it. Guarantee of the continuity of life, of immortality, the realm of art is offered as a replica of life, as a transcendence of life, as a miraculous object of desire, which is simultaneously the extinction of all that is human, a place of death.

*

I have pursued these questions in such detail because Yeats's poems seem to me to make visible the difficulties which reside in an empiricist account of art and of language. Because of their tenacious struggle to find solutions, the texts throw into relief the impossibility of resolving the problems of writing and subjectivity from within that discourse. The issues they confront are precisely the issues which for that reason have precipitated new discourses, new ways of understanding the nature of the subject and new approaches to textuality.

The notion of art as autonomous, autotelic and thus finally immobile, is one projected solution to the problem of mimesis. There are others. I have drawn on post-structuralist theory to mobilise Yeats's image of Byzantium almost against itself, in an attempt to demonstrate that the plenitude and the immobility it defines are inevitably synonymous in the end with absence and death. A mobilising critical practice probes the text for what it cannot say, or says reluctantly, since a criticism which rejects the possibility of mimesis also refuses to settle for sharing the experience of the poet. Meanwhile, a mobile and mobilising *textual* practice might equally refuse the conventional project of art, ceasing to define itself in relation to life, by its imitation of and thus its increasing distance from life.

I began with three terms extracted from the texts. They were change, art and death. As a solution to the problem of change the poems I have considered variously celebrate death, then art, and finally art-as-death. I have wanted to suggest that while death is not a very positive solution to anything, the notion of 'art' is not a solution either, but one of the problems.

Possibly, however, change is not a problem after all. Perhaps the time has come for us to repudiate immobilising concepts of art and of criticism, and to commit ourselves to the celebration of change.

# DOUBLES, SHADOWS, SEDAN-CHAIRS AND THE PAST: THE 'GHOST STORIES' OF J. S. LE FANU

PATRICIA COUGHLAN

Man has not been able to describe himself as a configuration in the *episteme* without thought at the same time discovering, both in itself and outside itself, at its borders yet also in its very warp and woof, an element of darkness, an apparently inert density in which it is embedded, an unthought which it contains entirely, yet in which it is also caught. The unthought (whatever name we give it) is not lodged in man like a shrivelled-up nature or a stratified history; it is, in relation to man, the Other: the Other that is not only a brother but a twin, born not of man, nor in man, but beside him and at the same time, in an identical newness, in an unavoidable duality. This obscure space so readily interpreted as an abyssal region in man's nature, or as a uniquely impregnable fortress in his history, is indispensable to him: in one sense, the shadow cast by man as he emerged in the field of knowledge; in another, the blind stain by which it is possible to know him. In any case, the unthought has accompanied man, mutely and uninterruptedly, since the nineteenth century. Since it was really never more than an insistent double, it has never been the object of reflection in an autonomous way . . . For though this double may be close, it is alien, and the role, the true undertaking, of thought will be to bring it as close to itself as possible; the whole of modern thought is imbued with the necessity of thinking the unthought . . . of ending man's alienation by reconciling him with his own essence, of making explicit the horizon that provides experience with its background of immediate and disarmed proof, of lifting the veil of the Unconscious, of becoming absorbed in its silence, or of straining to catch its endless murmur.

Michel Foucault, *The Order of Things*

Le Fanu's supernatural stories number about twenty-two, and are dated between 1838 and 1871. This paper starts from the premise that these haunting-tales form a coherent *oeuvre*, and deserve to be discussed as one. I shall not engage in a lengthy commentary on in-dividual stories, but shall proceed by identifying and interpreting some of the stories' most striking and frequently recurrent narrative motifs. These are: the domestic interior and its furniture; the *doppelganger* and shadow; and landscape as the locus of an otherness which is frequently apprehended as a buried layer of the past. Within the body of Le Fanu's haunting-tales these motifs form a constellation of significance; I shall try to suggest where it lies by discussing a few representative instances in each case, and generalizing from those. My purpose is to suggest that this body of work is not adequately described as a scattered series of slight, whimsical contributions to the genre of the Victorian ghost-story, but rather that it has a unity of purpose and meaning and that it may represent Le Fanu's most significant achievement. I propose that it would be more appropriately interpreted as being in the European genre of the metaphysical and psychological *nouvelle*, a genre whose characteristic strategy is to frame — within super-natural plots of various kinds — important questions about the concept of the self and the constitution of what is called reality.

Le Fanu began writing in a literary climate which was extremely receptive to the influences of German Romanticism. Recent German literature was enthusiastically and copiously translated and discussed in Irish periodicals in the 1830s.[1] It is likely that i.s peculiar combination of the perspectives of science and occultisin had a strong, though equivocal, influence on Le Fanu. The boundaries between the two were then far less clearly drawn than in later periods. Subjects in the trance cast by hypnotists using the newly discovered 'animal magnetism' seemed to reveal the possible existence of other personalities within the self, and in fact the development of psychology towards the discoveries of the psychoanalysts did happen as a curious combination of rational and avowedly surrational inquiry. The status of dual or multiple personality and of apparent haunting and visionary experiences of all kinds remained uneasily undefined throughout Le Fanu's period: such experiences might be attributed to electrical or magnetic activity in the body, or to otherworldly intervention in the traditional way. These issues were discussed by James Clarence Mangan and by Henry Ferris in the *Dublin University Magazine* in 1841, 1842 and 1845.[2] The *D.U.M.* articles arose chiefly from the work of Justinus Kerner, author of *Die Seherin von Prevorst* (1829), an investigation of a 'ghost-seeress', a case of alleged psychic experiences in a German town. Le Fanu indeed invents a scientist, the pompous Dr Hesselius, somewhat along the lines of Justinus Kerner the 'ghost-craftsman', to introduce a batch of his later haunting-stories in the guise of case-histories: the superb 'Carmilla', as well as 'Green Tea' and 'The Familiar', is framed in this way. Hesselius's limitations are clear to the reader, and though he is himself quite confident of the validity of his point of view, he is fairly savagely undermined by irony. Seen against the psychological experiences they claim but fail to account for, Hesselius's positivist explanations compound the problematic nature of the mind and thus represent a formal analogue to the smooth surfaces in the troubling of which I discern the chief project of these stories. The most important feature of Le Fanu's work in this genre is his insistence on keeping open the question of the origins or causes of psychological malaise, and not letting it collapse into glib explanations, whether moral or medical. In this indeterminacy lies one of the greater strengths of Le Fanu's haunting-stories; he knew that 'to explain was to explain away', as Beckett puts it, and therefore frequently gives a plurality of explanations, which cancel one another out. It seems clear that this indeterminacy represented his own real state of mind before the phenomena of apparent hauntings; this is evident in the questionable status enjoyed in his novel *Uncle Silas* by Swedenborgianism, another tradition combining the occult and the scientific.[3]

Like the German tale-writers, Le Fanu uses legend and folktale motifs quasi-allegorically, to go behind the apparently calm face of contemporary assumptions about the psyche and explore states of discontinuity, intolerable psychological strangeness (such as is captured by the notion of ghosts), and especially the fragmentation of the self. Le Fanu repeatedly and very effectively uses the motif of the double or shadow, a motif which was brought to prominence in Jean Paul Richter's *Siebenkas* (1796) and Adalbert Chamisso's *Peter Schlemihl* (1814), as well as in a large number of Hoffmann's stories. This motif is particularly expressive of some of the psychological concerns of the first and second generations of Romantics. Le Fanu's repeated use of it reveals his capacity to introduce highly individual variations on those themes.

The German Romantic tale not only used contemporary psychological experiment and study but also had, particularly in its form, another source of inspiration, from outside official literary tradition: the folk or fairy tale. In Chamisso's highly influential *Peter Schlemihl* (1814), for instance, the story of the man who barters away his shadow to a devil-figure then lives to regret it, is narrated in a naive and whimsical style which handles marvels of all kinds deadpan. Yet the effect of the story is very remote from that of genuine folktale: it is evident to the reader that allegory is intended, and that one is called upon to consider whether it is political, moral or epistemological, or a combination of these. The clarity and apparent simplicity of the folktale provided these writers with a narrative means of breaking the moulds of existing literary forms, and therefore of implicitly challenging the prevailing psychological assumptions embedded in those forms.[4] Further, in folklore marvels and metaphysics — magic journeys and feats, demonic lovers and bargains, haunting-plots of all kinds — was found a rich source of images of disturbance and strangeness, which could be used metaphorically to explore the concept of the individual self, newly problematic in the post-Enlightenment period.

Le Fanu had the stimulus not only of foreign literary appropriations of folk and fairy tales but, in common with his Irish contemporaries of various ethnic backgrounds, he had the opportunity of direct contact with folk material. He put that opportunity to very good use, most obviously in the trio of folktale retellings he published in 1870 — 'Stories of Lough Guir', 'The Child that Went with the Fairies', and 'The White Cat of Drumguinniol'. But the whole body of his ghost stories shows deeply the impress of the folk material he assimilated, partly in his childhood and youth in Co. Limerick, and partly through his friendship with the Dublin folklorist Patrick Kennedy in the 1870s. Of his remaining eighteen or so haunting-stories, at least five contain a demonic bargain of some kind, four a demon-lover who tries whether successfully or not to carry off a young girl, and six an otherworldly double or shadow, generally malevolent. Many stories combine several of these with one another and with other recurring story motifs.

That material underwent certain transformations in its assimilation into his fiction, as folklore necessarily must in being drawn into literature. The analysis of those transformations may be made to lead towards the formulation of pertinent questions about Le Fanu. The primary way in which the transformation of folk story material can be seen in Le Fanu is in the relations between the level of *discourse* in his work, and the level of *story*, or between *sjuzhet* and *fabula*, as it has been formulated by modern narrative theory.[5] On the one hand we have the narrator communicating with the reader, both rational and modern people, sophisticates, probably city-dwellers, certainly middle-class. On the other, there is the world of the stories: removed in place and generally also in time from that implied reader. Far from attempting to conceal this gap, Le Fanu frequently thematizes it in his stories. Here is an example from the opening of 'Ultor de Lacy' (1861):

In my youth I heard a great many Irish family traditions, more or less of a supernatural character, some of them very peculiar, and all, to a child at least, highly interesting. One of these I will now relate, though the translation to cold type from oral narrative, with all the aids of animated human voice and countenance, and the appropriate *mise-en-scène* of the old-fashioned parlour fireside and its listening circle of excited faces, and, outside, the wintry blast and the moan of leafless boughs, with the occasional rattle of the clumsy old window-frame behind shutter and curtain, as the blast swept by, is at best a trying one.                    (*BGS* p. 444)[6]

This passage contains a constellation of features important in Le Fanu's work. It proposes two sets of contrasts which are of the greatest importance for any interpretation of the story which it introduces. First, there is the opposition between the present occasion of narration and reception, and those of a posited original occasion: for the reader, from animated and excited faces to cold type and solitary passivity; for the writer, from past to present, youth to maturity, listener to narrator. The circumstances of oral narration are presented as an idyll of participatory communality, and the impossibility of recreating them as a sad loss. But within this passage there is also another opposition: between the warm company within and the winter wind outside. This is the tension characteristic of Romance and Gothic fictions of various kinds. As David Punter says in *The Literature of Terror* (1980):

Most ghost stories implicitly propose two alternate members of the audience, the second being by definition someone who is more credulous and thus more scared than oneself. This shadowy double is the residual form of Gothic's hypothetical previous audience, those people, conveniently located in the past but more probably in the lower depths of society, from whose fears Gothic is supposed to have arisen.[7]

This amalgam of safety and fear is, however, imputed by Le Fanu to both the kinds of audience he describes. It is true that the appropriation of Irish folklore by the institution of literature raises ideological problems; but Le Fanu's use of Irish folklore characteristically avoids the condescension sometimes shown to it by his contemporaries. He is aware of its difference from literature and its otherness from him and his class, but clearly he finds in it a mode of vision alternative and analogous to his own, which enables him to frame problems pressing to him too. It is evident not only from his use of so many folktale types and motifs but also from his reworking of the Earl of Desmond legends in 'Stories of Lough Guir' (1870) that he understood this material as a *langue* which carried an understanding of the world, and not as a quaint collection of outlandish or nugatory superstitions.

But in the passage quoted, though there is a doubleness, a dialectic of threat and safety in both kinds of social framework described, there is a difference in the apparatus of reassuring comfort. The fireside community of peasant oral narration is replaced by the more abstract and mediated order and sophistication of the bourgeois reader who feels safe enough to seek the sensation of fear in literature, and remains confident of his or her capacity to keep it within the proper bounds. The reader of Gothic and ghost stories is impelled by a half-shameful wish to transgress, to plunge virtually, but not actually, into strangeness. Hence the moralizing framework of most such stories, which is, however, no more than perfunctory and merely represents the putting away at the back of the mind of the temporarily prominent Other, rather as a very fancy party dress would be replaced in its drawer after a carnival occasion. Is Le Fanu's work any more than the pleasant diversion implied by this metaphor? Does he in fact preserve the security of the reader, by keeping his ghosts firmly in the realm of unreality? Or does he reveal that security as only a cover-up (in the sense of a corrupt deception)?

Schelling defined the uncanny as 'anything which ought to remain in secrecy and has become manifest'.[8] That 'ought' sounds like a moral imperative, but in the discourse of psychoanalysis it is revealed rather as the conscious mind's suppression of anxiety, which it may choose to call moral. Ludwig Binswanger describes the uncanny as:

. . . the original existential anxiety, which now 'has emerged'. The feeling of uncanniness is aroused by anything that causes that anxiety to emerge, anything that is apt to shock us out of our familiarity with 'world and life', as the (unwonted) recurrence of the similar, the *Doppelganger* . . . Through defensive measures, the existence tries to protect itself against the emergence of the Uncanny. Through them, it still finds some foothold in 'care', worrying, bargaining, being cautious, even though this caution serves exclusively to ward off the Uncanny, and completely spends itself in the service of the Uncanny.[9]

In the fiction of Le Fanu's period what we might call the order of the conscious mind is represented, in literary terms, by formally realistic works. Such narratives normally address themselves to the present, in time, and the proximate, in space. They make a claim to rationality in plotting and characterization and proclaim their distance from the enchantments of Gothic, folk and fairy tale, which they tend to represent as belonging to outgrown phases of mental development. As the name implies, realism sees itself exclusively as the form which confronts and holds the mirror up to actual social conditions, and aims to marginalize all other kinds of narrative and treat them as fantasy and decoration: the folktale as a toy for children, the ghost or horror story as mere entertainment. This is not the place for an extended justification of the seriousness of Gothic and romance narrative, a matter which has in any case been well explored in many recent discussions (for instance David Punter's *The Literature of Terror*, already mentioned). The old dismissal of it as a flight from social obligation has been replaced by a more mediated view which acknowledges the role of non-realist narrative forms in interrogating the status quo by tacitly rejecting its claims to full rationality. It is now possible to discern, as it was not in the period of realist dominance, in the practice and forms of other kinds of fiction, a challenging representation precisely of that which is excluded by realism, namely what Freud calls 'the dark, inaccessible part of our personality'.[10] He adds that it can mostly be known negatively, as a kind of shadow to the conscious part: a notion which is a challenge to the concept of the unitary and consciously structured personality on which realist narrative depends.

To use a metaphor: let us say realism is a house, in good order, with secure doors and windows, and fully furnished with wardrobes, cupboards, curtains, pictures, and hangings. In this well-regulated house is, however, a poltergeist, who (which?) bangs things around while no-one is in the room; on its walls are shadows or stains, suggestive of blood, which do not disappear in better lighting or when painted over. Strangers whom no-one remembers admitting wander about familiarly in the passageways, entering bedrooms and rummaging in drawers. The inhabitants are alternately scornful and terrified; they end by moving house. This is inconsequential (it is incidentally a plot-summary of Le Fanu's 'Authentic Narrative of a Haunted House' (1862)), and if one likes logic, and good sense, and finality, it is also somewhat irritating. In this metaphor the shadows, stains, traces, inexplicable noise, and puzzling visitors stand for horror and supernatural fiction, which do not so much set themselves up as alternatives to realism, as loiter darkly in its interstices, as if waiting to pounce. One might add (at the risk of making this building dangerous) that the idea of the fully conscious and rational personality is the house, and the stains and shadows represent its neuroses and dreams. In the 'Authentic Narrative' the head of the family takes all rational steps to try to solve the mystery:

I had . . . a most careful examination made to discover any traces of an entrance having been made by any window into the house. The doors had been found barred and locked as usual; but no sign of any thing of the sort was discernible. I then had the various articles — plate, wearing apparel,

books, &c., counted; and after having conned up and reckoned every
thing, it became quite clear that nothing whatever had been removed from
the house . . .                                              (*BGS*, p. 427)

But counting the spoons (a good example of Binswanger's *sorge*,
care, fuss, worry) is quite comically the reverse of appropriate;
something has been *added* to the house not taken away from it. The
other world of the unconscious is always already within (on the
level of *fabula*, of course, the crime has already been committed in
the house before they arrived).

It will be noticed that his idea of shutting in and shutting out is
also present in the 'Ultor de Lacy' passage. The 'shutter and curtain'
and the 'clumsy old window-frame' are set up as barriers between
within and without, between the controlled environment and the
Other, the uncanny, for which the sound of the wind is a
metonymy. What Binswanger calls 'the self-protection of the
existence' is represented in Le Fanu by the domestic interior. Le
Fanu is very interested in furniture. Most of it is a good deal more
substantial and elaborate than this, but its function in the stories
in general does not differ from that of this 'shutter and curtain': to
shut fear out, or sometimes in. Its solidity and weight stands for
that of the protagonists, for their status in the world and their confidence of its continuance; for their initial or outward certainties,
and against the past, retribution, moral debt. Furniture: great curtained beds, deep winged chairs, wainscot and wooden panelling,
ponderous oak or mahogany dressing-chests, and old family portraits. All are at once possessions and signs of their owners' claim
to permanence and control, and all become the ground of the undoing of control and the mocking of permanence.

Nearly all Le Fanu's protagonists are inhabitants of a time which
the reader can call the past — typically the eighteenth, but sometimes
the seventeenth century — and they are also almost invariably
members of the landed gentry. But in their emphasis on domestic
interiors the stories carry very definitely the impression of their contemporary readers', rather than their characters', social context.
The original possessors of those great beds and chests and ancestors'
portraits did not need to have them so obsessively noticed and
described; they are there for the Victorian middle-class reader, for
whom the domestic interior had a particular importance, as noted
by Walter Benjamin in his essay 'Louis Philippe or the Interior'.
Discussing the period beginning with 1830, he says:

For the private citizen, for the first time the living-space became
distinguished from the place of work. The former constituted itself as the

ʋ

interior. The office was its complement. The private citizen who in the office took reality into account, required of the interior that it should support him in his illusions . . . From this sprang the phantasmagorias of the interior. This represented the universe for the private citizen. In it he assembled the distant in space and in time . . . The interior was not only the private citizen's universe, it was also his casing. Living means leaving traces. In the interior, these were stressed. Coverings and antimacassars, boxes and casings, were devised in abundance, in which the traces of everyday objects were moulded. The resident's own traces were also moulded in the interior. The detective story appeared, which investigated these traces . . .[11]

At first glance the interiors in Le Fanu seem no more than a canny move to satisfy this bourgeois taste for grand antiques and 'pieces'. This is a deceptive impression. It can be shown that Le Fanu's interiors are as far as possible from mere decor. They have been fabricated for subversive purposes. (Max Ernst's delightful 'novel in collage', *Une Semaine de Bonté* (1934), with its grand rooms in which skeletons and monsters of equivocal gender and species ooze and peer out of heavy plush sofas and from behind brocade hangings, provides an analogy to this subversion.)

In the hall was placed, as was customary in those times, the sedan-chair which the master of the house occasionally used, covered with stamped leather, and studded with gilt nails, and with its red silk blinds down. In this case, the doors of this old-fashioned conveyance were locked, the windows up, and . . . the blinds down, but not so closely that the curious child could not peep underneath one of them, and see into the interior.

(Le Fanu, 'Mr Justice Harbottle', BGS, p. 270)

What the child sees in the 'interior' of the chair is the story's retributive ghost, waiting for the appointed hour of the judge's death, presumably in order — fittingly enough — to carry him off in his own sumptuous vehicle. Earlier in the story old Harbottle has had a grisly dream-trial while he waits, dozing in his carriage, for his drinking-companions. In both cases the terror intrudes upon him even though he has shut himself up in the security of his private domain. Neither his house nor his carriage turns out to be proof against the invasion, which lies in wait *within* the very conveyance which is the sign of his exalted status. Such heavy wooden pieces as these are rather like the symbolizing of law and conformity in another contemporary non-realistic fiction, Hawthorne's *The Scarlet Letter* (1850), by objects such as the iron-bound and studded prison-door, the brazen-clasped bible lying on its oak table, and the great suit of armour in the Governor's hall which distorts in its depths and hugely magnifies the scarlet 'A' worn by Hester Prynne.

In both cases the signs of apparent order and authority are revealed as a sham. Le Fanu's Judge Harbottle is cruel, arbitrary and corrupt, and clearly deserves his fate. The real interest of the story, however, does not lie in the moral come-uppance he gets, but rather in the projected sense of the infestation of a series of apparently secure interiors by alien energies, variously manifested.

These interiors are ostensibly domestic and material. On the level of the story, they are settings and possessions; but on the level of discourse the reader is impelled by the persistent foregrounding of what seem like mere details of decor, in tale after tale, to discover in them the trace of a theme. The concept of the interior has a domestic, but also a psychic, referent. Within is within the conscience, the mind, the consciousness, as well as within the cupboard, the chest, the bed.

The beds in Le Fanu are nearly always great curtained ones, like the one in 'Carmilla', down the length of which eerily slithers the heroine's vampire sweetheart; or the high majestic one in 'Madam Crowl's Ghost' on which the doll-like wicked old lady reclines, all dressed up to die; or the enormous one in 'Schalken the Painter' (1839) in the gloom of which the predatory figure of the plutocrat Death awaits the lovely Rose Velderkaust:

Abundance of costly furniture was disposed about the room and in one corner stood a four-post bed, with heavy black cloth curtains around it; the figure frequently turned towards him with the same arch smile; and when she came to the side of the bed, she drew the curtains, and, by the light of the lamp, which she held towards its contents, she disclosed to the horror-stricken painter, sitting bolt upright in the bed, the livid and demoniac form of Vanderhausen. (*BGS*, p. 46)

This early story brilliantly frames the problem in relations between surface and depths or appearance and reality. It is set in the studio of the seventeenth-century Dutch realist painter Gerard Douw, a highly successful painter of still-lifes, interiors and commissioned portraits. The historical Douw's pictures were famous for having a highly polished finish, a quality for which they continued to be prized until the Impressionists began to stress the uses of indeterminacy.[12] Le Fanu makes him smug about his profession and firm in his dealings with his niece: she may not marry his indigent pupil, Schalken, but must be preserved for a better match. The suitor Douw favours turns out to be Death, clinking with gold but bluishwhite about the face, presumably with putrefaction. The story shows the bourgeois solidity of Douw's paintings as the true expressive form of his acquisitiveness: and sure enough, in Schalken's horrific vision of the doomed girl in Death's chamber at the end, he finds she has led him

. . . to his infinite surprise, into what appeared to be an old-fashioned Dutch apartment, such as what the pictures of Gerard Douw have served to immortalize. (*BGS*, 46)

Earlier on, Douw has pooh-poohed Rose's objections to the ugliness of Vanderhausen-Death by reading her a moral lesson about not being taken in by mere appearances:

A man may be as ugly as the devil, and yet, if his heart and actions are good, he is worth all the pretty-faced perfumed puppies that walk the Mall. (*BGS*, p. 39)

For the reader this is full of ironies, verbal and other ('as ugly as *the devil'*): Douw proves himself to be taken in — and in part wilfully — by the most pleasant and substantial apparent good of the suitor's gold and fine clothing (a high surface polish, one might say). In the darker depths of the story, Rose is the victim of Douw's own hopeless sensual infatuation with material wealth. She is the price paid by Douw for his financial security. Her horrified lover, Schalken, is the author's stalking-horse, innocent and powerless witness of the business.

Le Fanu opens the story with the description of a painting, which the narrator says is the record of Schalken's haunted vision. This picture is double, like all pictures: a representation *of* something, but also an object, part of the furnishings, a family heirloom of the narrator's. The events of the *fabula* (story) are framed within this painting, unfolding from it and leading back to it at the end. Thus there are two descriptions of Rose, smiling and silent. Veiled and carrying a lamp, like a Truth-figure in traditional iconography, she leads Schalken towards the dreadful vision in the church crypt, which is itself done up like a Douw painting. But by the end the image of Rose, Schalken and the bridegroom Death has ceased to be a flat, possessable thing: the initial tableau with figures, complete with coyly mysterious gesture, has been invested with an intense and terrifying alien energy:

By the light of the lamp . . . she disclosed . . . the livid and demoniac form of Vanderhausen. (*BGS*, p. 46)

Just as death waits inside the curtained bed, so, as often in these tales, the images apparently safely fixed on canvas can take on a power related in some obscure way to the past, either of the individual or of history, and return upon the protagonist.[13] At the very beginning of 'Schalken' the narrator talks urbanely about 'the curious management of lights' as 'the chief apparent merit' of the painting, but adds:

I say *apparent*, for in its subject, not in its handling, however exquisite, consists its real value. (*BGS*, p. 29)

And from then on the tone alters from suavity to intense horror, as the detached 'pleasure in lights', or in fine surface gloss, is peeled away.

In Le Fanu the large-scale horrors of Gothic, the Gothic of Maturin, Lewis or Radcliffe, are absent. Terror in his work is a domestic matter, usually set back, to be sure, by a couple of generations, and mostly located in the countryside, whether of Ireland or Cumberland, but without the cosmic sweep of *Melmoth the Wanderer*, and eschewing exoticism of setting. The strangeness in his work is achieved by other means, and has largely different effects or purposes: it is to be met, as we have seen, inside the house, beneath the apparently straightforward surface and within the self.

This invasion may come from within, like the ghost sitting in the sedan-chair, or it may break or creep in from without by rationally inexplicable means. Another of the forms it takes is what Binswanger calls 'the unwonted recurrence of the similar', as in the motif of the double. The motif or device of the double has a long history in the tale-telling of many periods, but in its modern forms the tradition was instituted in German literature at the end of the eighteenth century; the word *doppelganger* was coined to name it by Jean Paul Richter. The double motif can take various forms.[14] The best known is that in which a character encounters a person exactly resembling him, but apparently with another quite independent existence. If one can isolate the main idea underlying the motif in its nineteenth-century versions, it is perhaps that the self is non-unitary and does not therefore present a single smooth surface to experience. This basic and highly subversive notion is usually masked or framed by an ethical motivation of the double's appearances and influence — as for instance in the case of the conscience-double, which accuses and retributively hangs about the protagonist — but it remains deeply disturbing to realist characterization, which depends on the notions of coherent and progressive personality development and full moral consciousness. The concept of the double has been suggestively compared to the hypothesis of the 'sleeping-soul', considered by Locke: that a man's complete unconsciousness of this thought while asleep may make him in effect into two separate entities.[15] Locke decisively rejects the idea of such a profound difference existing within the personality, but its close relationship to the fundamental hypotheses of psychoanalysis is obvious. The conscience-double, the gruesome phantom-double, and the Mephistophelean sidekick-double all embody the unsettling notion that whether by wickedness, or suffering, or as a result of a moment of inattention to some social or moral taboo, the self may undergo a process of fragmentation, and be ever after impossible to reunify. There is a brilliant social variant of this essentially psychological motif in Dostoevsky's early novel *The Double* (1846), which anatomizes the condition of rationalized bureaucratic man in the city. Wilde combined the legend of eternal youth with a double motif in *The Picture of Dorian Gray* (1891). Le Fanu shows interest in several varieties of doubling, with a particular emphasis on sibling- or cousin-doubling, on the Faust-Mephistopheles type, and on phantom doubles. His doubles are peculiar within the tradition of the motif in being often complementary halves of a notional pair rather than the more usual mirror-images; but they are perhaps all the more eerie for that. (He does have one highly effective use of the similar and supplanting double: in 'Mr Justice Harbottle', when the wicked judge is given a dream-trial and condemned by a dream-judge called Chief Justice Twofold.) Le Fanu's repeated use of doubles within the family — whether contemporary, or extended by the deployment of revivified ancestors, such as Carmilla — again reveals his stress on domesticity, and may even recall the Freudian emphasis on the family as ground for legendary reenactments. The first modern masters of the motif, Hoffmann, and Chamisso, were fond of using the shadow — also a folktale motif — or the reflection in a mirror as doubles. Le Fanu shows some suggestive traces of this, too; there is a very eerie one at the end of 'The Drunkard's Dream'. The drunkard's wife sees, on the night of her husband's death,

two persons, one of whom she recognized as her husband, noiselessly gliding out of the room. (*GSM*, p. 173)

The narrator suggests it may have been his shadow,

but she told me that the unknown person had been considerably in advance of the other, and on reaching the door, had turned back to reveal something to his companion . . . (*GSM*, p. 173)

What he reveals is presumably the way to the other world. This seems to draw on the primitive idea of the soul-double, as the

wraith or visible counterpart of the person, seen just before or just after, or at the moment of, his death.[16]

The double as used in nineteenth-century literature might be called, then, a submerged unconscious part of the personality; or sometimes

the insubstantial shadow of the truth, which a man prefers to reality.[17]

In Justinus Kerner (the 'ghost-craftsman' paraphrased extensively by Mangan in the *Dublin University Magazine*) it is used to embody 'the essential truth of affinity, of the predestined marriage of like souls'.[18] But what in Kerner is positive and uplifting, suggesting a cosmic harmony, in Le Fanu can combine desire and destruction. In 'Carmilla' (1872), which we shall consider at more length, the fairhaired Laura is wooed and preyed upon by the darkhaired vampire Carmilla. But though Carmilla is seen at story level to arrive from somewhere else — ostensibly — to the reader the elsewhere she represents is a hidden Other within the heroine and her father's house. She turns out to be the original of an old family portrait (a favourite motif of Le Fanu's) and she woos the innocent and bemused Laura with the promise of a common and mutual transformation in being:

> 'You are afraid to die?'
> 'Yes, everyone is.'
> 'But to die as lovers may — to die together, so that they may live together. Girls are caterpillars while they live in the world, to be finally butterflies when the summer comes; but in the meantime there are grubs and larvae, don't you see — each with their peculiar propensities, necessities and structure. So says Monsieur Buffon, in his big book, in the next room.'                                                          (*BGS*, p. 297)

Carmilla is the Other of desire. This is rare in Le Fanu; his other treatments of demonic-lover plots — such as 'Laura Silver Bell' or 'Ultor de Lacy' — do not attempt to show the lover to the *reader* as tempting, only to the object of seduction; in fact he goes out of his way to make those devil-figures clearly repulsive, and to show the victims as bewitched. The explanation for the extraordinary vividness and power of the character of Carmilla — unsatisfactory as her motivation would be if this were formal realism — may lie in Le Fanu's adaptation here of the *doppelganger* motif.

Carmilla is of an age with the heroine. They share, and have shared before Carmilla arrived, the same dreams. They do not resemble each other physically, but are presented as like two halves of a pair: Carmilla's dark colouring is the pendent to Laura's fairness, her vivacity to Laura's meekness: and her predatory nature to Laura's submissive one. It is never made clear in the story whether Carmilla is conscious of her vampire being; there are hints that she well understands it and is deceitful and cunning, and also indications that she is quite unaware of it, and is its prisoner. This uncertainty is one of the finest effects in the tale, and raises it well above the normal crude simplicity of vampire plots. It would seem that what Le Fanu is investigating is the recesses of consciousness; Carmilla and Laura are twin fragments of a complete personality, which it is somehow difficult to join or keep together. This effect recalls the lost shadows and reflections of the German Romantic writers: the reflection, for instance, which, in Hoffmann's story 'The Lost Reflection', the hero Erasmus Spikker leaves behind in sunny sensuous Italy with the demonic lover Giulietta while he goes back to his wife and baby in Germany. The point is that Carmilla stands for the suppressed, or perhaps unrealized, half of Laura. The story frames reality within unreality: because of the apparent remoteness from everyday social life of the supernatural and particularly of the vampire tale, Le Fanu could give Carmilla's seduction speeches an extraordinary directness. The sexual pleasure she promises to Laura involves an exquisite mutual yielding up of consciousness. This is to enable the metamorphosis from grub to butterfly: a clear metaphor for the attainment of adulthood, the state Laura, motherless and childishly dependent on her father, fights shy of. Pursuing this strand of interpretation, one might find that to give herself over to Carmilla's desires and learn to share them is Laura's best bet. One might, that is, but for the cross-strand which links Carmilla on the other hand to death, and makes 'when the summer comes' a moment in the other world. It is revealed at the dénouement that such moments are chimerical, and that the reality of Carmilla in her tomb is as follows:

The limbs were perfectly flexible, the flesh elastic; and the leaden coffin floated with blood, in which to a depth of seven inches, the body lay immersed.                                                                                                  (*BGS*, p. 336)

The peculiar version of the double motif which Le Fanu sets up in 'Carmilla' can be paralleled elsewhere among the stories. In 'Ultor de Lacy' there are two sisters: one fair, one dark; one saved, the other doomed to a demon lover (this time male, but also, like Carmilla, of the race of historical ghosts). The saved one, Alice, has nocturnal visions of the seduction of the doomed one, Una. When she confesses her fears, Una replies dismissively:

'Dreams, Alice. My dreams crossing your brain; only dreams, dreams. Get you to bed, and sleep.'                                                                                            (*BGS*, p. 464)

In 'The Haunted Baronet', the protagonist, Sir Bale Mardyke, has a kind of double in his kinsman Philip Feltram, illegitimate descendant of a woman wronged by an earlier Mardyke. In the course of the story the weakling Philip finds the strength, by means of an uncanny communicating with the past, to reverse Sir Bale's initial domination of him. Bale and Philip, like Laura and Carmilla, appear to the reader as two halves of a self which have somehow come adrift from each other: feeling and yielding in Philip, harshness and moral stupidity in Bale.

There is also another kind of unfixing of the bounds of the self in 'The Haunted Baronet'. At the beginning of the story there is a frame-passage set in the local village inn, all good English cheer and honest country folk. The wronged and drowned woman of a past generation is alluded to, but it is never made quite clear that the wrong really does belong to the past: the present Sir Bale seems to carry in the people's mind the guilt associated with his ancestor's evil deed. It seems that he is not quite fully an individual, but as well as being himself, in some sense *is* also his ancestor.

The two cousins in 'The Murdered Cousin' (1838) represent a variation on the double-motif: one girl is murdered by the villains in mistake for the other. This sinister and intriguing device was, significantly, dropped by Le Fanu in the later, more famous and more sentimental version, *Uncle Silas*. It is suggestively similar to the dénouement of 'Carmilla', in which also one half of a notional composite self must be sacrificed for the life of the other.

There are other Le Fanu stories which adapt rather differently the *doppelganger* motif, notably 'The Familiar' and 'Green Tea' (1869). Both are among Le Fanu's most skilled and brilliant work, both set in cities and in or near the present of narrator and original readers. This, especially 'Green Tea' (which uses Swedenborgian material) is as near as Le Fanu comes to a version of the motif which would explore the psychology of doubling at an individual level, in the characterization, in the realist manner.

Normally in his haunting-tales there is a large gap between the understanding of the characters, at story level, and that of the reader-narrator couple: if we take 'Carmilla' as an example, we can say that Laura and her father can only interpret the events of the story as a demonstration of the existence of vampires, whereas it is open to the reader to construe the material more metaphorically and find other, quite different meanings in it: that the Carmilla figure embodies Laura's fear of maturity, for instance, and that though Laura (the narrator) is quite unconscious of the fact, Carmilla represents a part of her, Laura's, self. In these stories it is as if the psychology of the protagonist is objectified, whether in a double-motif of some kind, or in the domestic interior, or, as we shall see, in the landscape. Le Fanu shows little interest in producing the effect of depth, or interiority, in characterization; his haunted characters do not reflect on their condition, or if they do we are not told about it. Instead their whole houses, or demesnes, become the ground of their inner conflicts, the stages of which are represented by haunting-episodes of growing intensity. A classic example of this is 'Squire Toby's Will', in which the protagonist has cut his elder brother off from his inheritance and is haunted by a type of conscience-double, in the shape of a dog, which attaches itself to him and follows him everywhere. Finally he has it shot by his gamekeeper. On story level, to him and his servants, the dog resembles his dead father, who thus seems to be accusing him; but to the reader, it seems the embodiment of the guilt he feels but will not acknowledge.

In Le Fanu the past, both personal and historical, leaves stains or traces in the world, or in our consciousness of the world (two things not easy to separate). Such traces are initially encountered as a residue, but actively lead back into that past. This is the case in 'Sir Dominick's Bargain' (1872), in which the 'rusty stain in the plaster of the wall's is made the starting-point of the story, which thus reverses the normal chronology and gives the ending first.

'Do you mind that mark, sir?' he asked . . .
'That's about seven or eight feet from the ground, sir, and you'll not guess what it is.'
'I dare say not', said I, 'unless it is a stain from the weather.'
' 'Tis nothing so lucky, sir,' he answered . . .     (*BGS*, p. 433)

And so the story is unfolded by the 'sharp-featured man' first encountered 'in the dark recess, deep in the shadow' of the castle window, as flashback from the present time of the detached frame-narrator who is an English visitor on business in rural Ireland. 'The Haunted Baronet' provides another more striking version of this stain-motif. The unwilling but desperate Sir Bale crosses the lake to seek the man he thinks is a gipsy fortune-teller. He is told he will find his way through the woods by scrutinizing the surface of a

broad druidic stone, that stood like a cyclopean table on its sunken stone props, before the snakelike roots of the oak.     (*BGS*, 133)

When he carries out the instructions and stares at the stone

it seemed not as if a shadow fell upon the stone, but rather as if the stone became semi-transparent, and just under its surface was something dark — a hand, he thought it — and darker and darker it grew, as if coming up towards the surface, and after some little wavering, it fixed itself move-lessly, pointing, as he thought, towards the forest.     (*BGS*, 135)

Perception has the task of interpreting such scars and traces. In 'Ultor de Lacy' (1861) the sardonic demon wooer can dematerialize before one's glance, passing back into the ancient building he inhabits: figure becoming one with ground, which means that ground must hold figure always eerily *in potentia*:

As Larry gazed, the figure somehow dissolved and broke up without receding. A hanging tuft of yellow and red ivy nodded queerly in place of the face, some broken and discoloured masonry in perspective took up the outline and colouring of the arms and figure, and two imperfect red and yellow lichen streaks carried out the curved tracing of the long spindle shanks. Larry blessed himself, and drew his hand across his damp forehead, over his bewildered eyes, and could not speak for a minute. It was all some devilish trick; he could take his oath he saw every feature in the fellow's face, the lace and buttons of his cloak and doublet, and even his long finger nails and thin yellow fingers that overhung the cross-shaft of the window, where there was nothing but a rusty stain left.

(*BGS*, p. 456)

Earlier in the story, the reverse happens: the apparently quite real castle fades away in the moonlight when the bewildered priest tries to visit it.

At last, sure enough, he saw the castle plain as plain could be . . . but when he emerged at the top, there was nothing but the bare heath . . . In a few minutes more he was quite close, all of a sudden, to the great front, rising gray and dim in the feeble light, and not till he could have struck it with his good oak 'wattle' did he discover it to be only one of those wild, gray frontages of living rock that rise here and there in picturesque tiers along the slopes of these solitary mountains.      (*BGS*, p. 452)

But for the tone, this would resemble nothing so much as Lewis Carroll's 'Mad Gardener's Songs' ('he looked again, and found it was a hippopotamus'), another apparently naive Victorian 'alternative' text.

But though the disappearing castle and the appearing ghost are motivated (sketchily, as usual, at the end) as historical retribution, the interest of such spellbinding moments in these stories surely does not lie in such motivation. When their editor, E. F. Bleiler (everywhere else a sensitive commentator) says they contain

a hidden, often diabolic morality, that will suffer evil to go unavenged or unbetrayed      (*BGS*, 'Introduction', p. viii)

he reverses the real interest of the matter. The numinous Other in nature and the past — the final motif we shall identify — usually functions retributively, it is true, at the level of *fabula* (story material). The haunted protagonists *are* evil, in the majority of cases. But the reader of more than one or two stories quickly sees that the working out of each individual damnation is hardly the point. Le Fanu's many repetitions of the same story-material confirm this perception; M. R. James was quite right to say that whatever the cause of such repetition, it was not poverty of invention.[19] The pleasure in the reading comes rather from the perception of larger patterns of psychic investigation than from the moralization of phantoms.

Le Fanu's construction of the Other in landscape and history owes a good deal to the influence of folklore, and is best examined by starting from the 1870 'Stories of Lough Guir'. This piece opens with a prefatory reminiscence by the narrator, in which he recounts his first hearing of the tales. The structure of this reminiscence is important: it presents the past as three successive levels, in a pattern strikingly replicated at least twice more in these stories. The most recent stratum is that of the writer's boyhood, when he says he first heard the stories, from a named source, Miss Anne Baily. The second is that of the Whig and convivial past of the Baily family, as implied by the great drinking-cup, engraved 'the glorious, pious, and immortal memory'. The third stratum is that of the Earl of Desmond, paradigm of the old ruined Norman-Irish aristocracy whose rule was supplanted by the English claim to sovereignty.

In his folklore existence this Earl subsumes at least two, and probably more, figures from actual history (the chief two are Gearoid Iarla, the fourteenth-century Desmond who is also an important Irish poet, and the last Earl, around whom gathered the resistance in Munster to the Elizabethan conquest of Ireland).[20] It appears at first that Le Fanu was evidently thinking of this last Earl, because he describes the castle beside the lake as

a stronghold of the last rebellious Earl of Desmond, which defied the army of the lord deputy . . .                                        (*GSM*, p. 145)

Yet the stories he then retells concern the Earl as a magical and otherworldly figure; the recession through the three stages of the past leads not just from his own childhood in this countryside to the 1688 Revolution, and thence to the Tudor conquest, but farther back, to a landscape from which the action of history has been elided.

The lake is the central symbol of this group of stories:

And beneath its waters lie enchanted, the grand old castle of the Desmonds, the great earl himself, his beautiful young countess, and all the retinue that surrounded him in the years of his splendour, and at the moment of his catastrophe.                                        (*GSM*, p. 145)

Out of those waters, it is said, he can emerge every seven years and attempt converse with the human world. The 'catastrophe' here mentioned is identified in this frame-narration as that of Desmond's political and military defeat; but within the first of the tales themselves, 'The Magician Earl', a quite different version is given, in which his imprisonment within the lake waters has been caused by his necromancy. Thus the reader is left with two incompatible versions of events, one history, one romance. Irish history being the echo-chamber it is, all this must, of course, have implications for Le Fanu's own political position, since, as Disraeli puts it in *Sybil*, ruins are 'the children of violence, not of time' and the picturesque is the Siamese twin of politics; but it is not as easy as it might initially seem to work out these implications.[21] It is not my intention here to try, but I shall point out that the 'Stories of Lough Guir' taken in its totality, frame-passages and all, does preserve both versions without deciding between them: in Le Fanu, hauntings take place apparently for preference in the best-furnished houses, and the past is always returning, usually retributively, on the present.

The threefold layering of the past which opens 'Lough Guir' strongly suggests a homologous layering of the self and of the landscape. We find it again in 'The White Cat of Drumguinniol' (1870), where, once again at the threshold of the *fabula* (which concerns the retributive haunting of a family by the ghost of a wronged woman), the reader's eye is led along the scenery, through personal childhood memory ('I have myself seen') and historical reference (the rapparees), to an otherworld entrance (the liss):

I have myself seen the old farm-house, with its orchard of huge mossgrown apple trees. I have looked round on the peculiar landscape; the roofless, ivied tower, that two hundred years before had afforded a refuge from raid and rapparee, and which still occupies its old place in the angle of the haggard; the bush-grown 'liss', that scarcely a hundred and fifty steps away records the labours of a bygone race . . . (*BGS*, p. 409)

In this dream-vivid landscape (which is always the same one, lovingly reconstructed over and over again in Le Fanu's stories) everything is encrusted, the trees 'mossy', the tower 'ivied', the liss 'bush-grown'. But these sedimentary layers, too, can be penetrated, as can those of the personal and historical forgetfulness whose action they mime, and as can the thick coverings and concealments of plush and tapestry and oak chests. The feline ghost (perhaps an albino double of Poe's contemporary black cat, who also likes to sit on dead men's faces) recurs through the generations and it seems cannot be eluded, even by the innocent.

The other place where this recession into time and space is rehearsed is in 'The Haunted Baronet', a story I have already mentioned in connection with the double motif. Several of Le Fanu's most important motifs are so skilfully interwoven in this story that it is difficult to unpick its fabric sufficiently to trace any one; so the discussion of landscape and memory will involve us again in traces, doubles and shadows.

When Sir Bale needs reliable racing tips, and ready cash with which to bet in order to save his estates, his half-double, half-sibling Philip Feltram leads him, as we have seen, to a source of both. To get there Bale must cross the lake and enter the forest. This forest, which is usually of aboriginal oak, makes repeated appearances in Le Fanu.[22] Sometimes it has suffered or is suffering denudation, which is the result and sign of evil-doing of some kind.[23] Many of these forests contain — are — the forest of the past. Sir Bale's version is the abode allegedly of the gipsy[24] but in fact of the malevolent ancestor who thereafter haunts him and is (once again, *to the reader*) a version of himself. Even before Bale's wife polishes up the old portraits near the end of the story and reveals this ancestor, he is throughout described as if he partook of an existence in some other dimension: part-human, part-avian predator.

To reach the forest Sir Bale must cross the lake. This he is extremely reluctant to do, for reasons he does not state in so many words, but which to the reader are both clear and full of metaphorical implication. The village people believed the lake is haunted by the drowned woman; but to Bale it represents another kind of barrier: he has not visited the woods on the far side since childhood, when they were his playground. His adult life has (outside the bounds of the story, as always in Le Fanu) been one of profligacy, dissipation and brutality; the crossing of the lake constitutes a confrontation with that earlier, innocent self, and hence within the landscape of Sir Bale's psyche it is truly a haunted and fearful place. Here again the personal and the ancestral past are made to coincide, as are the outer and inner scenery. When eventually he is forced by his pressing debts to make the journey, the landscape prompts in him an outpouring of reminiscence:

He looked round him as if in a dream. He had not been there since his childhood. There were no regrets, no sentiment, no remorse; only an odd return of the associations and fresh feelings of boyhood, and a long reach of time suddenly annihilated. The little hollow in which he stood; the three hawthorn trees at his right; every crease and undulation of the sward, every angle and crack in the lichen-covered rock at his feet, recurred with a sharp and instantaneous recognition to his memory.

'Many a time your brother and I fished for hours together from that back there, just where the bramble grows. That bramble has not grown an inch since, not a leaf altered . . .'                              (*BGS*, p. 131)

This hints that crossing the lake has led Bale into another dimension: a place which is changeless. In Irish folklore, lakes, like caves in hills, are frequently seen as otherworld entrances. Throughout 'The Haunted Baronet', the lake seems to Bale to menace him: he feels imprisoned in this ancestral landscape:

'There's nothing so gloomy as a lake pent up among barren mountains . . . We fancy the shore must look very pretty from a boat; and when we try it, we find we have only got down into a pit and can see nothing rightly. For my part, I hate boating, and I hate the water; and I'd rather have my house . . . at the edge of a moss . . . and an open horizon . . . then be suffocated among impassable mountains, or upset in a black lake and drowned like a kitten . . .'                       (*BGS*, p. 74)

For Philip, by contrast, the lake becomes a source of energy: he returns from his near-drowning in it as a changed man, who seems to have been invested with uncanny powers. After this event, when Bale sees him one evening standing on the steps of the house, in the evening sun, he is

throwing a long shadow that was lost in the lake.        (*BGS*, p. 129)

— a shadow that connects him with the other world of whose existence he now partakes, and to which he eventually brings Bale, through the agency of their common ancestor. When Bale asks him who is the source of the money he suddenly has to lend, he replies:

'A friend, who is — *myself.*'
'Yourself! Then it is yours — *you* lend it?' . . .
'Myself, and not myself,' said Feltram oracularly; 'as like as voice and echo, man and shadow.'                          (*BGS*, p. 118)

The lake in this story is a repository of the past and of guilt, inherited ancestrally and also perhaps incurred individually, though this is not clear. Together with the ancient house beside it, the fells surrounding it and the forest at the other, magical side of it, the lake forms the focus of the reader's and the narrator's attention. This landscape symbolically objectifies human consciousness; in it all the fragments of the Mardyke family are unified: Sir Bale, thinking himself safe behind the wainscot and stone of the great house; his malevolent ancestor, waiting within the forest and on the old canvas to be released into power; and Philip, who goes to encounter, within the lake waters, the slighted woman from whom he is descended. He undergoes there a transformation, fulfilling the prediction that he will 'but go in weakness to return in power (*BGS*, p. 94). This is evidently an inspired metamorphosis in Le Fanu's imagination of the Earl of Desmond's folklore life in the otherworld beneath Lough Guir. He, too, has undergone a transformation, and his life beneath the lake is structurally analogous to all those states of strangeness within the everyday which one encounters in various guises everywhere in Le Fanu: the Swedenborgian realm of the newly dead in *Uncle Silas*; the 'summer' of 'Carmilla' in which girls shall be butterflies; the aural wraith-life of Una de Lacy after her departure with her demon-lover (when she has dwindled to a voice singing in the glen). Those depths of the past and the Other are so profound, but also so completely subject to the laws of human history, that even the sound-stain of this ghost-voice will eventually wear away:

The apparition has long ceased. But it is said that now and again, perhaps once in two or three years, late on a summer night, you may hear — but faint and far away in the recesses of the glen — the sweet, sad notes of Una's voice, singing those plaintive melodies. This, too, of course, in time will cease, and all be forgotten.                           (*BGS*, p. 465)

Le Fanu's stories are haunted, then, not by phantoms from the realm of metaphysics, but by the various projections of otherness within the complexity of personality. Far from being amused essays in a trivial genre, they are forerunners of the revolutionary hypotheses of twentieth-century thought about human identity; forceful intimations of 'the element of darkness' described by Foucault as 'the unthought', revelations of the 'obscure space' in man, a tracing of 'the blind stain by which it is possible to know him'.

# NATIONAL CHARACTER AND NATIONAL AUDIENCE: RACES, CROWDS AND READERS

SEAMUS DEANE

'English literary history was shaped by the need for a definition of the superiority of the national character.'[1] This was true in the eighteenth century, when the first full-scale attempt to provide such a history was undertaken by Thomas Warton in his *The History of English Poetry* (1774–81). In that confused and confusing work, Warton chides the poets of the past for having failed to adhere to the linguistic norm of his own time; but he also regrets the disappearance of a society which, with its 'customs, institutions, traditions, and religion' was 'favorable to poetry'.[2] The first attempt at an Irish literary history, Douglas Hyde's *A Literary History of Ireland from the Earliest Times to the Present Day* (1899), is also concerned to distinguish between a nourishing Celtic past which was equally favourable to poetry and the impoverishing Anglicized present. Hyde's history restricts itself to the Gaelic language and has to accommodate itself to an internalised patriotism which opposes the 'Irish-speaking population . . . who . . . have . . . a remarkable command of language and a large store of traditional literature learned by heart' to the 'anglicized products of the National Schools'. To the bulk of the latter, in Hyde's view, 'poetry is an unknown term' and amongst them 'there exists little or no trace of traditional Irish feelings, or indeed seldom of any feelings save those prompted by (when they read it) a weekly newspaper'.[3] Between Warton and Hyde, the relationship which bound national character to language and literature had intensified as the political consequences of romantic nationalism ramified throughout Europe. In almost all the literature of nineteenth century Ireland, national character and the appeal of its various embodiments to a new national audience, is a constant refrain. Maria Edgeworth, Lady Morgan, Thomas Moore, Gerald Griffin, the Banim brothers, Mrs. Hall, William Carleton, Father Prout, William Maginn,

40

Somerville and Ross, the Young Irelanders, Standish O'Grady, the young Yeats, and Shaw (generally throughout his career as a professional Irishman, and specifically in *John Bull's Other Island*), all give it prominence.[4] It is important, however, that they tend to think of its fullest embodiments as belonging to the historical past (before 1782, before the rise of O'Connell, before the tithe war, before the coming of Christianity, of the Normans, of the English, before the Famine or the National Schools) or to a cultural recess (by remaining illiterate, ignorant of machinery, or of the law or of contemporary developments in any number of fields). Warton provides an early gloss on this species of appreciative condescension:

Ignorance and superstition, so opposite to the real interests of human society, are the parents of imagination.[5]

In Ireland, because of the vertical and horizontal divisions of creed, class, political affiliation and language, the idea of national character had to be either very flexible or very bland if it was to be inclusive; otherwise, it could only assert its purity and integrity by restricting itself to a particular group and indicting all the excluded as traitors, foreigners, rootless cosmopolitans or, more simply, as 'Anglicized'. Yeats often railed against this insularity when it involved the exclusion of people on grounds of political affiliation or religion, but it troubled him less to find it made on the basis of race or class. In his project for the 'Library of Ireland' he faced two problems. One was the definition of an Irish literary tradition, the other was the question of whom the definition was for. Yeats wanted to create an audience by inculcating a taste for genuine literature (as opposed to popular propaganda) which would also be definitively national. This was sufficiently difficult in itself; but the difficulty was compounded by the fact that his ideal audience would have to be recruited from the Irish-speaking people who had, as Hyde saw it, culture but were largely illiterate in English, or from the English-speaking people who were literate but uncultivated. By recording the oral culture of the Irish-speakers, he was, in effect, altering, even destroying it; although his admiration for Lady Gregory and Hyde was in part stimulated by that 'needful subtle imaginative sympathy'[6] with which they told the old stories.

Let us assume, then, that the writing of literary history is, in effect, a means towards the assertion of the supremacy or uniqueness of the national character and that it is therefore directed towards a specific audience which is in part created by such a literary history and is also in part a stimulus towards it. The purpose of such writing is fundamentally political. In the case of eighteenth century England, the aim of Warton (and of his many predecessors, particularly Dryden) was the validation, in literary terms, of England's claim to liberty. Thus, the extravagance of Shakespeare, Spenser and others was a typically English reaction to the hide-bound rules and prescriptions which governed the practice of more despotic and less fortunate nations.[7] Yet literary history, even when it is as miscellaneously compiled as Warton's, always has a teleological bias. This usually involves the writer in the claim that everything which came before culminated in the present; or that everything that came before would culminate in a future which would soon replace the dilapidated present. Thus Warton found it difficult to see Pope as a poet in the sense that Spenser was one; but equally he found it impossible to see Spenser as the exponent of an ideal linguistic norm, such as Pope represented. His confusions and indecisiveness are notorious; it is small wonder he did not complete the fourth volume of his work. But we may speculate now that one reason for his difficulty lay in his anxiety to demonstrate a theme of liberty for which the literary analogue was exuberant or extravagant language, and the consequent discovery that the orderly and polished language of Pope in particular seemed to make a nonsense of this demonstration.[8] So his literary judgement was governed by a political aim. It was a consciously pursued aim. Since Dryden's *Essay on Dramatic Poesy* (1688), it had been standard to depict English literature as a natural expression of the love of liberty characteristic of the English national character. The most famous contemporary political pamphlet which embodies this set of attitudes is John 'Estimate' Brown's, *An Estimate of the Manners and Principles of the Time* (1757, three editions in first year). Only a Coleridge, with his idea of a universal history of Poetry as such (not as the product of a nation or region) objected to Warton's premises — and, of course, with Coleridge it remained no more than an idea.[9]

In nineteenth and twentieth century Ireland, Hyde's literary history serves as a paradigm of the virtue attributed to national character. The Gaelic civilisation (which charmed Hyde as much as early English poetry charmed Warton) was taken to manifest a theme which it was the obligation of the present to revive. That theme was 'culture', a characteristic Victorian preoccupation translated into the service of a new myth. The Irish had it, the English and the Anglicized had not. The proof was in the language and in the sensibility which that language had helped to preserve. Therefore, the comparatively recent English-language past in literature could be deemed an aberration from the true path of Irish development, just as, in English literature, it was by then possible to think of the Augustans as an aberration from the great tradition of the Renaissance and the Romantics. The Irish situation was different, of course, in that the national character had taken a very severe beating in the popular press and in the higher realms of English writing, especially fierce in the crowded Anglo-Irish crises betweeen 1798 and the fall of Parnell. The Fenian bombing campaign in England and Parnell's contemptuous speeches in the House of Commons had brought this to a point of culmination; but the story is by now well known.[10]

In the seventy years between Gerald Griffin's *The Collegians* and Hyde's *History*, the politically dominant version of national character had come full circle from the pre-Emancipation apologetics to the post-Parnell revivalism. Whereas Griffin wished to persuade his audience that the Irish were, though different in some respects, sufficiently Anglicized to deserve Emancipation, Hyde asserted the need for complete de-Anglicization so that the Irish might recover their radical uniqueness. In the interval, the Irish national character had gone through a series of portrayals and embodiments; Boucicault's braggarts, Davis's anti-utilitarian rebels, Somerville and Ross's lovable rascals, Carleton's fiery and tender peasantry, *Punch* magazine's simian neo-Darwinian barbarians, Wilde's and Shaw's ultra-rational and cosmopolitan outsider-observers and, finally, Standish O'Grady's version of the Celt which was soon to be modified into later (largely Pearsean) versions of the Gael. Absorbing and reshaping all of these was Yeats, determined to create out of all these stereotypes a version of the Irish national destiny which would culminate in the present and would reveal the coherence of the Irish tradition in letters by providing room and explanation for them all.

It is commonplace to say that the various protagonists offered to the Irish reading audience in the period between 1880 and 1920 are so many *exempla virtutis*, designed to represent various modes of abstract virtue which had a particular national signficance. Cuchulainn, Fr. Gogarty, Stephen Dedalus, the Playboy, Juno, Tone, Shaw's Caesar or St. Joan are all versions of the legendary, historical or aesthetic personage defined against a world which is in sore need of their ignored or misunderstood gifts. Yeats is, of course, the greatest creator of such exempla. They constitute the dramatis personae of his poetry and they become, in a sense, his audience, it is quite proper that they should all find themselves in the Municipal Gallery, gazing upon their creator as he gazes upon them; just as, in 'The Circus Animals' Desertion', the fictive protagonists are reviewed and their effectiveness questioned. What is striking in Yeats's protagonists is their dependence upon a proper audience. In creating them, he tries to create the audience that will receive them. It could be argued that, in failing to elicit such an audience in Ireland, Yeats transforms them into his own audience, thereby transforming himself into the greatest of all his own *exempla virtutis*.[11]

One example may show the process in operation. On 14th May, 1892, Yeats published a letter to the Editor of *United Ireland*, which began:

Sir — One windy night I saw a fisherman staggering, very drunk, about Howth Pier and shouting at somebody that he was no gentleman because he had not been educated at Trinity College, Dublin. Had he been an Englishman he would have made his definition of 'gentleman' depend on money, and if he had been not only an Englishman, but a Cockney, on the excellence of the dinner he supposed his enemy to have eaten that day. My drunken fisherman had a profound respect for the things of the mind, and yet it is highly probable that he had never read a book in his life, and that even the newspapers were almost unknown to him. He is only too typical of Ireland. The people of Ireland respect letters and read nothing. They hold the words 'poet' and 'thinker' honourable, yet buy no books. They are proud of being a more imaginative people than the English, and yet compel their own imaginative writers to seek an audience across the sea. Surely there is some cause for all this and some remedy if we could but find it.

And later, in the same letter, he goes on to say that 'some method of reaching' the Irish people must be found; the *Nation* had done so before. The need is now greater because

Ireland is between the upper and the nether millstone — between the influence of American and the influence of England, and which of the two is denationalising us most rapidly it is hard to say. Whether we have still to face a long period of struggle, or have come to the land of promise at last, we need all our central fire, all our nationality.[12]

The point about this particular fisherman is that he represents a potential audience that must be reached. Yet he also represents an ideal of culture that must be realised. Yeats tried to reach him through organised efforts like the 'Library of Ireland' and the Irish Literary Society. He tried to realise him in his poetry, by presenting him as an idealised figure, an edifying icon of unspoiled, rustic life which also represented an unsmutched imaginative purity. The poem 'The Fisherman' from *The Wild Swans at Coole* is the obvious counterstatement to the drunken fisherman of his letter to the Editor. It is, above all, a poem about audiences. The fisherman is conceived 'In scorn of this audience' which beats down the wise

and great Art, both as an ideal in himself and as the audience for
whom the poet will hereafter write. Like Maud Gonne, Lady
Gregory, Synge, Major Robert Gregory, Hugh Lane and many
others, he is the image of perfection about which Yeats writes and
for whom he writes. His subject and his audience are one. He
created in his poetry an internal audience which was similar to the
internal audience of Hyde's history. It derived from living people,
but it was itself an icon of perfect culture. They both created an
image of the audience by which they were to be perceived. This was
what came of hoping 'To write for my own race'. De-Anglicization,
or de-Nationalization could not, as policies, make the Irish into an
audience; so they turned their idealised audience into a version of
the Irish. With O'Grady, Hyde and, above all, with Yeats, the
dream of national character is finally transmuted into the
*exemplum virtutis* who is also the ideal audience. As against this
virtual audience, there is the actual public, the mass crowd which
is without culture, without interest in books, beyond the reach of
any of Yeats's redemptive organisations. The programme of *The
Nation* had finally been surrendered. Poetry could not be popular,
therefore it must become especial, addressed to

> A man who does not exist,
> A man who is but a dream;

\*

Yeats was by no means original in his attempts to create a new audience through education. Young Ireland had anticipated him in
this and it had itself been anticipated in the various early Victorian
educational projects for the renovation of the educational
system.[13] Similarly, his sponsorship of a new aristocratic ideal,
and his vision of the new class of the professional intellectual as a
clerisy which would lead the people to a realisation of this ideal,
had been widely promoted in England since the 1820's.[14] What
was new in Yeats was his determination to combine these notions
with the relatively new theories of race and religion which were fast
gaining ground from the 1880's. The theories of race allowed him
to propose a spiritual idea of Irishness shared by peasant and noble,
while the theories of religion enabled him to transcend the sectarian
divide between Protestant and Catholic by proposing an alternative form of religious belief, foreign to each but accessible to
both. Thus armed, he could make a virtue of almost anything Irish.
Economic underdevelopment ensured that in Ireland the old

intensities and beliefs of the race were more securely preserved than they could be in England. Spiritual depth was still possible in a shallow economy.

However, all of Yeats's attitudes relied for their vindication on the power of an elite to activate the consciousness of the people. In his anxiety to find a means by which this could be done, he sought for a language which would have the inwardness of the privileged group and the appeal of recognition to the slumbering mass. Such a langue had to be predominantly symbolic in its fusion of esoteric and exoteric gestures. Race had its symbols; so too did occultism. These had special meaning within the charmed circle of those who belonged, and a recognised significance among those who did not. The shamrock, the rose, the folk story, the seance, had a double appeal to the initiated and to those who were capable of becoming initiates. They constituted his audience. The symbolist movement in literature is, like the theories of race and religion, an organised system which gives privileged status to the esoteric because it believes that within the secret symbols lies a universal wisdom which will come to be recognised by those who have the ears to hear or, more likely, the memories to remember.[15] Poetry is, in such a view, a kind of seance in which certain gestures can bring, through the medium who presides, the voices of the prophetic dead to be deciphered by the entranced present. Race too is a kind of seance when it is gathered up as a concept and brooded upon by a Standish O'Grady or a Pearse. Out of their mouths come the voices of the legendary dead, Cuchulain, Colmcille and others. Yeats's heroic voices are much more numerous. Parnell, Casement, Swift join with many contemporary acquaintances and legendary borrowings in his pantheon.[16] But they are all members of that special group, that 'company of governing men',[17] who preach wisdom, redemption or apocalypse to an increasingly deaf audience.

The mutual attraction between racial and occult beliefs and the many varieties of symbolism has been observed before now,[18] but the consequences of the subsequent affairs have not been pursued with much vigour. In Yeats's case, these consequences have been viewed, by a whole range of commentators, from Conor Cruise O'Brien to Elizabeth Cullingford,[19] as separate from the question of his attempt to realise an audience in Ireland for his work. The attempt failed. The audience did not appear. Instead it rioted over Synge and O'Casey, it failed to provide Hugh Lane with the gallery he wanted, it killed Kevin O'Higgins as it had killed Parnell, it repudiated the Anglo-Irish tradition and replaced it by a system of censorship; it liked the wrong sort of plays at the Abbey, burned down the Big Houses and counted its pence and its rosaries; it turned viciously on the workers during the great lock-out of 1913; it was, simply, the lower middle-class. The heroism of 1916 was reduced by its seizure of power. It was hostile to heroic individuality, to personality; it sponsored mechanical institutions like the State, bureaucracy, the Nation, those things which were not, he said in 1937, 'worth the blade of grass God gives for the nest of the linnet'.[20] In other words, Yeats could not create an audience for his art because democracy had made the rule of the mob the law of modern life. In Burke's *Reflections on the Revolution in France*, to the rhetoric of which he is surely indebted, Yeats found the spectre of mob rule and the triumph of brutality counterposed against the traditional images of monarchy, family and the hierarchical order of chivalry. Like Burke, he appeals to an audience far removed from the unfeeling and abstract bigotries of the petit bourgeoisie, although Yeats seemed to regard these as characteristic of a cast of mind rather than of a class of people. For the moment, however, the essential point is that the domination of such an attitude or class in Ireland made the possibility of an audience remote indeed. In despair of such an audience, Yeats, in characteristically symbolist fashion, created within and for his poetry, an internal audience of exemplary figures whose virtue would appear esoteric in modern conditions but would, beyond these, have a more universal appeal. The failure of his educational project for the Irish people resulted in the creation of an alternative — a group of seers, members of an inner sect, aristocratic spiritual archetypes, a clerisy of occluded leaders — who were both audience for and subject of his meditations.

It is in this light that we should, perhaps, understand his authoritarianism. It is that of a symbolist rather than that of a Fascist or even of a Nietzschean. Mussolini and General O'Duffy were briefly admitted to his esoteric band, but they were quickly dismissed precisely because they were exponents of the idolatry of the State, not heroic individuals in themselves. There is, of course, a danger that, in saying this, we might domesticate Yeats's poetry and politics by rendering it as a fairly harmless version of the nineteenth century's chivalric ideal. He is indeed very distant from the spurious and naive posturings of those who adapted the gentlemanly ideal to patriotic or imperial purposes. Kipling and Sir Henry Newbolt are as different from him as contemporaries could possibly be. In their work, doctrines of race are guaranteed as made in and for England. Yeats's authoritarianism was of a different kind.

It was indeed, like theirs, founded on the idea of a ruling class or group for which the historical moment had come. The destiny of the English or of the Irish races, differently understood in each case, was, in effect, to introduce order where there was chaos, meaning where there was meaninglessness. But Yeats, partly, because of his Irish experience, did not find that the missionary destiny was aborted by the intensification of chaos — whether that took the form of the Somme or Passchaendale, the War of Independence, the Russian Revolution, the Irish Civil War. It was, in fact, ratified by these countervailing catastrophes. He wrote this into *A Vision* as into some of his greatest poems. It is not just a matter of acknowledging that he proposed, in his system of gyres and antinomies, the tension between Grecian presences in a Roman world or, more germanely, of Jacobite aristocrats in a Jacobin phase of history. The holy city of Byzantium and the sea that beats upon its shore are both, city and sea, emblems of something which is both other and more than either. The poet is the authoritarian of form, the producer of the 'artifice of eternity', because it is his assigned role in the theatrical conflict. To be authoritarian is his destiny; to fulfill it he must move through chaos. But words like 'form' and 'chaos' are themselves derivatives from a common source. That source is the individual self.

The 'self' in Yeats is distinct from all those versions of the psychological subject which underlie the projection of character in Victorian fiction.[21] For it is at once 'individual' and 'collective'. It is the point at which history and personality converge, where the distinction between private and public had not yet taken effect. His decision to become an Irish poet[22] enabled him to abolish the historical conditions which had given rise to the concept of the alienated self in the preceding literature. For Ireland was still a country dominated by two versions of the self — the Protestant or Ascendancy self, characterised by solitude, and the Catholic or peasant self, characterised by its collective (folk) nature. All his heroic figures, including his own various personae, either combine these versions of self, or embody one of them, or seek reconciliation between the two. The same is true of his idea of the 'company of governing men'. This elite group has the characteristics of an isolated and of a communal group. The instances are easily encountered. Maud Gonne, essentially solitary, gives herself over to a false version of the communal; Synge, another solitary, discovers a true version of community; the lonely Parnell becomes the community's uncrowned king; Cuchulainn, the embodiment of the heroic community, yields to a tragic solitude. Common to all is oscillating conflict which reproduces Ireland's internal divisions while universalising them as modes of a fundamental conflict. Race and even sectarian division are thus used to establish the form of our trouble, but are denied to have any claim on its substance. A more radical role is reserved for occultism or magic, since it contains within itself a symbolic rendering of the principles which require that conflict be the natural destiny of man. But magic too assumes the inevitability of a personal solitude which seeks to overcome itself by an investment in the communal wisdom which its rites and symbols represent and preserve. Authoritarianism, then, is not, in this context, a primitive version of fascism. It is a gesture of reconciliation, fiercer and less ironic than that term might imply, an imperative which demands that we find a balance between the individual and the collective, between solitude and community.

> I balanced all, brought all to mind,
> The years to come seemed waste of breath,
> A waste of breath the years behind
> In balance with this life, this death.
> ('An Irish Airman foresees his Death')

Yet there is no doubt that individuality might be surrendered to individualism and that community might be vulgarised into mob democracy. The authentic drama has its anti-self in inauthentic posturings. Yet in Ireland, in the early thirties, Yeats came to believe that the debased national character and its attendant vulgar symbols might be transformed by a new spiritual, charismatic leadership, represented at first by De Valera and then by General O'Duffy and finally by no one individual but only by a desire for that fusion of solitude and community which he celebrated in 'The Statues'. In 1932, he looked at the Parnell monument, and decided that it

. . . was transfigured; it was a most beautiful symbol; it had ascended out of sentimentality, out of insincere rhetoric, out of mob emotion.[23]

In this mood, as Elizabeth Cullingford has shown, he could see De Valera as the new Swift; soon after he succumbed to the belief that O'Duffy might be the new saviour; and, very soon after that notion had failed to survive a conversation with O'Duffy, Yeats extended the poem 'Parnell's Funeral' (first published 1932), to include the fourth stanza and second section in which he sees the contemporary leaders — De Valera, Cosgrave, even O'Duffy — as false inheritors of the Swift-Parnell tradition of solitude.[24] For they had been

infected by 'the contagion of the throng' and had become thereby
inauthentic. Democrat and fascist had the same educational
background, the same audience, unlike Parnell;

> Their school a crowd, his master solitude.

Yeats was dismayed to see that Fascism, rather than representing
the 'despotic rule of the educated classes',[25] stood for mob rule:

> What if the Church and the State
> Are the mob that howls at the door!
>
> ('Church and State')

All the audiences he imagined he had found or founded in Ireland
— the audience for the Irish Library, for the Irish Literary Society,
the Abbey Theatre, the National Literary Society, the 'audience
like a secret society' for his proposed 'unpopular theatre', the
audience for his late ballads, including the fascist marching songs
as well as the early 'Down by the Sally Gardens', a marching tune
of the Free State Army, 'first published with words of mine, words
that are now folklore'[26] — were the achievement as well as the
recipients of art. He quoted Victor Hugo;

A nation should be like an audience in some great theatre, — 'In the
theatre', said Victor Hugo, 'the mob becomes a people' — watching the
sacred drama of its own history.[27]

It would seem, then, that Yeats believed that art could transform
a crowd or mob into a community or people. To do so it must itself
be at once solitary and communal, aristocratic as well as
democratic, Protestant as well as Catholic. In an early formulation,
he spoke of the need to 'find an audience for whatever is excellent
in the new or the old literature of Ireland' in order to overcome a
situation in which 'one half Ireland has received everything Irish
with undiscriminating praise, and the other half with undiscriminating indifference'.[28] He wanted to educate the Irish out
of provincialism and sectarianism so that they would be prepared
to rediscover, through the agency of art, their true national
character and destiny rather than the mixture of buffoonery and
tragedy which O'Connell and Parnell, in their antithetical ways,
represented.

　　In effect, in his search for an audience, Yeats was attempting to
find some way of reconciling the Irish Catholic and Protestant
traditions in a manner which would preserve the primacy of an elite
leadership while abolishing the sectarian basis upon which it had
hitherto been justified. To stem the democratic tide of uneducated,

Catholic dominance, he sought for an alternative to that 'many-headed foam' in the notion of an Irish national character and destiny which became incarnate in heroic figures who in turn transformed the mob or crowd into a people. He failed, in most senses of the word, to find that audience. It, like his fisherman, did not exist, was but a dream. But it is the acknowledged failure of his audience in the face of heroism or apocalypse which makes his poetry so theatrically effective. The lower middle classes, the Protestant ascendancy, the Free State Government, the Blueshirts, are all failed audiences, groups that have lost the power to consolidate themselves into the needful contemporary version of the national character. As against these, are Yeats and his literary friends and sometimes his political friends — from the Fenian O'Leary to the men of 1916 to the political leaders of the new state. The nature of this internalised heroic audience determines the nature of the mob or crowd to which they are opposed and of which they are often the scapegoat victims. Thus Yeats 'discovers' audiences in his poetry which reveal the failed audiences which do not receive it. His élite is a secret society of symbolists, which finds itself misunderstood in a literal world, practitioners of magic in an empirical wilderness, those who have

> . . . understood, what none have understood,
> Those images that waken in the blood.          ('Hound Voice')

In 'The Statues', the internal audience mutates from the young men and women of the Greece of Phidias — a culture threatened by the Persian mob — to 'We Irish', faced by the failed audience of the 'filthy modern tide' and seeking to ascend the spiral gyre or staircase of history to find its proper and occult esoteric darkness in which the new art can be formed and the old enemy defeated. The national character of the Irish in this poem has become a secret discipline; 1916 is a successful seance in which Pearse invokes Cuchulain; and 1939 is the prelude to a new apocalypse in which the Irish have become the initiates into a new form of art which is also an old form of wisdom. His friends and his race are the twin poles of his audience; when he internalises them in his poems he is indicating the loss of an ideal audience in the world beyond, while still creating for his poetry the possibility of a dialogue which is, in part, for the happy and included few and which yet contains promise of ultimate rescue for the benighted and excluded many. Like the great warrior Cuchulain surrounded by the convicted

cowards in the underworld of 'Cuchulain comforted', the poet faces
the crowd and, in this other world, becomes the audience to their
song.

> They sang, but had nor human notes nor words,
> Though all was done in common as before,
>
> They had changed their throats and had the throats of birds.

# GARNERING THE FACTS: UNRELIABLE NARRATORS IN SOME PLAYS OF BRIAN FRIEL

GERALD FITZGIBBON

In his introduction to the recently-published *Selected Plays of Brian Friel* Seamus Deane has observed that Brian Friel continues to have a 'fascination with the human capacity for producing consoling fictions to make life more tolerable'.[1] The variety of these fictions offers a surprising range of challenges to the interpreter of Friel's plays.

A look at *Philadelphia, Here I Come!* illustrates the point. The emotional and dramatic crisis in that play comes when the divided hero, Gar, tries to share with his father the one memory Gar possesses of real warmth between them. Gar's sense of family bond and, by implication, his decision to emigrate to America hang on the outcome of this attempt at emotional contact with his father. Gar is the central character in the play. He is the focus of the action; his decision to emigrate is the play's key issue; he is the only character to soliloquize — even when the soliloquy is disguised as dialogue by the fact that Gar's inner and outer self are represented by two actors. In an earlier discussion between the two voices of Gar, that one memory of total happiness has been identified as the character's emotional lodestone:

Private: . . . it was an afternoon in May — oh, fifteen years ago — I don't remember every detail but some things are as vivid as can be: the boat was blue and the paint peeling . . . and you had given me your hat and had put your jacket round my shoulders because there had been a shower of rain. And you had the rod in your left hand — I can see the cork nibbled away from the butt of the rod — and maybe we had been chatting — I don't remember — it doesn't matter — but between us at that moment there was this great happiness . . .          (pp. 82–83)

By this means the play's audience, whose sympathies have already been bound to Gar by having a share in his inner life, have now been enlisted on the side of Gar's attempt at communication.

Although his relationship with his father has become difficult

53

and taciturn since then, the memory of that simple event shines out as an unique moment of past harmony between father and son. Gar recognizes this, and that the attempt to repossess that moment and authenticate its meaning in the present has the potential to undermine either his past or his future, but he is goaded forward by the restless Private self. The play has already exposed the thinness in the fabric of Gar's relations with those around him — priest, teacher, friends, girlfriend have all failed to justify the psychic investment he has made in them — so the quest for one powerful bond which would give meaning to his decision to go or stay becomes the focus of the whole action. When it comes, the result is tragicomic bathos:

Private: Now! Now! he might remember — he might . . .
Public: (*With pretended carelessness*) D'you know what kept coming into my mind the day?
S.B.: Eh?
Public: The fishing we used to do on Lough na Cloc Cor.
S.B.: (*Confused, on guard*) Oh, aye, Lough na Cloc Cor — aye — aye —

\*

Public: D'you remember the blue boat?
S.B.: A blue one, eh?
Public: I don't know who owned it. But it was blue. And the paint was peeling.
S.B.: I mind a brown one the doctor brought from somewhere up in the —
Public: (*Quickly*) It doesn't matter who owned it. It doesn't even matter that it was blue. But d'you remember one afternoon in May — we were up there — the two of us — and it must have rained because you put your jacket round my shoulders and gave me your hat —
S.B.: Aye?
Public: — and it wasn't that we were talking or anything — but suddenly you sang 'All Round My Hat I'll Wear a Green Coloured Ribbono' —
S.B.: Me?
Public: For no reason at all except that we — that you were happy. D'you remember? D'you remember?
(*There is a pause while S.B. tries to recall.*)
S.B.: No . . . no, then, I don't . . .
(*Private claps his hands in nervous mockery.*)
Private: (*Quickly*) There! There! There!
S.B.: 'All Round My Hat'? No, I don't think I ever knew that one. It wasn't 'The Flower of Sweet Strabane', was it? That was my song.
Public: It could have been. It doesn't matter.
Private: So now you know: It never happened! Ha-ha-ha-ha-ha.
S.B.: 'All Round My Hat' — that was never one of mine. . . .

(pp. 94–95)

Gar's attempt at contact is defeated, it appears, by his father's amnesia. Whatever epiphanic radiance the moment had for Gar, it clearly had none for his father, and the father's efforts at response only intensify the comic painfulness of the scene and provoke more and more scorn from the Private voice which, having prompted the confrontation in the first place, now mocks at Gar's stupidity in even attempting to communicate his feelings. The inter-action of Gar's two voices — a private voice that is mobile, inquisitive and superficially urbane; a public voice that is dull, monosyllabic and repressed — provides much of the urgency and theatrical fun in scenes that would otherwise be straightforwardly naturalistic and so allows the dramatist the luxury of emotional ambivalence. Every sentimental gesture is undercut by the voice of mocking self-consciousness. But in this scene, in the midst of the mockery, the Private voice offers the more disturbing thought: 'it never happened'. The comment could be ironic but it offers the possibility that Gar's remembered 'fact' is simply an unconscious fiction.

The import of this is not immediately clear.[2] In several earlier encounters in the play characters create blatant fictions which allow them to live with themselves: the old schoolmaster talks of the offer of a big job in a college in Boston; Gar's pals rave on about their wild, exciting, erotic adventures; Gar himself fantasises about his new life in America. But in these encounters it is invariably Gar, in one of his manifestations, who provides the voice of dispassionate 'truth'. In this final scene it is the 'truth-teller' himself who is attempting to establish a fact, however personal that fact may be. And to further emphasise the failure of this attempt, directly after that conversation the father himself tries to share with Madge, the housekeeper, *his* treasured memory of bonding with Gar:

Father: D'you mind the trouble we had keeping him at school just after he
    turned ten. . . . And he had this wee sailor suit on him this morning —
Madge: A sailor suit? He never had a sailor suit.
Father: Oh, he had, Madge. Oh, Madge, he had. I can see him, with his
    shoulders back, and the wee head up straight, and the mouth, aw man,
    as set, and says he this morning, I can hear him saying it, says he, 'I'm
    not going to school. I'm going into my daddy's business' — . . . I had
    to go with him myself, the two of us, hand in hand, as happy as larks . . .
                                     (pp. 96–97)

The rhythm of this uncharacteristic emotional revelation almost overwhelms Madge's interpolation, but there it stands: 'He never had a sailor suit' (p. 96).

It seems then that the effect of this final scene is to suggest that the key emotional 'fact' of the play — the suppressed love of Gar and his father — can find no embodiment in the details of a shared past and that the authority of Gar's perspective, so crucial to his position in the play's structure, is unreliable. The play as a whole is less about failure of communication than about the futility of the attempt; in this play experience is inescapably private and there is a treacherous difficulty in establishing any moments of genuinely shared feeling.

There is no figure directly equivalent to the Private Self of Gar to be found in any other of Brian Friel's plays, but he frequently uses narrative reminiscence as a means of exploring the different versions of reality carried by different characters. In *Aristocrats*, his most naturalistic play, based on the decline of a well-to-do family, our attention is repeatedly directed towards the divergent opinions the O'Donnell family have about themselves and each other. The play's naturalistic framework tolerates, even demands, that these views will vary from one character to another, but the progress of the play, instead of offering increasing certainty about the 'facts' from which we, the audience, can judge the individual views, progressively undermines our confidence in the possibility of establishing with certainty any facts at all. Casimir, the only one with apparently unequivocally fond and detailed memories of the old home life, reveals himself as a complete fictionaliser. His accounts of the visits of famous persons — Yeats, Chesterton, Cardinal Newman, . . . — become outlandishly coincidental; snatches of dialogue attributed to one famous personage are just as confidently transposed to another; finally, inconsistencies with the known chronology of these famous lives force Tom Hoffnung, the American academic who is trying to compile data about the family, to realize that Casimir is not the reliable source of information he had seemed to be. Even those events that fall within the present tense of the play change quite radically according to which account is heard:

Casimir: Today was almost . . . festive, by comparison, wasn't it? Every shop shut and every blind drawn; and men kneeling on their caps as the hearse passed; and Nanny sobbing her heart out . . .    (p. 309)
Casimir: Did you notice — the whole village closed down.
Alice: For the minute it took the hearse to pass through. And as Sister Therese would say: 'The multitude in the church was a little empty, too.'
Casimir: I thought the requiem mass very moving.
Alice: Until Miss Quirke cut loose. For God's sake, did nobody tell her it wasn't the wedding?    (p. 313)

The introduction of a relatively arbitrary outsider who comments on the central events — Sir in *Living Quarters*, Dodds in *The Freedom of the City*, the commentators in *Lovers* — modifies the plain naturalism of several plays. In *Aristocrats* the presence of

Tom Hoffnung — the academic researching the historical position of the Catholic big house — clearly signals that the play is at least partly concerned with the gap between the purely personal narrations and the disinterested pursuit of verifiable fact. That Hoffnung is so easily misled by the idiotic Casimir may be no more than the dramatist's mischief. It seems important, however, that Hoffnung's clumsy attempt to set Casimir straight on the historical facts provokes another character to comment that 'there are certain things, certain truths, . . . that are beyond Tom's kind of scrutiny'. On one level this may be no more than an expression of solidarity among fictionalisers but the play as a whole validates their view: that the central experience is to do with emotional tones and a partly shared family mythology rather than with anything that could be contained within the academic/intellectual concept of 'history'.

In *Faith Healer* the only vestige of such shared mythology is the ambivalent belief of the characters in Frank's 'gift'. It is a play built totally on narratives, yet the narratives cross, contradict and subvert each other continually. Frank identifies Grace as his 'mistress' and implies they were never married; Grace claims they were married, but that Frank often introduced her as if they were not; Teddy apparently believes that they are married (p. 354). Frank says nothing of Grace's still-birth, but fleetingly comments in Act IV that she was 'barren'; Grace talks of two miscarriages; both Grace and Teddy give graphic though divergent accounts of a still-birth (pp. 344–5, 362–5). All three give quite different accounts of the sequence of events leading up to Frank's death. Here the deviations on the level of fact are unmodified by any profound sense of shared purpose, even of shared faith. The variations are important. They keep the audience at a kind of judgmental distance even while the bleak tangled story invites a degree of sentimental identification. On one level all these characters share is a van, a pointless journey, and fragments of a story; on another level they share a life. They are neither enhanced nor enriched by Frank's gift; they are just bound together. If this is Friel's portrait of the artist, it is an extraordinarily bleak one.

The play that most nakedly confronts the problem of 'garnering the facts' is *The Freedom of the City*. The play is based closely on the events of Bloody Sunday in Derry, January 30, 1972, and uses at its outset a resonant contemporary image — a crouching priest holding up a white handkerchief, making his way through the gun-fire in the streets to reach the dying. This reconstructs in a dramatic context a picture that had been seen so often in newspapers and

newsreels that it had acquired in itself a certain emblematic poten-
cy. At the time public outrage intensified as the subsequent tribunal
of enquiry proceeded. So in its contemporary and local context the
play was naturally interpreted as an exposure of the process by
which political powers, through the law, give their particular fiction the authority of historical 'fact'.[3] Since then the view of the
play as being simply concerned with the gap between the human
fact and the official lie has been variously modified, most notably
in Seamus Deane's suggestion that the play splits the fictions into
two kinds:

The voice of power tells one kind of fiction — the lie . . . the voice of
powerlessness tells another kind of fiction — the illusion. (p. 18)

Yet the closer we look at it, the more it appears that the characters
do not divide as neatly as that dichotomy suggests and that the
divergent accounts show curious subtleties and gradations.

Initially the play demonstrates two stark sets of assumptions.
The judge who presides over the tribunal of enquiry, while proclaiming his open-mindedness, effectively establishes the para-
meters of possibility in his frame of reference:

The facts we garner over the coming days may indicate that the deceased
were callous terrorists who had planned to seize the Guildhall . . .; or the
facts may indicate that the misguided scheme occurred to them on that
very day while they listened to revolutionary speeches . . .
(pp. 109–110)

Shortly after this, in the dramatist's presentation of the 'actual'
events of the demonstration, one of the soldiers yells 'the fucking
yobbos are inside the fucking Guildhall' (p. 117). To the soldier, on
the day, all demonstrators are 'fucking yobbos'; to the judge they
were either 'callous' or 'misguided' — terrorists or delinquents. As
symbols of military and judicial power, both these figures are easy
dramatic targets. What suggests a darker purpose on the
dramatist's part is that the army's version is immediately enlarged
upon not merely by gossips and balladeers but also by the (RTE)
news-reporter who relays reports that 'fifty armed gunmen have
taken possession of the Guildhall' (p. 117). The play develops in a
welter of comment and speculation, each version masquerading as
an account of 'the facts', each based on false or partial information
and highly coloured by the status, function and language of the
bearer.

The extent to which the various narratives are unreliable may be
easily demonstrated by comparing any two accounts, but even

more so by examining the tonal and interpretative variations found within the different accounts by one character. The Priest is a witness who would seem to be on the side of the victims — his attempt to give them the last rites verifies this. His first formal response to the deaths is emotionally loaded. He speaks of 'numbing grief':

Priest: Why did they die? . . . They died for their beliefs. They died for their fellow citizens. They died because they could endure no longer the injuries and injustices and indignities that have been their lot for too many years. They sacrificed their lives so that you and I and thousands like us might be rid of that iniquitous yoke and might inherit a decent way of life.                                                      (p. 125)

There are no facts here, only interpretation. And by later the same day the thrust of this interpretation has changed fundamentally. Following the introductory pieties about 'numbing grief', the same question is asked. The answer is different: The 'injuries and injustices and indignities' have become 'certain imperfections in our society'; 'the iniquitous yoke' (traditional nationalist rhetoric for British domination) is no longer to blame, but 'evil' Communist infiltration of the Civil Rights movement; the three are no longer heroes but victims; most important, the resolve to 'carry on where they left off' has been replaced by a doctrine of quiescent patience: ' "Blessed are the meek for *they* shall possess the land" '.

Dodds, the academic sociologist, is cool and impartial, culturally and emotionally equidistant from the passions and the parties involved. But somehow the choric detachment fails to deliver anything resembling the events that *we*, as audience, have witnessed. The dead become part of a statistical accumulation, data for a thesis, no more than minor seismic tremors in the rumblings of a global volcano. At one point there is a glimpse of correspondence between Dodds's theory and the 'facts' we see. Commenting on the worldwide phenomenon of ghetto violence, Dodds says:

. . . once they [the people of the ghetto] become aware that their condition has counterparts elsewhere, from that moment they have broken out of their ghetto sub-culture. . . .                                        (p. 111)

Later in the play, Skinner, the most articulate, volatile and perceptive of the three in the Guildhall, explains to Lily why she was on the march:

Skinner: Because you live with eleven kids and a sick husband in two rooms that aren't fit for animals . . . Because for the first time in your life you grumbled and someone else grumbled and someone else, and you heard each other and became aware that there were hundreds, thousands, millions, millions of us all over the world, and in a vague groping way you were outraged.                                    (p. 154)

At first it seems as if Dodds's theory is receiving authentication of a kind, but despite its eloquence, Skinner's analysis is just another theory, and is soon demolished by Lily's illogical, apolitical explanation:

Lily: He's not just shy, our Declan. He's a mongol. And it's for him I go
   on all the civil rights marches. Isn't that stupid? . . . Sure I could march
   and protest from here to Dublin and sure what good would it do Declan?
                                                                  (p. 155)

Structurally and thematically this play continually juxtaposes (a) the 'actual' story of how Lily, Skinner and Michael came to be in the Guildhall, what they did there, and how they died; and (b) the multiple distortions of those events as they become enshrined in and interpreted by a wide variety of official and unofficial cultures. Of the distortions, the play most clearly indicts those of a political and judicial system that so blatantly filters, misinterprets and falsifies the evidence so that it may conform to its own vision. But none of the commentators is immune from such indictment: priest, newsman, balladeer, sociologist, expert witness, all display their own professional preoccupations and ideologies rather than their broader human sympathies.

But two other points are to be considered. The 'actual' events as presented show us that even the three central characters have no shared sense that they 'knew what they were doing' either on the march or in the Guildhall; their values, assumptions and purposes are widely divergent. The second point is that the structural design employed by the dramatist repeats on a larger scale the mode of enquiry of the tribunal he so indicts, interrogating a wider range of witnesses and imaginatively reconstructing the possible course of events. The humour, colloquiality of idiom, and apparent spon-taneity of the dialogue in the Guildhall scenes momentarily hide the dramatist's hand, but he *is* constructing an alternative fiction, for his own purposes, determined by *his* system of thought, feeling, dramatic vocabulary. And in case we missed this important dimen-sion of the play the dramatist deliberately dismantles the naturalistic basis of the central characters just before the climax of the action. At the beginning of Act Two, Lily, Skinner and Michael step forward and give their accounts of the moment of death, but they, or, rather, the actors playing the parts, speak *'calmly, without emotion, in neutral accents'* (stage direction, p. 149), and the highly individualised 'character' idioms are dropped in favour of an educated 'standard' style. The technique is reminiscent of Brecht's instructions to actors on the achievement of the 'alienation' effect and seems to have a similar end in view — that of forcefully reminding the audience of their presence in a theatre, witnessing not 'the facts' but a skilful fiction.

While he consistently exploits the emotive potential of naturalistic characterisation, Brian Friel consistently denies his audience the comfort of easy identification with the characters, or easy identification of the issues. He achieves this by repeatedly confronting audiences with divergent accounts of the 'facts' on which the plays are based, forcing them to observe the effects on any narrative of the speaker's assumptions and capacities, and undermining repeatedly any facile assumptions regarding the reliability or otherwise of witnesses. I do not think that this is, as Fintan O'Toole would have it, an exploration of 'the Catholic mind . . . a mind with no clear grasp on a positive reality',[4] a phrase which suggests that somehow there is a 'non-Catholic mind' which has no problem whatever in gaining a clear grasp on reality. Brian Friel's vision seems broader. Observation of his characters suggests that the search for absolute 'fact and reason' is futile, that no individual narrator has access to 'the truth'. Within their systems of language, thought and feeling, and with varying degrees of integrity, the characters invent whatever versions of reality they can live with. It is a moot point whether the commentators in *Winners* can be taken as characters at all, and the opening stage directions claim for them a kind of detached omniscience:

Their reading is impersonal, completely without emotion: their function is to give information. At no time must they reveal an attitude to their material.[5]

Their use of the past tense and the burden of narrative they carry places them — and, by implication, the audience — at a temporal remove from the events of the play, but within a short time their neutral tones are contaminated by value-judgement and emotional colouration and 'facts' give way to speculation. Several plays go on to suggest that agreeing about 'the facts' may be over-rated as a verification of 'what happened' and it is clear that in *Philadelphia*, for instance, the emotion that underlies the final scene exists in its own right, even though the characters have failed to find a shared narrative that will contain it.

To dismiss the introduction of various detached commentators — sociologist, chorus, academic . . . — as 'neo-Expresionistic (sic)

crutches and neo-Brechtian gimmicks'[6] and suggest that the plays
would be naturalistically happier without them misses the point of
their presence. These figures ghost around the dramatic action,
commenting, interpreting, misinterpreting, observing, very much
as the dramatist imaginatively ghosts around his subject. But the
real dramatist behind them almost always draws attention to the
fragmentary and fallible nature of their commentary, so that,
although they appear to have a detachment denied the other
characters, they are actually bound by the same limitations of
vision. In so doing the dramatist makes clear that they, and, by implication, he, have neither the omniscient capacity to view nor the
uncontaminated language to embody the subject matter concerned
in the work. In drama there are no reliable narrators. Even when
it appears that the dramatist is establishing a narrative base of
axiomatic 'fact' on which the present action relies for intelligibility
and coherence, our consciousness of the partiality (in both senses)
of the speaker qualifies the information. That qualification is
heavier when, by internal cross-reference, the narrative emphasises
the individuality (emotional colouration, unreliability, falsehood,
judgement . . .) of the speaker's perspective and purpose. In *Faith
Healer* and *The Freedom of the City* Brian Friel completely exposes
to the audience the process by which they surrender their own
judgement to characters in a fiction.[7] He does not merely show us
characters who survive by making fictions; he repeatedly reminds
us that the author too survives in this way. Where 'the facts' are
presented, by Sir in *Living Quarters* or by the commentators in
*Lovers*, the imaginative gap between the written historical record
and the complex experience of the characters involved emphasises
the discontinuity between the different versions of events and
undermines the final authority of any one account. However,
though the 'facts' may be unattainable, the later plays suggest that
it is possible to get closer to the heart of the matter by exploring
the emotional, cultural, intellectual and political languages in
which approximations to the truth are realized.

# FATHERS VANQUISHED AND VICTORIOUS — A HISTORICAL READING OF SYNGE'S *PLAYBOY*

RUTH FLEISCHMANN

The rural society revealed to us through the exposition of the *Playboy* is, as Micheál MacLiammóir puts it, 'an ancient world in flame and ruins',[1] a world subsiding after terrible convulsions into slow decline and stagnation. There are still eruptions that cause streams of people to be driven from their homes: migrant workers, the evicted, 'the poor girls walking Mayo in their thousands' (p. 110),[2] the soldiers disbanded from the army, the tinkers and the 'thousand militia' (p. 81), roaming the province after 'the broken harvest and the ended wars' (p. 85). It is a terrifyingly open society — open to famine and eviction, to destitution and vagrancy, to the asylum and the workhouse; it is open to the prisons for those arrested, in areas proclaimed after agrarian unrest, by the 'looséd Kharki cut-throats' (p. 89) and convicted by juries that 'fill their stomachs selling judgements of the English law' (p. 107); it lies open to the four quarters of the earth, with its people now scattered and 'walking all great states and territories of the world' (p. 95).

Conditions in the west of Ireland at the turn of the century were squalid, brutal and perverse. The paradoxes of the *Playboy* make them stand out in relief. In the play, a man dying in a ditch is feared and avoided; a killer is welcomed and employed as protector against the police and other violent elements. This is the dramatic quintessence of the situation. In the 'congested districts' the destitute were too numerous to help — an official said in 1901 that the half million living there might be divided into two classes, the poor and the destitute.[3] The whole western seaboard still depended on the potato, fifty years after the Famine, and people still starved whenever the blight struck as it did in 1890, 1894, 1896 and 1897.[4] The concessions and reforms which the British government had been making since the Land War (the various Land Acts, the setting up of the Congested Districts Board, the replacement of the landlords' County Grand Juries by elected County Councils, etc.) could not inculcate among the people a respect for the law, which

63

had been seen for centuries in action as a terroristic instrument upholding landlord interests against a desperate and starving peasantry, and in recent times against the political organisations of the rural middle class.

When in the play the girls drink a toast to the slayers, the two vanquishers of patriarchal authority, Christy and the Widow Quin, they include them among the other wonders of the western world,

. . . the pirates, preachers, poteen-makers, with the jobbing jockies; parching peelers, and the juries fill their stomachs selling judgements of the English law. (p. 107)

They celebrate those who defy the law, such as the distillers engaged in guerilla warfare with the police, or the pirates of the old days like Grace O'Malley and the Flahertys' namesakes, the chieftains who, driven from their ancient territories during the Tudor wars, retreated to Aran whence they terrorised Galway in the sixteenth century[5] — people of whose spirit Pegeen has inherited not a little. But the girls also celebrate those who have the cunning to augment their meagre incomes by becoming blind, lame or eloquent at the opportune moment. And they include the preachers among this colourful and dubious company as they in a sense also live — and not only by 'making sermons' — 'on the villainy of man' (p. 86). So both defiant rebels and corrupt opportunists will flourish and be admired in communities where the law cannot command respect. And corruption thrived as the strong farmers, shopkeepers and publicans jockeyed for positions on the new councils, for allocations of land from the Congested Districts Board, and for political influence in the nationalist organisations. AE, who worked with Horace Plunkett to develop the co-operative movement in the West, encountering heavy opposition from the rural middle classes and the Catholic church, had reason to know them:

In the maps of ancient Ireland we see pictures of famous chiefs standing over their territories. . . . In maps of modern congested Ireland pictured in the same way we should find swollen gombeen men straddling right across whole parishes, sucking up like a sponge all the wealth in the district, ruling everything, presiding over county councils, rural councils, boards of guardians, and placing their relatives in every position which their public functions allow them to interfere with. In congested Ireland every job which can be filled by the kith and kin of the gombeen kings and queens is filled accordingly, and you get every kind of inefficiency and jobbery. They are all publicans and their friends are all strong drinkers. . . . All the local appointments are in their gift, and hence you get drunken doctors, drunken rate-collectors, drunken J.P.s, drunken inspectors — in fact round the gombeen system reels the whole drunken congested world, and underneath this revelry and jobbery the unfortunate peasant labours and gets no return for his labour.[6]

The *Playboy* also shows us the new Ireland emerging out of the wreckage of the old. The Flahertys are prosperous people, by local standards. Pegeen is able to order a new outfit from the town for her wedding, though she remains close enough to poverty and its attendant nuisances, as the last item on her list, the fine-comb, reminds us. Her father is a licensed publican who also runs a small shop and is involved in the only industry which has flourished in the west since the seventeenth century: illicit distilling.[7] He sells his customers poteen instead of the highly taxed 'parliament whiskey'. He maintains the necessary good relations with the police, 'decent, drouthy poor fellows, wouldn't touch a cur dog and not give warning in the dead of night' (p. 90), whose thirst he no doubt slakes in return for the warnings given in advance of raids. He owns land and employs occasional labour on it. He is related to the strong farmer, Shawn Keogh — a dispensation is required for Pegeen's marriage — and 'a good bargain' has been made (p. 77) according to which he will give Pegeen in return for a 'drift of heifers' and Shawn's 'blue bull from Sneem' (p. 139). Property ranks high with Michael: when, towards the end of the play, Pegeen has rejected Shawn and Christy threatens to kill him if he does not leave, Michael's only thought is that his illicit drink might be found and confiscated if the police came to investigate a murder:

'Is it mad yous are? Would you go making murder in this place, and it piled with poteen for our drink tonight?' (pp. 138–9)

But he is himself too fond of the drink he sells to be able to make the most of his property and advance in the world as his cousin Shawn does. He does not seem to be a gombeen man, that is to act as money-lender to the small tenant-farmers: we once see his daughter refusing credit (p. 97), and there is no indication in the play that the neighbours are in debt to him. Such debts, could he have afforded to let them mount up, would have opened the road to prosperity: they would have allowed him to overcharge his debtors for food and seed, for they could not leave him without paying up, and in the event of their becoming bankrupt, he would have been able to buy up their livestock and leases for a song.[8]

Shawn, the man of property who accumulates and does not drink, is a caricature of the weak, timid and unscrupulous rural bourgeois that since the Famine had begun to creep deviously into minor positions of money and influence. Shawn's servile deference to authority secular and ecclesiastic earns him the contempt of the community: the quaking pillar of the church is the joke of the countryside, yet his property prevails and he is to be given the fine Pegeen, the parish priest supporting the alliance between strong farmer and publican.

It is made clear before Christy appears on the scene that Pegeen has only accepted Shawn for want of something better. Like the Widow Quin and the daughters of the poor tenant-farmers, she is dissatisfied with rural life: the women have neither property rights to lure them upwards, nor may they find solace and stimulation in the heavy drinking to which the men are addicted.[9] Pegeen speaks with admiration and nostalgia of the days of the Land War:

Where now will you meet the like of Daneen Sullivan knocked the eye from a peeler; or Marcus Quin, God rest him, got six months for maiming ewes, and he a great warrant to tell stories of holy Ireland till he'd have the old women shedding down tears about their feet. Where will you find the like of them, I'm saying? (p. 79)

But the blinders, lamers and political agitators of the 1880s are gone[10] and only the blind, lame and crazed remain in the stricken country from which the strong seem to have fled:

. . . you'll meet none but Red Linahan, has a squint in his eyes, and Patcheen is lame in his heel, or the mad Mulrannies were driven from California and they lost in their wits. (p. 79)

This is the setting which allows a parricide to be welcomed as a hero. It was difficult and perplexing fare for a nationalist audience in 1907 used to pictures of rural Ireland after the manner of *Knocknagow*, the novel written in 1876 by the Fenian, Charles Kickham, in which the cheerful, patient people live in a simple, homely world the harmonious, wholesome and peaceful nature of which has remained miraculously untouched by the depredations of the landlords so often described.

Perhaps not unlike the first audience of the play, Pegeen expects a hero to come from an old Irish family, especially as Christy has a fine 'quality name'. But, though a thousand years earlier the Mahons of Munster 'were great, surely, with wide and windy acres of rich Munster land' (p. 91) having re-established their ancient dynasty, and though they lived 'like a king of Norway' when Mahon defeated the Norse king of Limerick and drove him off to Wales,[11] the present Mahon rules only over 'his cold, sloping, divil's patch of a field' (p. 105) and over one unfortunate son, having driven the stronger ones to the four corners of the earth. He only 'contends' with the women of Limerick (p. 93) and embarks on mad, drunken struggles with the elements and the forces of law and order, for which he is periodically locked up in the county asylum.

Christy's conflict with his father results from a greater degree of subjection than was usual in rural Ireland. The normal issues of contention with a father which could lead to violence in the family were, according to the Widow Quin, 'asking money of him or making talk of getting a wife would drive him from his farm' (p. 105). But such things have never occurred to Christy; he is being driven into marriage, is in danger of being sold for gold to an elderly widow by the father, who has drunk himself out of house and home. It is horror of the woman which makes him revolt, and which renders him eloquent in the presence of the girls.

The picture which emerges of rural life in Kerry is as sombre as that of Mayo — there, too, farms are small and stony, marriages rare, widows living alone, their children dead or gone; there, too, madness is prevalent and alcoholism rife. Christy can offer no 'gallous story' of ruling the roost at home; but his account of the loneliness and depression of the life he led in subjection to his wild, drunken despot of a father is articulate enough to impress Pegeen.

Christy's eloquence when talking to Pegeen of his feelings for her — which wins her, together with the public proof he gives at the sports of his physical strength and dexterity — draws on his experience roaming the countryside. When living with his father, he found a refuge there going poaching at night, nature providing him with a limbo on the borders of his domestic hell, where solitude was welcome relief from the company of a tyrant. His wandering as a fugitive 'walking wild eleven days and waking fearful in the night' (p. 91) makes him acquainted with the country as a place of torment for the lonely vagrant, so that when (in Act II) he thinks Pegeen is driving him away, he can describe with intensity the desolation of the solitary outcast:

. . . it's a lonesome thing to be passing small towns with the lights shining sideways when the night is down, or going in strange places with a dog noising before you and a dog noising behind, or drawn to the cities where you'd hear a voice kissing and talking deep love in every shadow of the ditch, and you passing on with an empty, hungry stomach failing from your heart. (p. 110)

Having discovered for the first time what love is, and having, as he thinks, lost Pegeen, he can imagine the anguish of looking from afar at 'women and girls the way the needy fallen spirits do be looking on the Lord' (p. 110). Then, after his triumph, he imagines wandering 'on the sides of Neifin or the Erris plain', no longer 'like Esau or Cain and Abel', but in Pegeen's company, the rapture of which would make even the highest of the Fathers — the bishops, prophets and God Himself — long to exchange their paradise for his.

In the countryside which Christy describes with the sensitivity of the old Irish poets,[12] the farmers and shepherds of Israel at the time of the patriarchs do not seem in the least out of place. The people's world stretches, because of emigration, from California to the eastern world; because of their preoccupation with history and politics, it encompasses the wars of the Danes and those of the Boers; because of the poets and hedgeschoolmasters they sheltered and honoured, the tales of the beautiful ladies and gallant warriors of Egypt and ancient Greece are as familiar as those of the saints. But this mediaeval, cosmopolitan folk-culture is on the verge of extinction: the young girls no longer get their stories from the old people, but from the newly founded popular press with its endless store of sensational novelties, from the incident of 'the man bit the yellow lady's nostril on the northern shore' (p. 103) to the accounts of murders and how the murdered 'do bleed and drip'.

Pegeen succeeds in creating a hero out of the unlikeliest of creatures, out of a poor fellow who, in the beginning, bears a close resemblance to Shawn Keogh, but who grows in stature according to the interest and admiration given until he fits the image held up to him. His apparently successful revolt against his father is followed by easy victory over his rival and over Pegeen's father, who reluctantly agrees to the alliance with a propertyless outlaw, reverting to the dynastic thinking of his ancestors as a face-saving device. But this victory is as deceptive as is the defeat Christy must undergo before he can prevail.

The growth of Christy's self-confidence and the blossoming of his innate abilities and qualities resembles that of the nationalist movement during the period of the Irish Revival. The image of Ireland held up by advocates of colonialism such as Froude or *Punch* was just as shaming and distorted as that which old Mahon presents to the Widow and the men of the simpleton son he scorns: both contain elements of truth, but the cartoonists have chosen to eliminate the strengths and to ignore the reasons for the weaknesses. The interest taken by Anglo-Irish men of letters in the peasantry and its culture (after their families' incomes had been seriously diminished in the wake of the Depression and Land War) led to a flowering of literature of the first order in the small backward colony on the edge of Europe which was every bit as astonishing as the flowering of Christy's eloquence when inspired by a splendid young woman. That the legitimate need to find a past which is admirable and uplifting could lead to other, no less grotesque distortions, much of the popular nationalist literature of the time documents; that it could lead to addiction to flattering self-images the reception of the *Playboy* was to demonstrate.

The rejection of the hero who has just proved his mettle in word and deed is no less paradoxical than his welcome. Hailed as a saviour when discovered to be a murderer, he is derided and faces expulsion when 'exposed' as a non-killer; he is abused by those to whom he responded as they desired.

The second assault on the father allows the people to see for themselves that, like the first, it is done in self-defence. Christy is shown to be gentle, terrified, and refused the help he begs for. He sees two possibilities before him — slavery, or destitution on the roads and progression through the workhouses:

Christy: (*looking round in desperation*) And I must go back into my torment is it, or run off like a vagabond straying through the unions with the dust of August making mudstains in the gullet of my throat; or the winds of March blowing on me till I'd take an oath I felt them making whistles of my ribs within? (p. 142)

He has no thought, at this stage, of impressing Pegeen by his deed: the two dreaded fates to be avoided are uppermost in his mind; there is no trace of a calculation of what might be won. He is furthermore provoked beyond endurance by his father. Christy asks the jeering crowd:

(*getting up in shy terror*): What is it drives you to torment me here, when I'd asked the thunders of the might of God to blast me if I ever did hurt to any saving only that one single blow?

Mahon answers for them:

If you didn't, you're a poor good-for-nothing, and isn't it by the like of you the sins of the whole world are committed?

An attack made in desperation on a man who vilifies the weak and derides his victim is justified, but it is not presented as being heroic, and Christy becomes farcical while he labours under this delusion, which is soon scorched out of him.

Though Christy already knows that his father is alive, he relives his astonishment over it, so that it is obvious that he has not been lying but was mistaken about the old man's death. Pegeen's fury is due to fear of ridicule and wounded vanity:

Take him on from this, for I think it bad the world should see me raging for a Munster liar, and the fool of men.

Her pithy saying about the difference 'between a gallous story and a dirty deed' does not give the measure of the issue. Christy's assault on his tyrannical father is neither 'gallous' (in the sense of 'great' or 'fine'),[13] nor is it totally sordid: like all acts of revolt, it has elements of both. Pegeen remains as blind now to the justification of Christy's deed as she was before to its sordidness. Nor does she become loath to see violence herself — the girl who appreciates gallous stories of the revenge taken on landlords by hamstringing their sheep now proceeds, for all her awareness, to the very dirty deed of torturing and laming a human being.

Christy must do without the recognition that was essential to his first stage of growth to counteract his father's contempt. He now grows in stature in the face of ridicule and contumely: he no longer needs mirrors held up by others, but has the maturity to judge for himself independently of and even contrary to the opinion of the public. He learns again from the behaviour of the crowd: this time, that it is to be ignored. But he holds to his estimation of Pegeen in spite of her rejection, and defends her against the girls. He will not ask her help, he says

. . . for there's torment in the splendour of her like, and she a girl any moon of midnight would take pride to meet, facing southwards on the heaths of Keel. But what did I want crawling forward to scorch my understanding at her flaming brow?

There is no wounded vanity here, nor is his love a narcissistic one. His 'infinite admiration' (p. 111) remains, and he accepts her right to banish him as unworthy from the garden of Eden as the angels banished Adam with their flaming swords. But when she commits her third betrayal and tries to deliver him to the hangman by applying a flaming sod of turf to his leg at the suggestion of the crawling worm, Shawneen, she extinguishes 'the love-light of the star of knowledge' (p. 120). She has half-heard and closed her ears to the evidence of Christy's integrity. In her first reaction, the most understandable, she echoes the mocking crowd and dismisses him. When, at the suggestion of her father, who fears that ruin might be brought on his property, she drops the noose on him so that he can be handed over to the law, he offers to go and to live 'like the madmen of Keel, eating muck and green weeds on the faces of the cliffs' — on the same splendid heath of Achill where he has imagined Pegeen wandering abroad, a fitting companion of 'the moon of midnight' and whose effect on those under her influence is no less

injurious than that of the moon on lunatics. But now, when she acts
as the agent of Shawn, she destroys that influence.

Old Mahon rises twice from the dead; Christy rises three times
from helplessness and fear to strength. But the third time he is reborn to a sombre kind of glory. Having lost 'the light of the seven
heavens' (p. 134), he determines to glory in the darkness. Hence-
forward he adopts the mechanism used by his father to turn trouble
into defiant triumph. The old man can recount the tale of an en-
forced stay in the asylum as pauper lunatic as a gallant exploit of
how he confounded science when he was

. . . a terrible and fearful case . . . screeching in a straightened waistcoat,
with seven doctors writing out my sayings in a printed book (p. 131).

Christy takes a similar defiant pleasure in painting the dark fate in
store for himself or which he can inflict on others. He now has the
match of his father's venomous wit. Before the first attack, Mahon
threatened to flatten Christy out 'like a crawling beast has passed
under a dray' and to 'having the divil making garters' of his limbs
that night (p. 106). Christy now threatens Shawn:

If I do lay my hands on you, it's the way you'll be at the fall of night, hanging as a scarecrow for the fowls of hell. Ah, you'll have a gallous jaunt,
I'm saying, coaching out through Limbo with my father's ghost. (p. 147)

He then depicts his trial, condemnation and execution:

If I can wring a neck among you, I'll have a royal judgement looking on
the trembling jury in the courts of law. And won't there be crying out in
Mayo the day I'm stretched upon the rope, with ladies in their silks and
satins snivelling in their lacy kerchiefs, and they rhyming songs and ballads
on the terror of my fate?

This is not the ignominious end of a criminal, who indeed sits in
'royal judgement' on the 'trembling jury' — it is the victory of a
man remaining unbroken to the end, who faces defeat intrepid.
This tragi-comic spirit of defiance is related to the tragic ferocity of
the ruined poets of the seventeenth and eighteenth centuries, to the
'heroic desolation and grandeur' of their best work.[14] Christy's
ability to turn rout into victory was shared by all politicians of the
nationalist movement since the Famine, the greatest magician being
Padraig Pearse, whose blood-sacrifice theory and its practice in the
Easter Rising of 1916 brought the apotheosis of the vanquished
become victorious.

Being now master of all images, Christy can now become 'master
of all fights' (p. 149). He is strong enough not to have to attack the
father physically, but can impose his will on him permanently

without resorting to violence. The fighting spirit when Pegeen admires and misses has been re-kindled, and is powerful enough to subdue that of the wild 'heathen', old Mahon, the déclassé spurred on to destruction by vague memories of former splendours and of injustices. But Christy's presentation of himself going off 'romancing through a romping lifetime' is surely another example of a defiant re-interpretation of defeat. He has vanquished his father, but remains without the fulfilment of his romance. Is he not going off into the loneliness he has so often described? May his fate not resemble that of the landless man unable to marry whom Michael spoke of, when he gave his assent to the union between Pegeen and her champion, as a poor fellow 'eating a bit in one house and drinking a sup in another, and he with no place of his own, like an old braying jackass strayed upon the rocks' (p. 140). Christy has prevented the alliance his father tried to force on him, which would have allowed the ruined tenant-farmer to find a roof over his head in the widow's hut and opened a last source of money for drink. But the alliance planned regardless of property considerations by the young people comes to nought, the propertied girl being willing to disregard property if need be, but not loss of prestige. So the vanquisher of his father moves off, victorious; but the road which took him from the poverty of his small stony Kerry farm to the shebeen in Mayo now leads him out of it, and into the wide-open world where the doors ahead may be those of the workhouses and the end, maybe, destitution, however defiantly borne.

The fortunes of the other father, who was in the process of rising from poverty to relative prosperity, are checked by his daughter's final rejection of the business alliance which would have laid the foundation for his future as a grazier. Yet, just as old Mahon submits with some pride to the rule of his son, Michael is not likely to take this set-back too seriously — provided he can be sure of having peace for his drinks (p. 149). These men's lives will go on much as before. Shawneen, the strong farmer with the weak character, will continue to defer abjectly to his spiritual father, and he will no doubt find another, if not a 'radiant' lady, 'with a drove of bullocks' (p. 138), even if the resulting offspring may be 'puny weeds' (p. 140). The drunken, congested world will continue to drink, to let its destitute die in the ditch or in the workhouses, and to send its more spirited children to America. In so far, these fathers remain victorious; but the world they rule is a broken one.

Synge presented his nationalist audience with some disconcerting political propositions. In the play the people succeed in making a man out of a 'stuttering lout'; but they fail to appreciate their

creation and drive him away in his moment of weakness. Creating
heroes is an achievement; living up to them, maintaining them, an
even greater one. He presents the tragi-comic, shattered world of
the demoralised fathers (as Sean O'Casey was to do in *Juno and the
Paycock*), not the tragic one of the abandoned mothers. He shows
them either reeling wildly into destruction and driving their
children to hatred, flight or violence, or else crawling meanly after
money and trying to barter their children for cattle. He indicates
that, if the young people are to find a life worth living in rural
Ireland, they will have to follow up the revolt of the older generation against the landlords with another against the tyrannical, corrupt and parasitical among their own class. The play contains little
hope, however, that this will happen. The poorest, most violent
(and therefore weakest) of the fathers is subdued; but as he cannot
be cured, only controlled, the relationship between father and son
continues to be one of master and slave, the roles now reversed. No
decisive impact has been made on the stronger fathers. It is also
made clear that violence is the last resort of the weak, that it will
inevitably ensue if conditions are violent; that it is damaging and
sordid, can be justifiable, and cannot provide solutions, though it
may help to bring about conditions in which they could be found.

It was the *leitmotif* of revolt which Padraig Pearse found so
disturbing in the *Playboy*. He defended the play in 1907 against the
attacks made on it, which he called 'puerile' and 'inept'. The charge
he brought was 'graver':

. . . it is not Ireland he libels so much as mankind in general, it is not
against a nation he blasphemes so much as against the moral order of the
universe. . . . In 'The Playboy of the Western World' . . . he has produced
a brutal glorification of violence, and grossness, and the flesh. In these
. . . plays humanity is in savage revolt.[15]

But by 1913 Pearse had come to a very different view:

Ireland, in our day as in the past, has excommunicated some of those who
have served her best, and has canonised some of those who have served
her worst. We damn a man for an unpopular phrase; we deify a man who
does a mean thing gracefully. The word is ever more significant to us than
the deed. When a man like Synge, a man in whose sad heart there glowed
a true love of Ireland, one of the two or three men who have in our time
made Ireland considerable in the eyes of the world, uses strange symbols
which we do not understand, we cry out that he has blasphemed and we
proceed to crucify him. When a sleek lawyer, rising step by step through
the most ignoble of all professions, attains to a Lord Chancellorship or to
an Attorney-Generalship, we confer upon him the freedom of our cities.
This is really a very terrible symptom in contemporary Ireland.[16]

He had come into contact with Larkin and Connolly and had seen what tyranny Irishmen can exercise over Irishmen — another 'sleek' citizen, William Martin Murphy, had just organised the employers to smash the union to the wretchedly paid, unskilled workers of Dublin. He had come to perceive the brutality of hunger and of poverty. And he had begun to organise that revolt the fate of which was to be in many ways so similar to Christy's. Pearse, a hero-worshipper rather like those of the play, grew into the role of the hero himself. The rising, planned as a desperate last stand to remind a people already thoroughly anglicised and bound by manifold 'ties of self-interest . . . to the Empire'[17] of their national distinctiveness and possibilities, was first reviled as a dirty deed, then hailed as the most gallous of exploits. Out of the defeat of 1916 came the victory of 1921. But then the Shawn Keoghs and the Father Reillys rose up out of the ashes and established themselves as the pillars of the Free State (gentlemen in essentials not dissimilar doing the same on the other side of the new border). For a long time to come the licensed premises would continue to flourish, the Mahons in their 'straightened waistcoats' to perplex the doctors, the widows and the Pegeens to remain unmarried, and the Christys to be sent to America in their thousands.

# 'IT IS MYSELF THAT I REMAKE':
# THE SHAPING SELF OF W. B. YEATS'S
# *AUTOBIOGRAPHIES*

MARGARET. E. FOGARTY

A few years ago a salutary and timely caution appeared in *The New York Times Book Review*, that 'art is not technology, and cannot be "mastered". It is an endless access to revelatory states of mind.'[1] The nature and process of that 'access' is pivotal in any consideration of the aesthetics of literature. For Yeats, such 'access' is gained via articulation — an articulation which, as Shirley Hazzard asserts, ' . . . is central to human survival and self-determination, not only in its commemorative and descriptive functions but in relieving the soul of incoherence'.[2] Both quotations have a direct relevance for the argument I wish to present concerning Yeats's *Autobiographies*: namely, that it is a multi-faceted artefact in which the Self, the mysterious Other, is the agent of design, the predominating and shaping architect of the work. For in *Autobiographies* Yeats articulates precisely the errant and aberrant primary self of his life, *and* that other Self, the (literary) symbol of that which is at once his 'double' and 'The most unlike, being [his] anti-self'.[3] In reckoning with self and Self, Yeats passes, however, from the 'commemorative and descriptive' pattern of mere autobiographical recall, to probing speculation about Art and the Self that generates or shapes it. Particularly manifest in Yeats's volumes of prose essays is the insistent need of the poet to articulate the artistic act, to explain the invading thoughts, images and spiritual impulses of his mind. *Autobiographies* reveals some of the toil, disillusionment and endless reckoning of that particular bid for '. . . relieving the soul of incoherence'.

It may justly be argued that all autobiographies wobble along this tight-rope of self-explanation, hence Freud's denunciation of them as being, in Sarah Kofman's paraphrase, 'All . . . untruthful, for they are written from the standpoint of retroactive illusion and with a view towards idealization'. But Yeats augments and 'object-ifies' the I of his text by frequent resort to the pronouns 'we' and 'our' — at those very moments when he becomes imbued with a 'revelatory state of mind'. He takes no stand to idealize his contingent, existential life; instead, his text ponders self seeking fusion with its Ideal, which is always Art. The descriptive *process* may be idealized; but then, one must argue, so is all thought, all creativity, born as they are out of speculative intuition, with no means of empirical verification *at origin*. The shaping Self of *Autobiographies* not only relieves Yeats of incoherence, but redeems *its* self from the trap of illusion — as this paper aims to demonstrate.

Much excitement is currently being generated in literary theory circles by discussion of the (philosophical) complexities of the autobiography. The notion that autobiography may be seen as a genre has been discredited for some years, by theorists such as Paul de Man, Paul L. Jay and Robert Elbaz (*inter alios*).[5] Now, more exactingly, the identity of the 'I' is investigated, the integrity of the process of recall and retrospective imaginings queried, and the view taken that since 'I am not myself', the autobiographical writer embarks on work that, ideologically, philosophically and fictionally speaking, is grounded in many artful, if not spurious precedures. Many theorists, by way of exemplifying their arguments, cite texts as disparate as Augustine's *Confessions*, Sterne's *Tristram Shandy*, and Nietzsche's *Ecce Homo*. Noticeably few have attempted to confront Yeats's *Autobiographies* — a peculiar omission.[6] For Yeats's lengthy work is neither (merely) confessional, chronological, purely retrospective or fictionalized, nor a set of memoirs: it is all of these and none of them.

The first problematic of signification in Yeats's text is located in the plural of the title.[7] How is one to conceive of subject-as-author when the reader is alerted from the outset to that author reviewing self in not one consecutive text, but a clutch of texts that sometimes overlap information, that are each written in a collection of anecdotal shards, that are sometimes essays and sometimes diary jottings? Furthermore, each section of *Autobiographies* is in a real sense a separate unit, holding a certain completeness, while information or speculation contained in one is sometimes repeated in another, or taken up in more detail. In the dating of the units there is indeed a very general chronology, the opening *Reveries* having first appeared in 1914, and the concluding 'Bounty of Sweden' in 1926. But this 'chronology' refers to manuscript and publication dating,[8] rather than to the sequence of Yeats's life; indeed, *Autobiographies* alone provides the reader with slim information, overall, about Yeats's life and work. The purpose and integrating factor of *Autobiographies* must therefore be sought elsewhere: namely in the role and power of the Shaping Self of the text, in the bid for an identity that is both aesthetic and seismic (or in Yeatsian terms, attuned to the Daimon). Yeats's autobiographical texts are retrospective *only* insofar as certain events help to demonstrate how his thinking has come about; only insofar as past explains present; only insofar as past and future are subsumed in (his) present attitude to imagination as transforming agent in creativity. In this fashion, *Autobiographies* appears to display the 'more elliptical and purely discursive' qualities Paul Jay sees as typifying some first-person texts.[9]

In order to demonstrate the uniqueness, as literary work, of *Autobiographies*, it is necessary first of all to show what it is *not*, and to come to terms, albeit briefly, with some of the theoretical principles currently surrounding the literary form, autobiography. Francis Stuart's autobiographical novel, *Black List, Section H*, shares with Yeats's the aspect of quest — but in Stuart's text the quest occurs 'within the context of the development of a creative mind' and by the conclusion of the novel that quest '. . . has been completed'.[10] In Yeats's text, on the other hand, narrative (and therefore quest) remains unclosed, while the creative mind is sought less in the internal self than in the *other* Self — the Image, the Mask, the antithesis:

When a man writes any work of genius, or invents some creative action, is it not because some knowledge or power has come into his mind from beyond his mind? It is called up by an image, as I think . . . but our images must be given to us, we cannot choose them deliberately.

('Hodos Chameliontos', p. 272)

And as I look backward upon my own writing, I take pleasure alone in those verses where it seems to me I have found something hard and cold, some articulation of the Image which is the opposite of all that I am in daily life, and all that my country is; yet man or nation can no more make this Mask or Image than the seed can be made by the soil into which it is cast.

('Hodos Chameliontos', p. 274)[11]

Thus far, one may find oneself in agreement with Marc Eli Blanchard's talk of 'the autobiographer's search for a satisfactory image to produce', of the circularity of autobiography and its (necessary) associative process(-es), of 'a metonymical approach to the past' and, especially, autobiography's '. . . prescription of an ongoing present of the mind'.[12] The only, but most obvious, point of departure or difference, however, is that Yeats's quest for the satisfactory Image is *not* for the image that will make the auto-biography. Rather, in his autobiographical ponderings he searches for, speculates and propounds on, that Image which will govern his *proper* literary work — in poems and plays especially: that is, in all that appears *outside* the *Autobiographies*. From this position one sees already some of the implications of Paul de Man's assertion that, 'Empirically as well as theoretically, autobiography lends itself poorly to generic definition . . . '.[13] However, the further argument is less credible:

We assume that life *produces* the autobiography as an act produces its consequences, but can we not suggest, with equal justice, that the autobiographical project may itself produce and determine the life and that whatever the writer *does* is in fact governed by the technical demands of self-portraiture and thus determined, in all its aspects, by the resources of his medium?[14]

Inspection of Yeats's discourse reveals little of the mimetic figuration implied here; for while his text documents movements in his life in *general*, such recall is designed to record, for close friends, how his entire poetic and dramatic career took shape. That *'shape'* is of the essence of Yeats, not the factual tale — even though his friends might have seen it differently;

I have changed nothing to my knowledge; and yet it must be that I have changed many things without my knowledge; for I am writing after many years and have consulted neither friend, nor letter, nor old newspaper, and describe what comes oftenest into my memory.
I say this fearing that some surviving friends of my youth may remember something in a different shape and be offended with my book.
                    (Preface to *Reveries Over Childhood and Youth*, p. 3)

While 'Shape' is rendered here out of remembering, the final composite text can in no sense be regarded as an autobiographical novel.

Rather, in his discussion of the autobiographical works of Paul Valéry and Roland Barthes, Paul Jay arrives at a description of their texts that could as well be provided for Yeats's *Autobiographies*:

In their texts the writer's life remains central, but the 'life' is no longer thought of strictly in terms of a chronological or historical series of events which are (or even should be) narratable. Rather, the 'life' in the work of each comes more and more to be thought of not as exterior and chronological, but as interior and dispersed, not separate from the time of writing, but constituted in and by it.[15]

At issue here is the problematical 'relation between the self-as-author, and the self-as-subject'. That problematic, however, seems naturally to disperse in Yeats's text, where the I remains dominantly author-subject, only shifting signification when that I speculates on the source of its inspiration from 'beyond', as already cited. Then the 'I' becomes 'one' or is transposed to the plural subject, 'we'. For Yeats's discourse, thus, the ultimate other (the opposite pole of I) is that 'beyond' mediating vision through the anti-self. This position is in line with, though an interesting and perhaps hitherto unexplored variant of, Marshall Grossmann's claim, built on that of Émile Benveniste, that the I,

. . . must posit another person to whom its discourse is addressed. Thus *I* and *You* are necessarily produced as the poles of any communication, and one cannot be conceived apart from the other: 'This polarity does not mean either equality or symmetry: "ego" always has a position of transcendence with regard to you'.[16]

Ideation, in this article by Grossmann, centres on the function of the subject and the 'rhetoric of the self' in narrative discourse (which here includes certain forms of poetry). Yeats's text, however, while indubitably literary and narrative, is not intentionally fictional (as is Joyce's *A Portrait of the Artist as a Young Man*, for example).

Nevertheless, one may readily agree that the *Autobiographies*, like (fictional) narrative, is '. . . a response to specific demands that grow out of the perceived discontinuities between self and world, and, indeed between self and self'.[17] Of this there is much evidence in *Autobiographies*; for example:

To oppose the new ill-breeding of Ireland . . . I can only set up a secondary or interior personality created out of the tradition of myself, and this personality (alas, only possible to me in my writings) must be always gracious and simple. It must have that slight separation from interests which makes charm possible, while remaining near enough for passion.

('Estrangement', p. 463)

The knowledge of reality is always in some measure a secret knowledge. It is a kind of death.                    ('Estrangement', p. 482)

These notes are morbid, but I heard a man of science say that all progress is at the outset pathological, and I write for your good.

('The Death of Synge', p. 502)

Am I going against nature in my constant attempt to fill my life with work? Is my mind as rich as in idle days? Is not perhaps the poet's labour a mere rejection? If he seeks purity — the ridding of his life of all but poetry — will not inspiration come? Can one reach God by toil? He gives Himself to the pure in heart. He asks nothing but attention.

('The Death of Synge', p. 522)

The latter excerpt in particular, takes one to the heart of Cyrus Hamlin's notion of the 'transcendence' occurring in autobiographical narrative, where, *inter alia*, there occurs,

> . . . a recognition that the ultimate referent for that discourse remains indeterminate and beyond the limits of signification. The narrator as subject submits to . . . [an] awareness of indeterminacy by allowing the displacement of the narrative to occur. The success of that displacement as ironic structure of communication will depend on the reader's willingness to participate in it to an equal degree. We must share in the emptying out of the sign so that the narrative itself as verbal structure can communicate to us an understanding which, according to the necessary dialectial [sic] form of negativity, replaces all subjective certainty of the self with a genuine ethical concern for an indeterminate and unknown otherness.[18]

A Freud's 'illusion' is thus a Hamlin's 'transcendence'. The ancient cry, What is Truth? reverberates still; but since all imparted theory, knowledge, fiction or poetry, is but the fruit of necessarily subjective observation, one might argue with Altieri that it is specious to speak of 'Truth', that only 'truthfulness' may be acceptable.[19] Perhaps the circularity Altieri and Elbaz see as typical of the autobiography, because it ends in its beginning, endorses this view.[20] Yeats's text, as earlier intimated, shows all the lineaments of such circularity. But amongst theorists James Olney would seem to be closest to the literary (as opposed to mere theoretical) point:

> . . . however much they [structuralists, post-structuralists and deconstructionists] talk about genre or linguistics or deep-lying structures, what they are still troubling about is the self and consciousness or knowledge of it, even though in a kind of bravura way some of them may be denying its possibility . . . the heart of the explanation for the special appeal of autobiography . . . is a fascination with the self and its profound, its endless mysteries and, accompanying that fascination, an anxiety about the self.[21]

The mystery, the fascination and the 'anxiety about the self' are epitomized in Yeats's reflections in his sectionalized text. The shifter I moves less, if at all, from a subject I to an object you, than from a social, voluble, primary self, to a speculative, questing, artistic other Self. Seen in this way, the Self of Yeats's discourse is not polarised but antithetical. It may be argued that antithesis, of its nature, establishes an immediate and automatic construct of polar opposites. For Yeats, however, the antithetical was fundamentally *the other face of the same*; and the contraries, via their self-generated force-field, inexorably sought and finally achieved unity. It was here that Yeats envisioned the greatest art being actualized. For Bernard Levine, the nexus in this achievement is the Self, 'the transpersonalizing (though not impersonal) voice behind the flow of images'.[22] According to Levine, Yeats sought an art that '. . . was purified of everything that did not lead to a realization of Self and to an awareness of "spiritual reality" ';[23] he bases this deduction on Yeats's assertion that:

The more a poet rids his verse of heterogeneous knowledge and irrelevant analysis, and purifies his mind with elaborate art, the more does the little ritual of his verse resemble the great ritual of Nature, and become mysterious and inscrutable. He becomes, as all the great mystics have believed, a vessel of the creative power of God.[24]

F. A. C. Wilson considers Yeats's theory of the Self as not only significant in its time, but a marked uniqueness in Yeats's thought, for whereas 'Religious thought at the turn of the century had attached itself to the concept of an externalized God . . . Yeats almost alone perceived this truth ['the godhead within us'] for himself fifty years before the metaphysicians, and defended his isolated position with consummate integrity all his life'.[25] Yet, it should be noted, Yeats's concern with the Self was not (mere) concern with theory that exists apart in some esoteric domain. In the *Autobiographies*, at issue is the self as artist, the son of an exceptional painter become the father and artist too: the self as bearer of Mask and Daimon, and bent on the song of speech. *Autobiographies* ponders the cadences of that speech, agonizes over imperfect writing coming from a lack of congruency in Self, and asserts:

I know now that revelation is from the self, but from that age-long memorised self . . .; and that genius is a crisis that joins that buried self for certain moments to our trivial daily mind. There are, indeed, personifying spirits that we had best call but Gates and Gate-keepers because through their dramatic power they bring our souls to crisis, to Mask and Image . . .

('Hodos Chameliontos', p. 272)

Self and revelation thus act in full, harmonious accord in the generation of the art work. Additionally — in reflexive interaction — the rendering of art is a rendering, a 'shaping' of the Self. The Shaping Self is thus both creation and creator. In an untitled poem, Yeats declares:

> The friends that have it I do wrong
> When ever I remake a song,
> Should know what issue is at stake:
> It is myself that I remake.[26]

The I of Yeats's discourse thus projects not a fictitious or illusory self as some theorists would claim, but *an extension of Self* in another, the completed work of art. Mediating in this extension, is revelation, the 'intrusion' of yet an-other force or power from 'beyond the mind', as already noted. The paradox in Yeats's system is as notable as that of contraries seeking resolution in Unity; because for Yeats the 'articulation of the Image . . . is the opposite' of all that he is 'in daily life', yet only in that precise articulation is his inner self most appropriately transmuted — or transpersonalized as Levine has termed it. Recalling Yeats's explanation of the ending of *The Cat and the Moon* (1917) — 'When the lame man takes the saint upon his back, the normal man has become one with his opposite' — Richard Ellmann comments: 'Thus self and anti-self were reconciled . . . Regardless of the presence of the saint, the reconcilement of opposites was for Yeats a secular miracle, the key to his verse, his private system, and his life.'[27]

Such achievement did not come readily to Yeats. All his life he found writing the greatest, most onerous labour. He had to learn that discipline was needed to temper daimon, if creativity was to burn steadily, instead of vanquishing all, in a brief outburst:

Dowson or Johnson, or Horne or Symons . . . had taught me that violent energy, which is like a fire of straw, consumes in a few minutes the nervous vitality, and is useless in the arts. Our fire must burn slowly, and we must constantly turn away to think, constantly analyse what we have done, be content even to have little life outside our work, to show, perhaps, to other men, as little as the watch-mender shows, his magnifying-glass caught in his screwed-up eye. Only then do we learn to conserve our vitality, to keep our mind enough under control and to make our technique sufficiently flexible for expression of the emotions of life as they arise.

('The Tragic Generation', p. 318)

This passage is an important, and intimate, depiction of Yeats the social man wrestling with the demands of the artistic I. It is somewhat ingenuous in its simplicity, yet for that reason, perhaps, far more evocative of that 'truthfulness' earlier touched on. However, a stylistically important feature is also in evidence here, and that is the shift from the personalized 'I' to the distanced 'our': the temporary grammatical employment of the plural not only accommodating Dowson, *et al.*, but all artists or writers. When Yeats is more consciously objectifying his speculations on the creative process, the shift invariably occurs from the direct autobiographical 'I' to the rhetoric of unanswered questions — the device frequently employed in some of his greatest poetry. By this leap of the interrogative as I choose to call it, Yeats transcends the limits of the purely personal, and ambushes the most hardened empiricist theoretical approach to literature. For in these interrogative passages, he poises on the threshold of his active artistic intuition, at the doorway of mystery. While it is modish for contemporary theorists to decry the notion of mystery in the arts,[28] for Yeats all that *lacked* mystery was not art:

Does not all art come when a nature, that never ceases to judge itself, exhausts personal emotion in action or desire so completely that something impersonal, something that has nothing to do with action or desire, suddenly starts into its place, something which is as unforeseen, as completely organized, even as unique, as the images that pass before the mind between sleeping and waking? . . . In 1895 or 1896 I was in despair at the new breath of comedy that had began to wither the beauty that I loved, just when that beauty seemed to have united itself to mystery.

('The Tragic Generation', pp. 332–3)

But for the initiate to the portals of mystery, the apprenticeship is always exacting:

A writer must die every day he lives, be reborn, as it is said in the Burial Service, an incorruptible self, that self opposite of all that he has named 'himself'.

('Dramatis Personae', p. 457)

With this in mind, Yeats determines on setting up, as already seen, 'a secondary or interior personality created out of the tradition of myself', a personality, he affirms, that is 'only possible to me in my writings'. Then, in the kind of astonishing linkage one comes to associate with and expect from Yeats, he aligns discipline, theatrical sense and the 'second self'. He goes even further, asserting not a mere alignment but a *necessary* connectedness:

There is a relation between discipline and the theatrical sense. If we cannot imagine ourselves as different from what we are and assume that second self, we cannot impose a discipline upon ourselves, though we may accept one from others. Active virtue as distinguished from the passive acceptance of a current code is therefore theatrical, consciously dramatic, the wearing of a mask. It is the condition of arduous full life.

('Estrangement', p. 469)

Yet all is not arduous, and nothing in art is accomplished by mere action:

We artists suffer in our art if we do not love most of all life at peace with itself and doing without forethought what its humanity bids it and therefore happily. We are, as seen from life, an artifice, an emphasis, an uncompleted arc perhaps. Those whom it is our business to cherish and celebrate are complete arcs. Because the life man sees is not the final end of things, the moment we attain to greatness of any kind by personal labour and will we become fragmentary, and find no task in active life which can use our finest faculties. We are compelled to think and express and not to do.                    ('Estrangement', p. 475)

As insight matures, and acceptance grows, so for Yeats 'The soul becomes a mirror not a brazier. This culture is self-knowledge in so far as the self is a calm, deliberating, discriminating thing . . .' ('Estrangement', p. 477). Even when, through pressure of public and political matters, Yeats found that sense of self faltering, he insisted on his own endurance, believing, determining, that 'Whatever happens . . . there may be a man behind the lines already written . . . I cast the die long ago and must be true to the cast' ('Estrangement', p. 485). Here, unequivocally, soul, self and anti-thetical self, are merged in one even though, as Yeats points out, in societal terms, 'We are never a unity, a personality to ourselves' ('The Death of Synge', p. 503).

Finally, bereft at the death of Synge, Yeats is prompted to con-sider again the role of the artist in relation both to society *and* to himself. Creativity, he concludes, arrives eventually at that point where self has somehow been effaced but where an antithetical Self lives on in perpetual renewal:

I think that all happiness depends on the energy to assume the mask of some other self; that all joyous or creative life is a rebirth as something not oneself, something which has no memory and is created in a moment and perpetually renewed.                    ('The Death of Synge', p. 503)

In creativity, thus, the Self is articulated, restored, renewed, perpetuated. For Yeats the I is perpetually poised between interiority of existence and external re-presentation, whether in the process of recall or in the Other of meditation. The *Autobiographies* are vocal on the tension of that poise, the difficulty and discipline entailed in maintaining equilibrium, the energy required in the remaking — from self to Self, or from self to its Image in the Mask. The 'infinite pain of self-realization' is paradoxically temporary; but its mirror-ing in Art, permanent. That permanence was sought in the symbol, something Yeats saw as '. . . more powerful than an emotion without symbol' ('Estrangement', p. 487). Levine comments that 'The Self represents the one perfect symbol the poet can evolve: the selfless image the poet makes of himself . . . that image, or symbol, comes to signify absolute dissolution of the self as an object and as an object-oriented form of consciousness'.[29] The Shaping Self is therefore *the* determining feature of the *Autobiographies*, as also in the entire corpus of Yeats's work, whether prose, poetry or drama. Defying theory and ideology, the Shaping Self 'wither[s] into the truth',[30] declaiming:

> . . . I seek an image, not a book.
> Those men that in their writings are most wise
> Own nothing but their blind, stupefied hearts.
> I call to the mysterious one who yet
> Shall walk the wet sands by the edge of the stream
> And look most like me, being indeed my double,
> And prove of all unimaginable things
> The most unlike, being my anti-self . . . [31]

# THE CRITICAL CONDITION OF ULSTER

JOHN WILSON FOSTER

The critical condition of Ireland at the present time seems undivorceable from the condition of criticism in Ireland. The failure of Irish society is the failure of criticism. First of all, the failure of objectivity, of the generosity that permits objectivity, of the sympathetic faculty that impels generosity. Secondly, the failure of reflection and self-examination. Thirdly, the failure of an intelligent assertion of legitimate sectarian interest, heritage and identity possible only when objectivity has been striven for. It is surely telling that whereas the island has an enviable canon of literature, a critical canon would be difficult to conjure into existence.

The reasons for criticism's poor showing occur to me as they occur to you: throughout the island a powerful and ancient church permitting, if I may borrow a phrase from Matthew Arnold, as much play of the mind as may suit its being that; in one corner of the island a Dissenting church dangerously confusable, as Arnold claimed, with philistinism; the presence on the island of several homogeneous groups religiously and otherwise distinctive and bent on power and survival in ways that lead to petty, occasionally forceful forms of absolutism (and criticism cannot breathe the air of absolutism). To these we might add the unnecessarily but understandably disabling effects of class-consciousness, province-consciousness and colony-consciousness, all imposed by the association with England. I hesitate to add that quality of life Yeats attributed (or misattributed) to us when he relished the remark: 'We Irish cannot become philosophic like the English; our lives are too exciting.'

What recognizable criticism we have had in Ireland was conducted by writers for whom England and Ireland represented, discursively, a unified field: 'critical unionism', we might say. Yeats and the Irish Revivalists attempted to disrupt that with an anti-bourgeois, nationalist universe of discourse. To this extent the Revivalists were Partisans (interested proponents of a view of Ireland as she ought to be), yet in their recoil from political factionalism, sectarianism, and practicality, in their cultural umpirage, they resembled 19th century Sages, or Olympians as I would call them. (We watch Olympian and Partisan jostling for position in Yeats's 'Easter 1916', for example.)

That public sphere from which the Olympian detached himself but upon which he depended, passed with the Revival, with the Anglo-Irish, leaving a discourse vacuum. In Ireland at the present time there is no genuine critical sphere. (Outside Ireland, of course, there is, as this conference bears witness; for in a sense this conference is not taking place in Belfast but in an international academic setting. The international Academic plies a valuable trade in Irish literature, but tends to take his cultural and political cues from the writers under examination.) The passing of the Anglo-Irish has at once fractionalized, simplified and deadlocked the issue by leaving the field to two antagonistic Irelands in need of education. These two Irelands, Catholic and Protestant, Southern and Northern, Nationalist and Unionist, have up to now supported little criticism that wasn't Partisan.

Circumstances of course have not been felicitous. The earlier Troubles were solved when the Anglo-Irish capitulated (the metamorphoses of identity by which the leaders of the Revival disguised their capitulation became the chief works of that movement). This led the majority culture to suppose that by an internal domino principle Ulster Protestantism would follow suit.

Because this did not happen, because the differences in Ulster seem unbridgeable, and because Ulster defended its integrity with injustice, the critical faculty, unused in Ireland to objectivity, is baffled. Over it Ulster seems to cast a dangerous spell. I want to demonstrate this actually happening when some of the liveliest minds in Ireland today contemplate Northern Ireland, the critical condition of which occupies me here. These are the New Partisans: inheritors of a cultural identity and political stance pulling them one way, but academic practitioners of a discipline whose various imperatives and currencies pull them, by gravity of intellect, another way. Despite the confusion this creates over Ulster, a confusion of rhetorics but ultimately of politics, I take heart from the discursive plurality, seeing in it an unprecedented promise of a genuine critical sphere in which we will one day discuss Ulster without rancour, sectarianism, radical prescription, or atavism.

I have taken as my test the pamphlets put out by the Field Day Theatre Company of Derry, a most significant critical enterprise, all of whose implications even its directors may not recognize.

*

In *Heroic Styles: The Tradition of an Idea* (pamphlet No. 4), Seamus Deane claims there are two dominant ways of reading Irish literature and history: the Romantic way and the Pluralistic way. He means also that there are two modes of Irish writing, since the first is represented by Yeats and the second by Joyce. Neither is capable of addressing satisfactorily the Northern crisis in his opinion, which he sees (in deference to current critical theory) as a linguistic or stylistic crisis. Both the Romantic and the Pluralistic modes are, he argues, at base nationalistic, fuelled by the nationalist notion of restored vitality.

In the Romantic mode, 'the restoration of native energy to the English language is seen as a specifically Irish contribution to a shared heritage'. 'Cultural nationalism', writes Deane, 'is thus transformed into a species of literary unionism.' To this extent, Deane allows no difference between Yeats and Ferguson, since both beat the strategic retreat of the Ascendancy from political and cultural supremacy. Whereas Catholic Ireland could provide Yeats with a language of renovation, the art and civilization of Yeats's new Ireland came from the political connection between England and Ireland. Deane writes: 'An idea of art opposed to the idea of utility, an idea of an audience opposed to the idea of popularity, an idea of the peripheral becoming the central — in these three ideas Yeats provided Irish writing with a programme for action. But whatever its connection with Irish nationalism, it was not, finally, a programme of separation from the English tradition.' Deane then quotes from Yeats's 'A General Introduction for My Work' to exemplify what he calls 'the pathology of literary unionism'.

With some of this I am in agreement. The problems arise when Deane seeks to import his categories into Ulster where in its special air they disintegrate (and indeed, his argument in part requires that they do). He wants to use the old categories to explain Ulster but senses that they no longer apply: a critical point in his thinking, I believe. Since we are told that 'the cultural machinery of Romantic Ireland has . . . wholly taken over in the North', the equation of Romanticism with unionism cannot hold here (unless Ulster Catholics are seen as unionists at heart), for *both* communities, it seems, cherish a Romantic millenial faith in their eventual triumph. And if the equation is just between Romanticism and Nationalism, that might work for Paisleyism but not for Official Unionism. Indeed, Deane has to cut corners to demonstrate that the Ulster

Protestants resemble the Anglo-Irish (though this stage of the argument requires that Ulster Catholics do too) in seeing themselves as an élite people, even as a lost tribe. This might be true of politicized fundamentalists (and Terence Brown and Marianne Elliott — of whom more anon — confirm this), but when applied to thoroughgoing bourgeois and yuppy unionists, of whom there are thousands, it is obviously nonsense. For Deane, Paisley IS Ulster, embodying as he does 'violence, a trumpery evangelicalism, anti-popery and a craven adulation of the "British" way of life'. The recourse of Deane's argument to caricature (of Ulster Protestants, not Paisley) betrays a reluctance to admit that Protestantisms need not be identical, to admit the possibility of an authentic, appositive culture.

Joycean separatism is not an acceptable alternative, it seems, to the romantic nationalisms (or unionisms) of Ulster, because it leads to cosmopolitan pluralism, to what Deane eloquently calls 'the harmony of indifference'. Superficially attractive though this is to Deane's critical theory, it is rendered unusable by his residual cultural nationalism. This critical theory and that cultural nationalism conspire to reject in Joyce what might have been at least entertained vis-à-vis the North: individualism (which Deane might be confusing with cosmopolitan anonymity), realism, and a liberal humanism earthed in tolerance and compassion. Instead, Joyce is seen as having become disenchanted even with the privacy of the individual consciousness though he is yet seen as nostalgic (in some vaguely nationalistic way) for the lost vitality of community.

Meanwhile, and despite resisting the claims of realism, Deane calls for a rejection of the romantic mystique of Irishness. To accept this mystique 'is to be involved in the spiritual heroics of a Yeats or a Pearse'. Yet to reject it 'is to make a fetish of exile, alienation and dislocation in the manner of Joyce or Beckett'. But although they represent worn oppositions, there is 'little room for choice', apparently, between the hot and cold rhetorics of Yeats and Joyce. Indeed, they are 'inescapable'. Against this defeatism, it is difficult to know how to entertain Deane's request that we re-read (i.e. rewrite) all our politics and literature, and that we compile 'a comprehensive anthology of what writing in this country has been for the last 300–500 years'. Such an anthology, we are told, would expose the ultimately political stereotyping of Irish national character. The request is cast in some doubt since Deane himself is not averse to stereotyping when he addresses Ulster Protestantism. Still, such an anthology is worth a try, and Field Day might consider assembling a group of potential editors under the leadership of Seamus Deane himself. I myself would be willing to participate, just as long as the all-Ireland anthology reflected the strong Scottish and English dimensions of Northern literary culture; the compilation, which might be epoch-making, must in other words have the comprehensiveness of political neutrality.

Deane castigates Yeats's literary unionism in order, one feels, to loosen the grip on contemporary Ireland of remaining Anglo-Irish thinking, ultimately of Protestantism and England, in fact of the British presence. Yet the real significance of his argument is that his attentiveness to contemporary critical theory has involved him in an attack on _any_ Irish nationalism that recalls us to a preferable past, relies on a mystique of Irishness, and defends itself on grounds of the restoration of vitalizing unity. Given Deane's background and eminence, this is monumental. Deane has broken with one of the two distinct discourses in which the republican movement speaks, according to Richard Kearney in Field Day pamphlet No. 5 (_Myth and Motherland_). The remaining discourse is 'the secular discourse of military action, political electioneering and social work', but on the subject of a united Ireland such a discourse has been so far unconvincing. Seamus Deane, this most influential of Irish critics, must now it seems abandon the nationalist position (including the realism of its secular discourse) and describe for us the alternative space to romantic nationalism and international modernism he believes his anthology would establish. Whether he does or not, _Heroic Styles: The Tradition of an Idea_ joins the lonely landmarks of Irish criticism.

*

In so far as Declan Kiberd's _Anglo-Irish Attitudes_ (pamphlet No. 6) offers a realist solution to the Irish problem, it is at variance with Deane's, but the Northern terminus of the argument is familiar.

'Antithesis', in Kiberd's opinion, 'was the master-key to the entire Victorian cast of mind, causing people to make absolute divisions not just between English and Irish, but also between men and women, good and evil, and so on.' Although as far as English and Irish perceptions of each other were concerned, this was a reciprocal arrangement, it is the English perception of the Irish that exercises Kiberd because England was the colonizing power and the Irish a minority group — like women and children whom the Irish (he provocatively tells us) were occasionally held by the English to resemble.

For some of the English, the Irish represented barbarism, a stereotype examined by Seamus Deane in Field Day pamphlet No. 3, *Civilians and Barbarians*. For other, Ireland represented pastoral beauty, emotional spontaneity and spiritual idealism. Yeats accepted the antithesis but reinforced the positive stereotype, though stereotype nonetheless. In the beginning of his pamphlet, Kiberd demonstrates with a supple intelligence how Irish dramatists from the late Victorian period onwards — notably Wilde, Shaw and O'Casey — turned the stereotypes on their heads in the service of a belief in an underlying human unity. Kiberd himself rejects and reverses the English stereotypes of Ireland. He agrees with Conor Cruise O'Brien that the Irish are not pugnacious but paralysed, not idealistic but pragmatic, not passionate but cunning. At the same time, nationality is itself something close to a stereotype to be jettisoned. Kiberd would seem to write approvingly: 'As an internationalist, Shaw had mocked "that hollowest of fictions", the notion of an *English* or an *Irish* man.' Kiberd's attack on antithesis and stereotype, behind which lie his feminism and socialism, would seem to incline him to a belief in essential unity underlying exploitive and divisive stereotypes.

Oddly, though, this manages to leave his nationalism and republicanism intact. Unity is all right, unionism is all wrong. His argument leads him to diminish cultural differences between England and Ireland, and also — judging by his rather unfair treatment of F. S. L. Lyons's *Culture and Anarchy* — *within* Ireland. Kiberd substitutes the unifying power of cash for the divisive power of culture which he sees the English as fostering.

To do so, he has to conjure out of existence Ulster Protestantism as a cultural entity. There is no Ulster culture because there is no Protestant imagination. Protestant culture is 'unionist culture'; it is in fact the Unionist party; no, it is (leaving for Kiberd a residue of admiration for the cash-conscious hard men) the Ulster Defence Association. How disappointing that someone so alert, so correctly alert, to the stereotyping of the Irish by the English should resort to the very mental process he deprecates in order to solve the Ulster question. The concept of androgyny, to which Kiberd seems attracted and which makes a nonsense of the binary opposition of stereotyped genders, rests on the equality and mutual respect of the constituent sexes, not on the caricaturing and absorption of one by the other. Yet this is what Kiberd's political androgyny does. One might have thought, moreover, that the political androgyny of the Ulster people, especially of the Ulster Protestants (part British, part Irish) would have aroused Kiberd's benign curiosity. Instead, his nationalist stance turns out to be the political equivalent of male chauvinism.

Kiberd ends his pamphlet by calling on English liberals to scrutinize Ulster unionism. We suspect why: he supposes that when they find out how hideous a movement it is they will lobby for British withdrawal. But I should have thought that the call is unearned until *Kiberd* has striven to understand 'Unionist culture', its history and dynamics. The antithesis in his mind between Unionist and Republican might saddeningly become real, but at least it would rest upon the awareness of unevadeable cultural differences.

Besides, his enviably well-argued belief in underlying unity, especially economic unity, of Britain and Ireland (that future Anglo-Irish talks might ironically uncover or cement) surely pushes him towards a federalist grasp of the British Archipelago! 'Opposition brings reunion', he approvingly quotes Giordano Bruno at the outset of his pamphlet, a quotation bearing some irony by pamphlet's end. When he laments — albeit for familiarly tactical reasons — that Unionist misrule has eroded many of the best features of British democracy, that nationalist argument threatens to backfire. The deconstructionist tendency of Kiberd's always lively criticism, enabling his attacks on antithesis and stereotype, and his contemporary feminism and older socialism ought, it would seem, to conspire to threaten his republicanism and nationalism as well as permit an attack on British colonialism; they do, I think, but not yet acknowledgeably. In the meantime, we do have a provisionally healthy plurality of rhetorics at work.

*

In each of these important pamphlets, then, there is a text splendidly handled for the most part. Seamus Deane wishes to demystify Irishness, a task compelled by the Romanticism of the Revival. Declan Kiberd wishes to dissolve racist, sexual and cultural antitheses, perpetuated by the Revival, and substitute the economic facts of predicamental similarity. In pamphlet No. 1, *A New Look at the Language Question*, Tom Paulin wishes to enhance our awareness of the linguistic unity of the island. Respectively, these are attacks on literary, cultural and linguistic unionism. To them we can add pamphlet No. 2, Seamus Heaney's *Open Letter*, a rejection of literary unionism by refusing the laureateship bestowed on him by Motion and Morrison in their anthology, *Contemporary British Poetry*.

In each case there is a subtext: repudiation of the political union of Great Britain and Northern Ireland. The Anglo-Irish are slighted, likewise (in the cases of Deane and Kiberd) the Ulster Protestants (except for the hard or wild men, praised, one suspects, as potential separatists and therefore potential republicans). The pamphlets are politics by other means, and as variations on the nationalist theme are chromatic and resourceful.

But in each case the logic of the text will not support the subtext. Deane's argument points us towards anti-nationalism, Kiberd's towards an undefined British federalism. Paulin's points us towards partition or UDI as convincingly as towards Irish federalism, but my claim will have to go unsubstantiated, I'm afraid. The moment at which the subtext threatens to surface is rather like the turn in a sonnet. In each case there is a brilliant octave on English-Irish cultural relations, followed by a disappointing sestet when Ulster is contemplated. Criticism flounders when political discourse subverts the splendidly deployed critical discourse of the octave. The process is repeated in Richard Kearney's *Myth and Motherland*. There, the *logos* of rational critique is distinguished from the *mythos* of irrational mystification (Kearney's example being the pervasive Irish myth of motherland). '*Mythos*', we are told promisingly, 'can never be insulated from the ethical critique of *logos* . . . We cannot afford to dispense with the difficult task of determining when myth emancipates and when it incarcerates.' The next stage is surely Kearney's own ethical critique of the Irish myth of motherland. In the meantime, his own lapse back into *mythos* — the language of sacrificial republicanism — does not augur well; 'The poets and [H-Block] prisoners', he says, 'are there to remind us that myth often harbours memories or expectations which established reason has ignored at its peril . . . if we need to demythologize, we also need to remythologize.' His pamphlet threatens to prove alas that the longest way round is indeed the shortest way home.

These provocative pamphlets have helped us reach a critical point in Irish cultural understanding. If these and other critics can honour the logic of their text, abandon subtexts, and maintain a critical discourse in wilful neglect of hereditary or acquired political discourse, we will see the emergence in Ireland of an authentic critical sphere, a critical unionism within the island, we might say. Success will require getting behind all stereotypes, not just disfavoured stereotypes, as unearned unitary thinking seduces us into doing.

'Culture, not politics' ought to be one of our slogans, 'Criticism, not politics' another, each implying the strategic pretence that these are separable activities. By politics I mean political and constitutional scenarios, prescriptions, blueprints, programmes — and an uncritical contempt for 'the other side'. We simply do not know enough at present to prescribe or forecast the political future of Ulster, certainly not an imminent united Ireland.

And so I echo Tom Paulin's regard for the dialects and languages of Ireland, but suggest we study them without yoking them to a political prescription. I echo Declan Kiberd's call for the study of Unionist culture, but let its positive as well as negative guises be studied, and by *Irish*, indeed, anti-Unionist, students of culture, not just English politicians. And I echo Seamus Deane's summons to dissolve the mystique of Irishness, but I challenge him to initiate this necessary task by seeking to dissolve through understanding the negative mystique of Ulster Protestantism. In Kearney's otherwise illuminating pamphlet, Unionist mythology receives one sentence, and whereas nationalism is a 'tradition', Unionism is a 'camp' (whose tents, he no doubt wishes, were folded). If my own summons seems one-sided, that is because critics of non-nationalist background have reciprocated in advance to the extent that they are sympathetic students of that Anglo-Irish literature dominated since Joyce by 'Catholic' and 'nationalist' writers.

The Free State came about only after forty years of cultural preparation. By 1920 Ireland had asserted a sufficiently different culture, according, that is, to the people who turned out to be the ones who mattered — including, let us take note, the Anglo-Irish who studied well (if not too wisely) a culture not their own. Consider the contrasting case in Ulster. There has been no cultural preparation for a united Ireland WHATSOEVER. That being the case, it is an impossibility outside its military imposition. And *that* being the case, I beg to differ with the New Ireland Forum *Report* which considers that any kind of united Ireland is preferable to the status quo and that a united Ireland is an urgent requirement. If there is anything it is not, it is urgent, unless we wish to witness the spectacle of civil war. Cultural fusion by force would result in sharper cultural fission than before. Those who wish to see a united Ireland by consent should let the cultural preparation commence, but it will require the altriusm of cross-sectarian studies.

What I am proposing is something different from, but not unconnected to, what I sense happening in Ulster this weather: reversion, the return to respective corners, the equivalent in the intellectual sphere of that increasing polarization we are witnessing in the political sphere. If one guise of this is the Field Day enterprise, another is the less apologetic stance by Protestant historians and critics, which we see, for example, in the *Festschrift* Edna Longley and Gerald Dawe have edited in honour of John Hewitt. Ian Adamson, who correctly I think accuses the Ulster intelligentsia of failing to promote a Northern identity, has taken the stance one step further, and in the book *The Identity of Ulster* tries to provide all of the Ulster people with an ancestry, a language, a culture — a mythic base for the political superstructure of a future independence.

The authentic critical space and time lie the hither side of Adamson's prematurely independent North. In the cause of understanding, we must probe (but not press) cultural differences as far as is incompatible with sectarianism or political prescription. 'The recognition of difference, especially by Irishmen themselves,' Lyons has correctly said, 'is a prerequisite for peaceful coexistence.' We might choose to interpret such work as an inducement to the change of heart Orwell found, in the work of Dickens, as revolutionary as the call for a change in society. It might even constitute the third phase of a familiar dialectic. In phase one, two groups are invidiously conscious of their differences, with one group enjoying supremacy. In phase two, there is a liberal assumption, especially by conciliatory members of the dominant group, that the two groups are equal because similar. In phase three, there is a mutual recognition, initiated by members of the oppressed group, that the two groups are equal and mutually dependent because *different*. This, I think, has been the pattern in the Women's Movement and, before that, in the Civil Rights Movement in the United States; it may with luck be the pattern in Ulster.

*

In achieving it, we might enlist, along with pooled cultural information, the kind of thinking pioneered for us by Deane and Kiberd but applied by them only to Anglo-Irish relations. In its alertness to the deployment of opposing stereotypes, we might call this thinking structuralist. Structuralism is heavily indebted to Saussure for whom in the linguistic system there are only *differences*, with meaning not immanent but functional, the result of a sign's difference from other signs. In Levi-Strauss, as we know, the differences become binary opposition, a state to which we in Ulster are daily accustomed. At the same time, for the structuralist the units of a system have meaning only by virtue of their relations to one another. This strikes me as an interesting avenue to explore, though we are not speaking of the liberal relief at finding underlying unity. To give but one example: to what extent is an Ulster Protestant an Ulster Protestant because he is not the Ulster Catholic of whom he is nevertheless incessantly conscious? Isn't the Ulster Catholic an inescapable element of his own identity? But if so, this is only because Protestant and Catholic stand in constant opposition to one another. The psychoanalytic (not just semiotic) implications of Self and Other couched in sectarian rather than sexual terms remain as far as I know unexplored.

For Roland Barthes, signs are deployed in codes with which we are in Ulster again daily familiar, along with a rich subtextuality of Irish discourse virtually inaudible to outsiders. 'O land of password, wink and nod', writes Seamus Heaney. 'The spurious mystery in the knowing nod', writes Derek Mahon, revising it later, with semantic if not poetic gain, to 'The hidden menace in the knowing nod', for of course such mysteries are not spurious. Barthes's musings on the class vocabulary of the French Restoration could be matched by our musings on the encodification of such words and phrases as 'the North', 'the people of Northern Ireland', 'The Six Counties', 'peace and stability of Ireland', 'cherish', 'aspiration', 'staunch', 'fervent', 'intransigent'. Among recent documents, the New Ireland Forum *Report* cries loudest for decoding.

We know, too, that for Saussure rites and customs, and for Levi-Strauss historical facts and even myths, partake of the nature of signs. Almost at random, one might consider the Irish implications of Levi-Strauss's claim that myths are logical techniques for resolving basic antinomies in thought and social existence, and of his reflections on the analogical processes of the archaic mind (which seems to have survived into modern Ireland).

*

To their credit, Field Day have chosen to honour a sense of difference by commissioning three pamphlets on Unionist culture by writers of non-nationalist background. Unfortunately, then, it is a case of Protestants on Protestants, not the cross-cultural studies I am calling for, but it is better than nothing. Indeed, I heartily recommend the pamphlets by Terence Brown and Marianne Elliott (Nos. 7 and 8 respectively) as contributions to our knowledge of Northern Irish culture and, especially, as evidence of a rich and honourable Protestant culture in the province. Moreover, in

these two pamphlets, the difference is in the end denied, one arguing for the desirability, the other for the possibility, of a unified
Ireland. Protestant culture, it is alleged (as though answering
Kiberd by being more truly nationalist than himself), is not
Unionist culture. It is unjust to accuse Brown and Elliott of some
wishful thinking on the matter of a united Ireland without giving
them a hearing, especially since cultural ignorance we most certainly can not accuse them of, but such I fear is the case, and the pamphlets are available for your scrutiny, perhaps as material for
discussion in seminar.

Given the limitation on time, I have opted to strengthen my
argument (and to obviate if I can any misunderstanding of my position) by glancing at the one Field Day pamphlet that advocates continued Union and partition. My argument is a simple one: inadequacy
in our cultural knowledge and our criticism vitiates our thinking on
Ulster, and is encouraged by political prejudgement. It is the principle neither of nationalism nor of unification that is at issue but
the concreteness of the relationship between these and cultural
reality.

The liberal (or Official) Unionism of Robert McCartney's *Liberty
and Authority in Ireland* (Pamphlet No. 9) completes the trinity of
Protestant viewpoints begun with Brown's Anglo-Irish perspective (cultural fusionism) and Elliott's United Irish perspective
(Protestant-led republicanism). As befits the author's status as
Unionist Member of the Assembly and Queen's Counsellor,
McCartney's pamphlet defends partition on the grounds that only
membership in the United Kingdom guarantees the liberty of the individual possible in a libertarian democracy. Unification of Ireland
is undesirable (and undesirable *only*) because the present Republic
is a theocratic state. Where Brown sees, since 1914, a monolithic,
occasionally irrational Unionist North, McCartney sees a would-be
pluralist state. Where Brown sees in the present Republic a state
pluralistic enough to assemble the New Ireland Forum, McCartney
sees a threatening and irrational monolith, a conspiracy of
nationalism and Catholicism, an authoritarian homogeny (and
hegemony) that violate the frontiers of private life and individual
freedom.

The dilemma of liberal Unionism, according to McCartney, is its
support for civil and individual rights while rejecting an Irish unity
which would entail the denial of those rights. Clearly, liberal
Unionism is itself McCartney's resolution of the dilemma which
that political position creates. For, in fact, the dilemma as he poses
it creates not one but two Catch-22s.

First of all, whereas the aspiration towards a united Ireland might be granted to Northern nationalists as a civil and individual right, that aspiration, if it is pursued too actively or successfully, will be opposed and the right rescinded. In *The Way Forward*, a recent Unionist Assembly Party discussion paper (one of the authors of which is McCartney), it is proposed that 'distinctively Irish cultural activities' be fostered in a pluralist, British Ulster. But for decades, the aspiration to unity has been part of the cultural ideology of a large part of Ireland. What Catholic nationalist believes that his culture would be sincerely fostered in a state which bases its opposition to a united Ireland partly on cultural grounds? This is a problem raised by my earlier suggestion that we strategically pretend that culture and politics are separable. Where the aspiration to unity is concerned, this could only be done if the aspiration were culturally processed as precisely that — the *aspiration* to unity. But Conor Cruise O'Brien has told us that in the Republic the aspiration has in fact already been transferred from the political to the cultural realm. If so, the status of the aspiration could conceivably change in Ulster (if it hasn't already), pending cultural preparations for its retranslation from the cultural to the political realm.

I seem to be helping McCartney solve a problem he hasn't even recognized. For the difference between North and South he labours to establish must surely hold in some sense between the Nationalist and Unionist populations of Northern Ireland itself. Unless he regards (like Adamson) Ulster Catholic and Protestant as mutually distinct from Southerners, then the overriding of minority and individual rights that McCartney deplores in the Republic must by definition happen — though to a lesser extent — in Ulster also. McCartney would not see the ironic parallel, since he does not see events in cultural terms. For him it is a simple question of legal rights originating in the secular democracy of the United Kingdom. Not only are Catholics and Protestants alike, but everyone is like everyone else, in desiring liberty; it is just that certain populations, for example Southerners, are denied liberty by powerful institutions, for example the Catholic hierarchy and their parliamentary puppets.

It is an unwarranted cultural assumption that everyone subscribes to the bourgeois liberal humanism McCartney tries to articulate. It is not just that Northern Protestants maintain certain democratic rights at the expense of those who do not recognize the democratic majority *as a democratic majority*, but that Ulster Catholics may not even subscribe to the values of the putative

majority. McCartney assumes that Southerners groan under a
political structure that isn't a full secular democracy on the British
model. But if they aren't so groaning, then perhaps their Northern
co-religionists are groaning under a political structure that impedes
full expression of a culture that does *not* produce or want to produce, a secular democracy. We don't know enough (or rather, I as
an Ulster Protestant do not know enough) about possible differences that might ironically underwrite partition but leave the
problem of Northern Ireland unsolved.

The second Catch-22 is this. The inability of Northern Ireland to
accommodate the active aspirations of many of its citizens is surely
one cause of its conservatism. But if Ulster cannot be truly liberal
because the Republic is an illiberal state, as McCartney maintains,
this is an implicit acceptance of the interconnectedness of North
and South. And if the rejection of unity is based *solely* upon objections to state restrictions on individual freedom in the Republic,
Irish unity is not being rejected in theory or principle but only in
practice, on grounds of present reality in the South. Of course,
McCartney believes that the theocratic nationalism of the South is
synonymous with that state's sovereignty and independence, making real changes impossible. But if we grant this, and if McCartney
desires a greater liberality in Ulster, would not a forceful statement
of unity as a goal and a good not encourage liberalism in the
Republic (a milder form of the Protestant re-colonization of Ireland
with which Elliott toys) since the prospect of unification would
endanger its future as a Catholic monolith? In turn, the pluraliza-
tion of the South would — using McCartney's own formulation —
lift the siege in Ulster, creating conditions for the greater liberaliza-
tion, not just of Ulster but of all of Ireland, bringing the island into
synchrony with mainland democracy. The principle of unification,
and practical discussion between North and South on its eventua-
tion, would, then, resolve the fundamental dilemma of liberal
Unionism. The only snag is that it is erased as a political position
in the very resolution of its dilemma.

Once again, criticism and culture, reason and reality, part company. It is not just that reason is imposing itself on someone else's
culture, but that it has lost touch with, shrinks from, the culture
that lies behind *it*. McCartney overlooks the possibility that
another reason for Ulster's conservatism might be the nature of
Ulster Protestant, his own, society. Besides the little-sung virtues of
this society (and we thank Brown and Elliott and the editors of the
*Festschrift* for bringing them to our attention), there are the repres-
sions and illiberalisms, even the theocratic impulses, rooted in a

culture that might or might not be very different were the nationalist siege lifted. McCartney's libertarian constitutionalism
seems not always relevant to the Ulster I know, even though Brown
implies that if the nationalist siege were lifted (through unification),
an historical freedom of belief and behaviour would return. But the
relationship might be there nevertheless. It is highly likely that
McCartney holds his views for cultural rather than strictly
philosophical reasons, that his philosophy is a rationalization and
defence, through inversion, of Ulster reality; the legalistic argument might be the best one, not necessarily the most sincere one,
McCartney can muster. Certainly his appeal to the rights of the
individual is important and is to be heeded, but it must be earned
*through* the past and the present in the way Gabriel Conroy in
Joyce's great story 'The Dead' earns his selfhood by confronting
and absorbing the cultural forces that seek to impede as well as sustain him.

*

　　The early Field Day pamphlets do not consider individualism as
any kind of solution to the Irish problem, crushed as it is between
the anti-individualism of nationalism and the anti-individualism of
structuralism. Structuralism has, of course, given way outside
Ireland to poststructuralism, and if poststructuralism finds the individual no more meaningful than its predecessor, at least it stresses
the plurality of meaning, an emphasis that has more in common
with liberal humanism than with structuralism, as Eagleton
remarks, more in common with multiculturalism than with the
homogeneous social state Barthes anticipated in *Writing Degree
Zero*. In structuralism is the wherewithal to understand the
systemic tensions of Ulster and Irish societies. But if we are
disssatisfied with the composition of these societies (and who is
not?), and if structuralism is too comfortably reconcilable with the
ideology of the status quo, then we can try to reveal the inherent
contradictions and assumptions in defences of that composition.
Deconstruction in particular seems, at least in its intention to
undermine binary oppositions, admirably suited to meet the
demands upon the critic of two looming realities in Irish life: sectarianism and sexism. 'For of all the binary oppositions which post-
structuralism sought to undo,' Eagleton writes, 'the hierarchical
opposition between men and women was perhaps the most virulent.'

In Ulster (and Ireland) they are joined by the opposition of Protestant and Catholic, as well as Nationalist and Unionist (and within Protestantism, of Ulster Loyalist and Ulster Nationalist). But all the cultural data (including the unpalatable data) must be factored into the process of decoding, else it will be an arid academic exercise. And it is surely possible without political prescription (veiled or overt). And yet it might be in the end a truly revolutionary criticism: to say 'this is the case' might be tantamount to saying 'is it right that this should *be* the case?' Revelation, we might say, *is* revolution.

Mine is, unashamedly, the old liberal humanism (Arnold's disinterestedness, even, but strategically courted) co-opting the methods of structuralism and poststructuralism, but prepared to entertain, though not permit, its own supersession. A critical programme for Ireland, after all, has to accommodate fear, brutality, unhappiness and violent death. You will recall David Lodge's character, the critical theorist Morris Zapp, surviving the ordeal of being a hostage, and expressing a revisionist belief in the individual. 'I thought deconstructionists didn't believe in the individual', he's challenged. 'They don't. But death is the one concept you can't deconstruct. Work back from there and you end up with the old idea of an autonomous self. I can die, therefore I am. I realized that when those wop radicals threatened to deconstruct *me.*'

Besides, the autonomous individual may be a bourgeois humanist fantasy, but many of us in Ireland would like to enjoy that fantasy, thank you very much. We have had the psychological feudalism, as it were of nationalism and oppressive religion: it would be foolish for us to embrace the psychological socialism of poststructuralism before reaping the rewards of psychological *embourgeoisement*. The anti-individualism championed by the Revival lingered long enough in much of Ireland to thwart the reactionary claims of the self staked by a line of writers stretching from O'Connor and O'Faolain to Brian Moore and Bernard MacLaverty. (And to Seamus Heaney, whose poetry richly displaces its recurrent desire into totem and taboo.) The celebration of self-realization, not just cultural similitude, is what I intend by Realism, and Realism in Ireland has not yet earned its own replacement, settling as we have had to for pathological realism, a literary mode that is nourished on its own impossibility, examining among other things how personalities are warped into what it pleases us to call 'characters'. 'Self, not system' should be another of our slogans, dangerous and outmoded in America but revolutionary here. I was gladdened to hear Declan Kiberd in Tacoma, Washington recently, in a characteristically pyrotechnical talk, defend individualism, referring to 'modern Ireland, whose writers, whose philosophers, and whose people have never had the opportunity to become themselves. And this is because, after the Easter Rebellion, they abandoned the Irish Renaissance as a search for personal freedom.' This is the line we must walk, skirting carefully cultural insult and insensitivity.

And if we bracket for the time being poststructural strictures on Realism, let us bracket likewise those on biography and autobiography. It is a plurality of voices we precisely need in Ireland in order to interrupt the tiresome duologue of recent history. I was heartened to come across this by Levi-Strauss:

Biographical and anecdotal history is the least explanatory; but it is the richest in point of information, for it considers individuals in their particularity and details for each of them the shades of character, the twists and turns of their motives, the phases of their deliberations.

One is tempted to exclaim: let ungovernable choirs of dissonant voices rain down on us in Ireland; let the forests be invisible for the trees! But of course the claims of sect and heritage will remain and remain legitimately, helping as they do to form this exclamatory self. To aid us in understanding *them*, let me suggest that Field Day organize a series of public seminars up and down the island devoted to examining our cultural diversity and constituent personalities, seminars popular enough in presentation to attract the intelligent unacademic, scholarly enough not to arouse the attentions of those with a political prescription in one pocket, a gun in the other. Before us we have the example of the Revivalists of what can be accomplished along these lines. But let us not like them prejudge the outcome of our deliberations, whose final political form none of us in any case will live to see. To those of us who wish to see a unified Ireland, it is an immense but necessary forbearance for us to accept, as I believe we must, words borrowed by Arnold from another context: the existing order of things till right is ready. And right is ready when objectivity, sympathy and generosity have been expended.

# THE POLITICAL UNCONSCIOUS IN THE AUTOBIOGRAPHICAL WRITINGS OF PATRICK KAVANAGH

EAMONN HUGHES

The autobiographical impulse is at the heart of much writing in Ireland, with an influence which spreads far beyond the formal and generic boundaries of autobiography into the novel, poetry and even drama. The obvious concern common to both autobiography and Irish writing is the issue of identity and it is to this shared concern which I wish to attend. What I propose to offer in this paper, therefore, is a consideration of the constituents of identity in an Irish context and an examination of some of the theoretical principles raised by the criticism of autobiography followed by a brief reading of Kavanagh's autobiographical work as an illustration.

To fix identity in an Irish context is an apparently easy matter. One chooses from a range of available terms, Catholic or Protestant, Northern or Southern, provincial or cosmopolitan, rural or urban, nationalist or unionist and so on, until one has identified oneself with a particular group or community. Ultimately, of course, the identity which is at stake is that of being Irish or non-Irish. It is for this reason that the issue of identity is such a contentious one, and the debate on the issue is not aided by the fact that the very terms in which the debate is usually couched are themselves sites of conflict. Consequently, when the debate considers those terms it usually results in a frightening circularity, as is evidenced by the cultural criticism of, say, Daniel Corkery, in which the Irishness of any writer can only be sanctioned if he or she fulfills each of the conditions which Corkery applies normatively rather than descriptively.[1]

I would suggest that this is evidence of a political unconscious in Irish writing and history despite the apparently politicised quality of both. This unconscious — political and social rather than personal and so beyond psychoanalysis — is due to the way in which the whole range of political thought and feeling has been appropriated to one particular type of politics. In Ireland politics are either nationalist or unionist or else they do not exist. That is to say, one can be nationalist or, its strategic rather than its ideological opposite, unionist, or else one is considered to be either apolitical or disillusioned with politics. Nationalism, by definition, must assert that it is an absolute and it is this quality which needs to be analysed.[2]

A defining characteristic of nationalism is that it must appear to be a monadic force. It is this characteristic which both resists and requires analysis. As an apparent monad, Nationalism cannot allow for the presence of dissenting, oppositional or even question-ing voices; consequently it presents itself as an absolute. This self-presentation operates in two ways. Firstly, Nationalism appears to be a coherent and unified totality. Secondly, Nationalism offers itself as a unifying force. The structures offered by Nationalism are undifferentiated; should questions to do with one's relationships, allegiances and identity arise they are all answered in the same way: one belongs to a national grouping. Under Nationalism this answer is supposed to satisfy all such questions. The power of Nationalism, its ability to provide a satisfying set of relationships, a focus for allegiances and an identity which meets the needs of many individuals cannot be denied. Nor should we forget that this power is derived, in part, from the fact that Nationalism is originally predicated upon certain cultural features common to individuals within a given society. However, while such common features cannot be denied, the effect of Nationalism is to alter them from a set of contingencies into an apparently natural totality. To do so, Nationalism inverts its own relationship with culture and attempts to control cultural activity. By doing this it presents itself as a natural way of organising a society and its culture with the consequence that it appears to be beyond human determination. Since the principal focus of Nationalism is the relationship of a society with other societies, more usually with one other, dominant society, Nationalism sanctions conflict with other societies while refusing to accept the possibility of conflict (in whatever form) within its own sphere of influence.

For this reason the undoubted power of Nationalism to satisfy needs and to explain experience must not be taken at its own valua-tion. That valuation — Nationalism as a natural order — denies history, denies the fact that Nationalism alters and fragments to accommodate itself to historical change while always attempting, often successfully, to present a seemingly changeless facade. In effect, Nationalism would deny that its roots are in human activity and that it is a nexus of — often conflicting — human practices. In fact, while it can satisfy certain needs, if it were really monadic, questions about relationships, allegiances and identity would not arise. That they do arise is a challenge to Nationalism, a challenge that it is ill-prepared to meet since its very appearance denies that such challenges can arise. Unionism is effectively the shadow of Nationalism. Like Nationalism it has changed and fragmented while presenting itself as a unity. Unlike Nationalism, however, Unionism is not an ideology but a strategy and as such it reacts in accordance with its perception of Nationalism — Stormont, not the Dáil, was the direct descendant of Grattan's parliament, and as such would have satisfied any of the major figures of constitutional Nationalism.[3]

The persistence of Nationalism and Unionism have skewed political, social and cultural debate in Ireland. However, neither Nationalism nor Unionism can satisfy the political unconscious which both seek to repress under a ready-made identity. The writing of autobiography is an act of that political unconscious, a refusal to accept the identity between the state, the nation, society, culture and the individual by which both Nationalism and Unionism seek to repress the political unconscious. That this is the case is evidenced not just by the large number of autobiographies produced in Ireland but also by the form which many autobiographical projects take. Many writers (like Yeats or O'Casey) produce serial autobiographies, a number of separate but linked volumes over a long period, or else (like Moore or Kavanagh) they involve themselves in a process of autobiographical experimentation. Common to both types of project is the constant need to question the supposedly unquestionable.

The criticism of autobiography, which I now wish to consider briefly, is comparatively recent. Autobiography had been discussed before the 1950s[4] but it was in the 1950s that it really came under critical scrutiny. Its criticism grew at a time characterised by new criticism and proto-structuralism and has remained marked by that time. Attention is most often focussed on major texts and a variety of formalist approaches has been used. The consequence of this is that, with some recent exceptions, the prime concern of critics of autobiography has been 'Western man' who goes under a number of aliases: Augustine, Cellini, Bunyan, Rousseau and Newman are some of them. This kind of approach equates autobiographies and autobiographers from a range of historical and cultural contexts in an effort to consider them in purely generic terms. Critics such as Shumaker and Pascal,[5] using this kind of method, have located the formal autobiography on a sliding scale of autobiographical writing, which is itself continuous with other forms of prose. The formal autobiography, they maintain, must be a unified meditation upon the individual avoiding both the over-emphasis on 'external' events of the memoir and *res gestae* and the fragmented form of the journal and diary. This seems to be a fair assessment of the genre. More recent critics, such as Avrom Fleishman,[6] have continued and elaborated upon this approach as have, in a slightly different way, those critics, like Jeffrey Mehlman,[7] whose concerns are determined by the post-structuralist crisis of the subject. It may seem odd to link this range of critics but what is common to all of them is that, despite the fact that they have done valuable work in establishing the credentials of the genre, they have also distorted the genre. The focus of their criticism, with its interest in the self and in writing, is more pro-perly called 'autography' rather than autobiography because all such criticism leaves the *bios*, the life, out of account. As a conse-quence, and given the transhistorical and transcultural nature of much of this criticism, autobiography is reduced to being yet one more example of textuality. It is simply to be regarded as another set of textual structures interacting only with other such structures and displaying a signal failure to refer to anything outside of those structures. Autobiography properly considered, however, scan-dalises this type of criticism. A consideration of the *bios* shows that autobiography is separate from the memoir and *res gestae*. Unlike them it is not concerned with events at which the writer was only fortuitously present. The *bios* represents a set of events and ac-tivities upon which both the *autos* and the *graphé* are contingent. As Karl Weintraub puts it: 'History of self and history of a world are inextricably linked.'[8] Criticism of autobiography must con-sider the autobiographer, his or her determined and determining activities, the life, and the ways in which those are evidenced by the writing. Such an approach would add to our sense of the textual sophistication of autobiography rather than detracting from it. It would also allow for the comparison of autobiographies with a shared cultural and historical background, and, in the context of Irish Studies, would enable autobiography to be seen as a genre which considers the relationship between a nation and the culture from which the nation is constructed.

This should not be mistaken as a plea for a return to any of the forms of traditional biographical criticism. I have taken my title from Frederic Jameson's *The Political Unconscious* and am interested particularly in his concept of the 'life' as 'an unconscious master narrative . . . a *fantasm* . . . an unstable or contradictory structure, whose persistent actantial functions and events . . . demand repetition, permutation and the ceaseless generation of various structural 'resolutions' which are never satisfactory . . .'.[9] These repetitions and permutations determine both life and texts in Jameson's terms. It seems to me that they are the mark of autobiography, especially autobiography constantly returned to, since it is the genre in which such repetitions and permutations are most blatantly, though still unconsciously, enacted.

Kavanagh's persistence as an autobiographer is one of the reasons I have chosen him for illustrative purposes. The others are to do with the period in which he worked. He followed the writers of the revival who had already established autobiography as a major form in Ireland, who had tilled the field, and he is also an influence on contemporary writers. For Terence Brown he is a writer of 'assured vision',[10] while for Seamus Heaney he is, despite certain reservations, a true writer of place and as such a touchstone and a continuing presence in Irish poetry.[11] In both cases it is his success which is important. My concern however is with Kavanagh's struggle, his recurrent theme of failure, and (the fortuitous resolution of the later poetry aside) his own eventual failure.

Kavanagh's writing is marked by anoesis, a condition of experience without understanding; his struggle was to understand that experience. The theme of failure in his work is linked with his continuing anoesis and his eventual failure was that, despite the length of the struggle, he never did come to an understanding of his experience, and could not comfortably assume an identity. The clearest sign of this is the number of autobiographical works he produced: *The Green Fool*, *Tarry Flynn*, *The Great Hunger*, *Self-Portrait* and the posthumous *By Night Unstarred*. With the exception of *Self-Portrait*, which is anyway not a continuous narrative, all of these works are set in the same period, roughly from the turn of the century to the 1930s. This is, unsurprisingly, also the time of Kavanagh's upbringing and early manhood and also the most significant period in Irish history. Kavanagh treats it in a particular, even peculiar, way. His autobiographical works treat of, but pay little attention to, the major events of those years: the apparent defeat of nationalist aspirations, their recrudescence and partial fulfilment after war and civil war, the establishment and consolidation of a state around that partial fulfilment, the massive redistribution of land and continuing rural depopulation. This strangely neglectful treatment of the great moments of nationalist history corroborates what Heaney says about Kavanagh:

Much of what he says is a plea for an ideal national culture but it is premised on the rejection of nationality as a category in cultural life.[12]

Kavanagh's stress in his autobiographical works is not on the changes brought about, in one way or another, by the nationalist movement but rather on the lasting qualities of life in his part of Ireland. In the face of the altogether slower and grander rhythms of history with which Kavanagh is concerned such changes are seen to be superficial. The community he describes is in decline, caught between the past and the present, subject to the inevitable forces of modernisation but still enmeshed in the social and economic structures of the past. His image of the very landscape reveals this:

From the tops of the little hills there spread a view right back to the days of Saint Patrick and the druids. Slieve Gullion to the north fifteen miles distant, to the west the bewitched hills and forths of Donaghmoyne; eastward one could see the distillery chimney of Dundalk sending up its prosperous smoke . . .[13]

Kavanagh rejects Nationalism as a structure of history; *The Green Fool* shows us a brief flirtation with nationalist politics quickly ended when it becomes obvious that such politics will not deliver the new Ireland which they have promised (*TGF*, pp. 104–9).

Not satisfied with this rejection of nationalist politics Kavanagh then sets out to scandalise one of the main nationalist pieties. Both *The Green Fool* and *Tarry Flynn* address the question of what the peasant community is like, and both come up with an image which is at odds with the more usual, contemporary images of that community. For contemporaries such as O'Connor and O'Faolain the peasantry represented an organic community into which the urban individual could escape from the individualism and alienation of the modern world. This image of the peasantry was also a major constituent of the ideological project of the Free State, serving in effect as a mask for the poverty of the social and economic realities of the new state, a project given cultural ratification by Corkery in his role as semi-official cultural apparatchik of that state. *The Green Fool* and *Tarry Flynn*, in language which establishes Kavanagh as a part of that community, explode this sentimental and politically useful image of the peasantry by revealing that they are disunited, litigious, spiteful, apathetic and bound by outworn rituals and conventions. What Kavanagh had achieved by the time he had completed *Tarry Flynn* was to have discounted any form of nationalism as a sufficient explanation for his own individual consciousness. This is a major, almost prescient, achievement given that O'Connor and O' Faolain would in their own later autobiographies rely heavily on those same received ideas as the explanation for their own respective identities. Having dismissed the stock fictions by which so many autobiographers in Ireland explain their identity Kavanagh was left with a major problem: how was he to account for his own identity except in those terms? There are two moments, one in *The Green Fool*, one in *Tarry Flynn*, which offer a synthesis of what Kavanagh was. In *The Green Fool* there is an image of the farm as a library in which every tree and hedge harbours a piece of writing (p. 208) while in *Tarry Flynn* clay, that most central of Kavanagh's images, is recognised as a substance which 'could produce a miracle of wings'[14]. In each case the tensions felt by Kavanagh, love of the land and the need for literature and escape, are balanced as active principles. Such moments, however, are rare; it is more often the case that the land is seen as an inertial force keeping him from poetry and escape, as is the case in *The Great Hunger*; at other times escape and literature are seen only in terms of the loss of the land which he loves.

To understand this tension fully we need to invoke the concept of the master narrative. All too often Irish literary autobiographers seek to explain their identities as writers who have been brought to birth by the nationalist movement and their autobiographies end as ratifications of state ideology, no matter what has gone before — I am thinking here particularly of O'Faolain. Kavanagh, once again, refuses this option. His autobiographical project seeks an explanation not just for the writer but for the whole man. Kavanagh was peasant, cobbler, farmer, poet, each of which is both an individual pursuit and a social function. As a poet he was set apart from his original community and yet the *parole* of his writing is very much a part of the *langue* of that community — which is to say that in practical terms his consciousness was a part of that community. That consciousness in its turn barred him from writing in a way which could afford him an easy social function. In terms of a master narrative such social functions are both determining of and determined by the tensions within the individual. The autobiographical writings seek not to smooth out those tensions but to understand them. *The Green Fool* gives us a full account of the elements which go to make up the fragments of Kavanagh's identity. *Tarry Flynn* attends more closely to the period in which the decision is made to leave the community. *The Great Hunger*, like *Tarry Flynn* a projection of the master narrative rather than autobiography proper, offers an enactment of what Kavanagh's life and identity may have been if he had not left. The first part of *By Night Unstarred*, editorially the most problematic of Kavanagh's

writings, offers another version of that same life. It is the only one
of his works which is about success and is a projection of what
Kavanagh might have been as a successful farmer. It is also the only
one of his works which suggests a way forward for Kavanagh after
he had left nationalist politics behind. In the first part of the novel
we have a projection of what Kavanagh might have been, based,
as is *The Great Hunger*, partly on his own experience and partly
on actual conditions. What this part of the work offers is a critique
of how indigenous capitalism arose in Ireland and how nascent
capitalists appropriated nationalist politics. To this end Peter
Devine, the central figure, is seen joining the Land League for
motives of self-interest rather than political ones,[15] doing no pro-
ductive work himself and deliberately alienating the labour of those
who work for him (*BNU*, p. 72). It is this which sets Devine apart
from Kavanagh who had from the first lines in his *Collected Poems*
sought an identity between the farmer and the artist which turned
upon the unalienated nature of their labour:

> I turn the lea-green down
> Gaily now,
> And paint the meadow brown
> With my plough.[16]

However, Kavanagh's analysis of Devine is compromised by the
evident admiration for him as a man with a vision, at times akin
to the vision of the poet (*BNU*, p. 104), who has ruthlessly and successfully followed through that vision. The Devine family are subject to criticism only because they have refused patronage to
another of Kavanagh's autobiographical projections, the poor poet
of part two of the novel.

Mention of this poor poet brings me to the end of this paper with
the reflection that, despite his achievements in refusing the easy
answers of nationalism and the beginnings of a real subversion in
*By Night Unstarred*, Kavanagh never wrote an autobiography
about a successful poet because, paradoxically, his achievements
rest on his own political unconscious and his need to continue his
autobiographical experiments. Such, indeed, is the motive for most
Irish autobiography.

# THE AUTOBIOGRAPHICAL IMAGINATION AND IRISH LITERARY AUTOBIOGRAPHIES

MICHAEL KENNEALLY

For a complex set of cultural and political reasons, critical response to Irish literature in English has gravitated towards biographical and historical rather than other theoretical perspectives. Nowhere is this emphasis more evident than in critical readings of Irish autobiographies. Several reasons unique to Irish autobiography account for this insistent seeking after factual truth and historical reliability. For one thing, most of the great twentieth-century literary self-portraits overlap in their reference to major political and social changes which occurred in Ireland during the 1890s to 1920s. The tradition was early established that readers of these texts, who themselves frequently appeared in them, questioned the validity of the facts and characters being described; thus we have Yeats impugning Moore's account of certain events or Padraic Colum calling into doubt O'Casey's portrait of specific individuals, such as Douglas Hyde. Later readers deemed themselves possessors of sufficient knowledge of the social, cultural and political development of these years, that they too could judge and compare, question and object to the materials preferred. Moreover, the biographical and historical approach is a product of conventional perceptions of the autobiographical mode. Broadly-based assumptions about the genre have led, with a few significant exceptions, to rather cursory treatment of works which not only constitute an integral and important achievement in Irish writing but are an impressive contribution to that wider body of literature which is concerned with literary self-portrayal. Preeminent among these are Moore's *Hail and Farewell*, Yeats's *Autobiographies*, O'Casey's *Mirror in My House*, and O'Faolain's *Vive Moi!*, but there are self-portraits by Frank O'Connor, Liam O'Flaherty, Patrick Kavanagh, Forrest Reid, Monk Gibbon, Austin Clarke, Brendan Behan and others.

It has only been within the last two decades that critics have begun to accord appropriate attention and investigative scrutiny to

111

this literary form. The results of this newfound critical interest are somewhat predictable; questions with regard to the use of language, the meanings of texts, and the roles of author and reader have been as critically vexing and sporadically profitable as when such issues are explored in other works of literature. As a result of this increased critical activity it has become fashionable to claim that each form of literary expression is autobiographical, that all writing (and here Goethe is often cited) constitutes a chapter in one's autobiography. Patrick Kavanagh expressed similar views in his brief *Self-Portrait* where, discussing the difficulty of finding a suitable literary means of self-disclosure, he says that the two most fully realised examples of self-revelation are *Don Quixote* and Joyce's *Ulysses*.[1] There is an obvious sense in which all literary expression is autobiographical, if only because it is a product of the author's imagination, and some writing — perhaps *Ulysses*, certainly the later poetry of Yeats — does indeed draw to a significant degree on autobiographical material. But the presence of autobiographical elements in such works does not necessarily make them autobiographies. To show how crowded and potentially confusing this corner of the literary landscape actually is, one has only to refer to such generic terms as the memoir, the confession or the autobiographical novel, or to juxtapose texts such as Newman's *Apologia Pro Vita Sua*, H. G. Wells's *Autobiography*, Francis Stuart's *Black List Section H* or even David Niven's *The Moon is a Balloon*. Despite this, it is my contention that what can be designated a literary autobiography is a genre in its own right, which, because of its own defining inevitabilities and its own criteria for success and failure, places special demands on readers. An expansion and clarification of this argument results from a consideration of the materials, structure and style of a literary autobiography.

It is symptomatic of the nebulous and complex nature of this form of literary expression that an effective means of positing some of its inherent principles is to point out distinctions from contingent genres such as the memoir, the confession and the autobiographical novel. Of these, a memoir is the most readily identifiable since it is essentially a record of one's participation in public events. The focus is directed outward to those incidents that have shaped the public persona, while personal feelings and responses are recounted to explain, clarify or perhaps justify actions in the external world. Assuming a knowledge of the self, the memoirist is concerned with providing the account of his or her participation in the social contract.

An autobiography, on the other hand, is ultimately focused

inward, to subjective states and feelings, to one's past relationship with reality, and, now, to one's contemporary perception of those former selves. The primary area of interest is not so much the social world but the private significance of public experiences, the role they have played in shaping individual consciousness developing through historical time. It should be observed that this kind of self-portrait is quite distinct from the conventional autobiography of statesmen, retired generals or celebrities; such works would more accurately be described as memoirs, concerned as they are with the public self, and never crossing into the realm where the well-springs of identity are plumbed, where beliefs, knowledge and perceptions of the self and its relationship to reality are confronted and probed. It should also be observed that while literary autobiographies are most frequently composed by writers, that fact alone neither precludes others from writing them nor, of course, does it mean that a writer will necessarily produce a literary autobiography.

There are no essential generic distinctions between a confession and a literary autobiography; what differences do exist have more to do with form than genre, since the subject of a confession, as well as its narrative procedures and structural elements, find echoes in that long line of works known as spiritual autobiographies. In fact, the autobiographical tradition may be seen originating in the introspection that is central to the Christian ethos, where one's relationship to God is personal and private. As prerequisites to defining that relationship, one must examine one's soul (a word which previously meant very much what we mean today by self), develop a sense of accountability and responsibility for actions, and explain the self to the self. In the paradigm of the confessional form, the narrative traces the protagonist's religious odyssey, the wayward journey to spiritual truth, the progression from the acknowledged sinfulness of past actions to the present state of grace and divine forgiveness. The author of the work confesses, the confession is made to God, the witness to the confession is the reader. St. Augustine's *Confessions* and Bunyan's *Grace Abounding* epitomize this autobiographical mode.

Even without the overtly religious dimension, vestigial structural and rhetorical characteristics of the confessional form continue to manifest themselves in autobiographical literature; in the eighteenth century we have Rousseau's *Confessions*, in the nineteenth, George Moore's *Confessions of a Young Man*, and, more recently, *The Autobiography of Malcolm X*. The key structural metaphor of the confessional mode is the conversion from false knowledge to truth, a moment elaborately prepared for, dramatically articulated, and subsequently confirmed by action and statement. In the triangular relationship between author, addressee and reader, the reader's role is to observe the honesty with which the self is examined; it is to witness the truth being discovered, the sins being acknowledged, and the newfound grace — be it social, political, religious or artistic — being described.

Even in those works which evince little similarity with the confessional mode, the trope or metaphor of the turning-point from ignorance to true knowledge can serve as an important structural device. O'Casey's autobiography, for example, hinges on his successive attempts to arrive at a personal ideology which would account for his past sufferings, explain his present literary and political frustrations, and hold out the promise of a future compatible with his deepest aspirations. The movement toward that moment of insight and genuine understanding of the self is prepared for in the first three volumes of the work, is articulated in the ringing prose of the fourth with his conversion to a vision of an international communist order, and is reaffirmed throughout the two closing volumes by periodic passages of praise for the Soviet Union, which is presented as the first tangible proof that the new Jerusalem will be manifest on earth. In *Hail and Farewell* Moore, in a more subtle and finely-woven fashion, employs a similar strategy by casting himself in the role of cultural Messiah who will save Ireland from the barbarisms of Catholicism. The progression from his misplaced interest in English art and literature, succeeded by his active commitment to the cause of Irish culture, followed by his inevitable rejection and separation, parallels the confessional mode in which the hero is finally at peace with himself and his God (in Moore's case, art) even if he is alienated from his own people.

As with the memoir, the essential distinction between the autobiographical novel and the literary autobiography is one of focus. Although autobiographical novelists freely plunder episodes from their past, their concern is with wider, supra-personal goals which have more to do with society than individual history, with aesthetics than the self, with literature than biography. In turning to personal history, the autobiographical novelist is involved in an act of imaginative liberation of the self, of sanitizing experiences so that they can be enlisted in the service of a truth whose validity transcends the personal. The literary autobiographer is also involved in an imaginative encounter with selected details of biography; this common characteristic is the source of the ambiguities and generic overlappings often perceived in literary self-portraits and autobiographical novels. Obviously, this imaginative dimension is intrinsic to all retrospective processes since earlier moments of existence and previous states of being are recalled across a gulf created by time and only accessible now through memory which, necessarily selective, often compensates for its failures and distortions through the use of imagination. In autobiographical portrayal, then, to recollect is often to imagine, to remember is frequently to create. Given those similar tendencies, the genres are ultimately distinguished from one another on the basis of how each author treats the outlines of personal history to bring the story to its inevitable conclusion. The autobiographical novelist can achieve narrative and imaginative closure unavailable to the autobiographer, whose story consists of a predetermined subsuming of past awareness into contemporary consciousness. No matter how disparate former images of the self are, an autobiographer must acknowledge a tenuous but nonetheless prefiguring relationship between them and later identity. Unlike the autobiographical novelist, the autobiographer writes under the burden of reaching a demonstrable accommodation between the created selves and their creator.

This is not to claim that an autobiographer views his text as being strictly mimetic. A literary self-portrait does not attempt a representation of quotidian reality with all its concrete details, objective historical facts and chronological sequences. While such information can help delineate the external self, while it may ground the public persona in place and time, the literary autobiographer is ultimately concerned with exploring private subjective reality. Thus, interest is evinced in factual and chronological exactitude only to the degree that it contextualizes thoughts and emotions and allows for the clarification of awareness and consciousness. As James Olney has observed, the life with which an autobiographer is concerned 'does not stretch back across time but extends down to the roots of individual being; it is atemporal, committed to a vertical thrust from consciousness down into the unconscious rather than to a historical thrust from the present into the past'.[2]

In addition, as the literary autobiographer involves himself in an imaginative interpretation of personal history, his ultimate focus is on himself as he does so; he is always his own observer, ever cognisant of his dual roles as subject and creator. Sean O'Faolain begins his brief autobiographical sketch with a disclaimer:

You ask for a self-portrait? Very well, in that case I must ask you to imagine me at this moment standing in front of a painter's easel, my right hand poised to make the first charcoal outline on the bare canvas. And you must also imagine that I am looking into a mirror placed a little to my left, because what I am about to execute is *A Portrait of the Artist as an Old Man*. I need hardly say that when I present myself to you as a portrait painter, I am using a metaphor. I am really a portrait writer, a very different person indeed, if only in so far as a painter of self-portraits is always the same age as his sitter, whereas a portrait writer is always older, always remembering, always looking back.[3]

O'Faolain might have gone on to say that, in fact, he required two mirrors, one to reflect the series of former selves lurking down the long corridors of memory, and the other to catch his reactions and responses as he views those earlier manifestations of identity. In *Shame the Devil* Liam O'Flaherty dramatically highlights the encounter between present and past selves by introducing a haunting figure from his past, his artistic demon, which enters into conversation with the side of his character struggling to live an ordinary, non-literary life. This device of staging an imaginary conversation between aspects of self is also to be found in, of all places, John Mitchel's *Jail Journal*, a work whose title does nothing to suggest the introspective analysis of motives which periodically characterizes the narrative. Mitchel sets up a conversation between different facets of self — what he calls The Ego and Doppelganger — to explore the premises of his nationalist ideology and examine the consequences of his political actions. In such balancing of mimetic and self-reflexive impulses a literary autobiography profoundly challenges many of our assumptions about the various tensions implicit in every act of literary creation. A written self-portrait is premised on a special relationship between objective and subjective realities, between author and text, between text and reader, and, finally, between reader and author. It is in the unique configurations of these relationships that the distinguishing features of a literary autobiography are to be found.

There is yet a further mirror phenomenon at work in the process of literary self-disclosure. If the autobiographer gazes into the mirror of his own past, and simultaneously consults the mirror catching his reaction as he does so, he is also confronted by the images of the self looking back at him out of the mirror of his own creation. Unlike the most introspective self-portrait by a painter, which is restricted to presenting the findings of self-observation and scrutiny, literary autobiography can not only render the dialogue between contemporary and former selves which yielded such findings but also the dialogue between the emerging self in the work and the autobiographer, between the created self and its creator, between text and author. This capability means that literary autobiographies are frequently characterized by periodic assessments of the emerging images of the self; the autobiographer becomes, as it were, a surrogate reader of his own text which, in turn, incorporates a discussion of its ongoing validity and effect. Such internal critical evaluation often produces adjustments in perspectives and shifts in emphasis.

In *Vive Moi!* O'Faolain gives an example of this dynamic process as he describes his idyllic childhood summers spent with cousins in Rathkeale. In his attempt to capture who he was in that far-off time, he tries to recount his experiences by asking: 'What did I do in Rathkeale? Nothing. I once described Rathkeale in a travel book as a dead, lousy, snoring, fleabitten pig of a town, adding that I can never think of it without going soft as a woman. Nobody ever came to Rathkeale unless he came there from his mother's womb or for business . . .' O'Faolain goes on in this vein for another half page, creating a picture of a silent, enervated Irish town where nothing happens — and does so with a deadening regularity. He abruptly stops, however, and decides that such a picture does not allow for the accurate portrayal of the self in that environment, it fails to suggest the complexity of his former connections with that charmed place. He writes: 'But no! This is the wrong style. This is the cowardly, evading style that fears the heart. Ask me that question again so that I may answer it simply and honestly. "What *did* I do there?" '[4] He proceeds to give a much more varied description of the town, and then goes on to trace the later perceptions, knowledge and feelings derived from his experiences there.

What this passage also vividly demonstrates is the obvious but nonetheless significant fact that an autobiography is much more an accurate reflection of contemporary awareness than a replication of past selves. The past is not some locatable object which can be bracketed and contained; it never existed as a separate entity which we have left and to which we can return as we might to a house or landscape of childhood. The past remains forever inaccessible simply because we are unable to obliterate the present. It is, therefore, always a function of present consciousness or, as one critic of the genre has put it, an illusion created by the symbolizing activity of the mind.[5] As a product of immediate affiliations, then, a literary autobiography is often a unique version of identity, evincing all the competing impulses and tensions of character at a given moment of life. As such, it is a projection of self which may not necessarily be compatible with an identity defined ten years before or after. Patrick Kavanagh in his brief *Self-Portrait* scornfully dismisses the stage-Irish image of self presented twenty-seven years previously in *The Green Fool* which, he now claims, was written

'under the evil aegis of the so-called Irish Literary Movement'.[6] It
is possible that certain writers, George Moore for example,
become obsessed with the evanescent nature of the self and, in
repeated efforts to pin down its changing, elusive qualities, per-
sistently return to the autobiographical mode. Incidentally, in this
regard, Moore's literary heir is Monk Gibbon, whose several
autobiographical volumes reveal a recurring desire to transform experiences into images of the self. Moore and Gibbon are reminiscent of Rembrandt (Moore would have been delighted with the
comparison) who, over his long career, painted more than sixty
self-portraits, all of them complete, all of them valid, yet none of
them final.

Each literary autobiography, then, will embody its own unique
purposes. In some works, the author's intentions may be annun-
ciated at the outset of the text; in others, additional motives may
be discovered by the author during the introspective process; in still
others, certain purposes may only be implicit in the text. An
autobiographer may start out secure in knowledge of the self, so
that the undertaking is one of self-definition and self-confirmation.
Or, the unfolding of palimpsestic layers of former selves may be
initiated for self-clarification or self-discovery; the retrospective
journey is begun by the individual on the premise that true contemporary awareness of the self is possible only when previous aspects
of identity are understood. Alternatively, an autobiographer may
begin self-representation secure in the conviction of contemporary
self-understanding only to discover in the very act of self-
disclosure, in the actual process of conjuring up former selves and
considering and reflecting on them with present insight and pre-
judice, a new perception of the relationship between those selves
and the self which is reflecting on them. Thus, what will have
begun as an assured process of portraying a self already known and
understood, can become one of insight and revelation, with past
selves, as it were, competing in dissonant voices for their own claim
to authenticity.

At the outset of *Shame the Devil*, Liam O'Flaherty announces his
suspicions that the fount of his literary inspiration has gone dry but
he ends the book by incorporating the short story he had been
struggling to write all through the self-portrait. In the opening
paragraph O'Flaherty writes that the work will have an ostensible
didactic aim because it will be 'the log of my folly, and as such,
perhaps useful to those of my species who are equally cursed with
original sin'.[7] But as soon becomes apparent, the autobiography
was undertaken to write his way out of a slump as a creative writer,

to restore his confidence in his capabilities as a literary artist. James Clarence Mangan begins his autobiography by stating: 'My desire is to leave after me a work that may not merely inform but instruct . . . that shall operate, simply in virtue of its statements, as a warning to the uneducated votary of Vice.'[8] However, in addition to these moral and didactic reasons, it becomes evident that an implicit purpose in writing the work is Mangan's desire to confess his sins and personal weaknesses not merely to God and the reader but to himself.

Self-explanation, self-justification, self-discovery and self-expression are some of the most common autobiographical purposes. Ultimately, all autobiographies are an attempt at self-communication; the process of literary portrayal, of imposing form on one's life, is a means of concretising that which has previously been amorphous and subjective, an act which proves to oneself as well as others that one has existed, and exists. It is an effort, however feeble, to break down the barriers of personal isolation, to liberate oneself from the restrictive silences of self-consciousness; all autobiographies are proclamations of existence, notes sent from the island of self to make contact with another. As such, they are also gestures toward immortality, proof that the self not only existed but has derived significance and meaning above and beyond the haphazard experiences of the fleeting years.

The competing intentions and essential themes of autobiography find expression in the designs imposed on the materials of exterior facts, in the metaphors of the self that are created. However, O'Faolain's scepticism about the difficulties of painting a picture with words reminds us that autobiography, like all literary texts, is dependent on language, with the attendant ambiguities, restrictions and distortions that such use entails. Autobiography is a verbal construct exploiting all the possibilities of literary composition to refer beyond itself to a putative self, modulating in a spatial and temporal world. Unlike a painter's self-portrait, a written portrait is fluid; it exists in time and space and can only be viewed, not from a static vantage point as a painting can, but over the period of reading the text. Equally problematic, it is a portrait which comes into existence anew for each reader; indeed, like all texts it attains its final meaning from the dynamic process by which the reader's active participation allows the words to achieve their full effect. Whereas a painting is an object of perception, a literary self-portrait is, ultimately, a product of the reader's conception. Just as the autobiographer is relentlessly confronted by the limitations of his medium, readers of the work must acknowledge that the images

of self proffered are the writer's creative response to the challenge
of language as a medium for approximating consciousness. Access
to autobiographical identity is therefore integrally bound up with
all aspects of the work as a literary construct: the choice of
materials, the formal patterns and structural tensions evident in
their emphasis and proportion, and the many narrative and
stylistic means of rendering them.

If we begin with the question of contents, we might take as our
guiding principle Oscar Wilde's observation that 'The truth is
rarely pure and never simple'. Indeed, that all those involved in
retrospective analysis harbour profound suspicions about the
possibility of being faithful to the truth is attested to by the frequent and contradictory statements on the issue found in the works
themselves. For example, Lady Gregory in her autobiography
chafes under the pressure to conform to factual accuracy by
quoting from her own play, *The Jackdaw*, in which the character
Mrs. Broderick complains, 'it's a terrible thing to be put in the dock
and be bound to speak nothing but the truth'.[9] On the other hand,
William Carleton opens his autobiography with the claim that 'in
the events which I am about to detail, especially those of my later
life, the reader may expect nothing but the strictest and most con-
scientious truth'.[10] Autobiographers who are acutely aware of the
difficulty, indeed the final inefficacy of persistent recourse to factual truth, usually adopt rhetorical strategies to deflect interest
away from this aspect of the work. They may attempt to preclude
the litmus test of accuracy by a direct admission such as Yeats's
statement in the preface to *Reveries Over Childhood and Youth*
that 'I have changed nothing to my knowledge; and yet it must be
that I have changed many things without my knowledge . . .'.[11] In
*Hail and Farewell*, Moore so weaves obvious fictional scenes, imaginary conversations, fantasies and dramatised events with actual
experiences that the whole orchestrated creation is intended to ob-
fuscate and undermine objective reliability so as to make impossible any appeal to historical truth. Others, like O'Casey, attempt to
distance themselves from the responsibility of being faithful to the
facts by writing in the third-person, thereby making explicit what
is inherent in the use of the more conventional 'I' of first-person
narrative — that the protagonist in any autobiography is a persona
created by the author.

It is obvious, then, that biographical and historical approaches
to literary autobiography offer little of critical value by observing
the inaccuracies and distortions resulting from a highly selective,
assuredly biased and frequently imaginative rendition of experience.

External information may be used, however, to determine the principles behind the re-alignment of events and the interpretive emphasis accorded them. Even so, while such critical procedures may prove salutary for an understanding of the self encompassed in the work, a much more vital, sensitive and illuminating perception of autobiographical identity results from reading the text as a coherent literary construct which, through strategies of composition and expression, yields possible conduits to that ultimately ineffable centre where individuating rhythms of consciousness shimmer and vibrate.

In addition to facets of identity suggested by contents, further insights into character are available through an examination of the formal and structural elements of the work. By virtue of his retrospective position an autobiographer tends to project a shape onto his materials. Indeed, several critics of autobiography have made the observation that the original sin of the genre is the assumption that life can be shown to possess coherence, if not actual unity, that it evinces cause and effect, and is open to rational explanation.[12] As O'Faolain says in 'A Portrait of the Artist as an Old Man':

> . . . every artist, of his nature, always wants to discover some sort of personal pattern in the apparently formless chaos of his life. Unfortunately there is no such consistent pattern in any man's life. Man is not a roll of wallpaper. He is not homogeneous. He is a multitude of particles, full of those contradictions, inconsistencies and incompatibilities that are our efforts to adapt to change, to chance, to fate, to unforeseen experiences, to new discoveries and to our own manifold mistakes.[13]

Compounding the potential distortions produced by the imposition of form are those produced by the pressure to encase experiences in the carapace of narrative; the requirements of plot, character development and satisfactory resolutions of conflicts can vitally affect the shape of the work. In autobiography, then, the desire, indeed one might say the necessity, to present life as story often plays havoc with the details of life as personal history.

The structure of an autobiography is influenced by yet another crucial factor. Unlike specific literary forms within a given mode of writing — for example, the sonnet or epic within the poetic mode, the tragic or comic within the dramatic —, literary autobiography does not appropriate any specific formal requirements. Nor indeed is prose the only narrative mode which might be used; Wordsworth's *The Prelude* is proof that structure and form are very much determined by individual predilections. An autobiographer may structure his or her work by following the traditional linear patterns of chronological sequence, by orchestrating materials around a moment of conversion, by following the chronology of the unfolding autobiographical act, or by responding to spontaneous mnemonic rather than temporal contiguities. For many autobiographers, an experimental, fragmented form produces a more accurate image on the representational plane of the fundamental structures of consciousness. Yeats's autobiography is a classic instance of the loose, inchoate structure that a written self-portrait can achieve. Because of its different compositional periods, the work comprises six distinct sections, one of which, *The Trembling of the Veil*, is further divided into five books which attempt to compartmentalize distinct periods in Yeats's evolution. But within this overall principle, we have rapid shifts in narrative perspectives, cryptic bits of dialogue, enigmatic musings, extracts from diaries, accounts of dreams, reveries and visions. Forrest Reid writes the penultimate chapter of *Private Road* in the form of a poem; Synge uses prose passages as transitions between scraps of poetry and diary extracts; and, as noted, Liam O'Flaherty includes his story, 'The Caress', as part of his text. Perhaps the strangest of all formal experiments in Irish literary autobiography is that of Joyce's friend J. F. Byrne (the model of Cranly in *A Portrait*) whose *Silent Years* concludes with several pages written in five-character code groups, climaxed somewhat incongruously by the coded rendition of a speech by Douglas MacArthur to the American Congress, on Asian policy.

Primary among the factors shaping the structure of an autobiographical portrait are the roles which the author creates for himself in his relationship with the external world. Because almost all twentieth-century Irish literary autobiographers had their formative or most active years in the dynamic period from the 1890s to the 1920s, their self-portraits acquired structural characteristics that transcend the mere fact of covering the same historical events. Thus, among others, Moore, Yeats, O'Casey, O'Connor and O'Faolain, armed with the retrospective wisdom that is the privilege of all autobiographers, turn to the events of recent Irish history as a means of authenticating their present identity. Common to all these works is that their contemporary perspectives — whether Moore's London of the early 1910s, Yeats sporadic vantage points from 1914 to 1938, O'Casey's two-decade compositional period, or O'Connor's and O'Faolain's position in the Ireland of the early 1960s — reveal a view of Irish life dramatically inconsonant with that envisioned and worked for in earlier years. Thus, the pattern manifested in these self-portraits is of the individual's initial optimistic, even idealistic perception of Ireland's future (whether perceived in cultural, social or political terms), his active participation in Irish life to see the realisation of that concept of nation, followed by disillusionment and disappointment in the reality which now confronts him. This perception of a special relationship between self and nation, the tendency to explore and define oneself in terms of patriotic values and national goals, to equate one's development with national destiny provides the central structural metaphor of twentieth-century Irish literary autobiographies.

O'Faolain in *Vive Moi!* makes what is perhaps the most overt equation between self and country. His stubborn commitment to the ideal of an Irish republic, even as the events of 1922 showed the hopelessness of such a dream, is evident in the claim that 'I was Ireland, the guardian of her faith, the one solitary man who would keep the Republican symbol alive, keep the last lamp glowing before the last icon even if everybody else denied or forgot the gospel that had inspired us all from 1916 onwards'.[14] Implicit in these self-portraits is a romantic image of Ireland's past, a shared belief in what might be termed the myth of national pilgrimage, a view of Irish history as a long, slow and painful journey from denial to fulfilment. With Ireland's past offering no readily identifiable or generally acknowledged moment embodying the many national ideals on which the future was predicated, this perception of history and destiny could evince all the eclectic, vague and composite qualities associated with a mythic image of nationhood. As each autobiographer attempted to define the role he or she played in Irish affairs, personal activities are justified and explained by conjuring up subjective versions of Ireland's past. And the legitimacy of one's vision could be attested to by references to symbolic and highly resonant touchstones in Irish history, legend and literature; events and figures from the past were commingled with actual figures and episodes from personal history to stand as models of behaviour, embodiments of patriotic aspirations, and confirmation of one's attitudes and decisions. In addition, references to a whole range of sacred Irish texts — whether songs, ballads, sagas, histories, or memoirs — could serve to clarify one's vision of Ireland's future. Thus, by linking personal identity with Ireland's quest for liberation and national fulfilment, each cultural nationalist, language revivalist, political patriot, could create metaphors of the self commensurate with aspirations and perceptions of identity.

Even more important, the evocation of myths associated with

Irish nationhood could confirm one's present alienation from Irish society, one's current role of outsider, one's estimate of Ireland's failure to achieve its true potential. In analysing the process by which dreams were shattered, O'Faolain describes how individuals were

> blinded and dazzled . . . by our icons, caught in the labyrinth of our dearest symbols — our Ancient Past, our Broken Chains, over Seven Centuries of Slavery, the Silenced Harp, the Glorious Dead, the tears of Dark Rosaleen, the miseries of the Poor Old Woman, the Sunburst of Freedom that we had always believed would end our Long Night and solve all our problems with the descent of a heavenly human order which we would immediately recognise as the reality of our never-articulated dreams.[15]

Yeats too looked to Ireland's ancient and mythic past as the source of his inspiration for that 'Unity of Culture', which would transform the Irish people into an 'enduring Nation'. The projection of self as national prophet is evident in Yeats's hope that

> a nation or an individual with great emotional intensity might follow the pilgrims, as it were, to some unknown shrine, and give to all those separated elements, and to all that abstract love and melancholy, a symbolical, a mythological coherence. . . . Might I not, with health and good luck to aid me, create some new *Prometheus Unbound*; Patrick or Columcille, Oisin or Finn, in Prometheus' stead; and, instead of Caucasus, Cro-Patrick or Ben Bulben? Have not all races had their first unity from a mythology that marries them to rock and hill?[16]

This identification of self with national destiny was possible, of course, only while the Irish nation was perceived as being in a state of becoming. Thus, an Ireland already awakened but not yet free could accommodate, if not pander to, a diverse range of national images: the urbane and artistically sensitive society of Moore, the Unity of Culture of Yeats, the socialist dreams of O'Casey, the Gaelic world of O'Connor, the ideal republic of O'Faolain. However, the Irish reality which began to emerge in the years from 1916 to 1922 and thereafter, forced a dramatic alteration in each individual's perception of Ireland's future. When the myths associated with Ireland's past were interpreted by others, when someone else's vision began to be translated into reality, an essential conflict occurred for all who had made personal identity commensurate with national destiny.

The impossibility of equating self with the emerging nation was reinforced by the deaths of the 1916 leaders. In their vision of Ireland's future, Pearse, MacDonagh, Plunkett and Connolly each had specific ideological perspectives on Ireland's past. By dying, they preserved the inviolate nature of their ideals, ensured that their perception of national destiny would be forever unsullied by the inevitable compromises and disagreements that freedom would have entailed. The dichotomy between the heroic circumstances of the Easter Rising and its fractured aftermath was interpreted by autobiographers such as Yeats, O'Casey, O'Connor and O'Faolain as confirmation of the discrepancy between the idealistic aspirations they associated with national destiny and the actual social and political reality of post-1916 Ireland. The bloody civil war and the eventual division of the country into two political jurisdictions made it obvious that no single vision of nationhood claimed unqualified support; consequently, those autobiographers who had worked for a specific concept of a liberated country could feel vindicated in not sanctioning a flawed version of national freedom. In ensuing years, the policies of successive bourgeois and church-dominated Irish governments supported the conclusion for autobiographers, especially those whose activities had been of a political nature, that it was no longer possible to identify self with country. And, of course, it was this increased sense of alienation that provided the perspective from which most of these self-portraits were written. For example, Frank O'Connor's *An Only Child* enacts the pattern of bitter discovery and uneasy adjustment. The second half of this autobiographical volume is organized around the process by which his patriotic fervor is undermined, until he is gradually forced to acknowledge his 'grave doubts about many of the political ideas I had held as gospel'.[17] At the conclusion of the book, his contemporary sense of disappointment is revealed when he narrates that, upon his release from detention camp after the civil war, his mother had claimed the experience had made a man of him. He observed that 'it took me some time to realize what Mother had seen in that first glimpse of me, that I had crossed another shadow line, and make me wonder if I should ever again be completely at ease with the people I loved, their introverted religion and introverted patriotism.'[18] However, despite the blighted hopes over Ireland's failure to achieve its full potential, to realize what each believed was its true national character, the disillusionment of Moore, Yeats, O'Casey, O'Connor and O'Faolain itself became a crucial means of structuring the presentation and clarification of their autobiographical identity.

The style of autobiography — its diction, syntax, idiom, imagery, metaphors, allusions as well as its shifting narrative postures, use of dialogue, presentation of characters and dramatised scenes — provides additional vehicles for self-definition and self-revelation. Even within a given work such devices will vary and modulate, vitally affecting the emerging images of the self. For example, childhood is usually evoked in an idealised manner, whereby the innocent and unsentient persona is encapsulated through descriptive and fleeting scenes, unstructured narrative, associative transitions and a wealth of sensory imagery. The autobiographies of Synge and Forrest Reid are notable in this regard, conjuring up as they do the wonder, exquisite happiness and blissful sense of freedom associated with younger years. In *The Green Fool* Kavanagh vividly creates the timeless, transformational quality of childhood in his account of picking blackberries at Rocksavage estate, an experience which is recollected as being of another order of reality, a totally self-contained and integrated realm of imaginative memory. Even for those who wish to stress the harshness of their youth, style can often belie such impressions by creating countervailing suggestions of joy and pleasure. Thus, an analysis of style can offer a more balanced and representative account of the ambiguity with which an author considers personal history.

Several aspects of Irish autobiographical style are noteworthy. The first of these stems from an inordinate concern with place, not so much in the just mentioned sense of private memories associated with location which is endemic to the genre, but with the sense of historical and mythical place. In Anglo-Irish autobiographies, this concern manifests itself in a stress on familial connections with the land; it is as if such individuals still possess vestigial feelings of alienation, of being an outsider if not a trespasser, and so strive to legitimize their claim to national identity by establishing the bond between self and setting, the historical plexus of genealogy and place. This emphasis is readily apparent in Moore, Yeats, and, in particular, in Elizabeth Bowen's *Bowen's Court*.

A second attitude towards place manifests itself on the opening pages of *The Green Fool* where Kavanagh, even before he gives the name of his village, provides a list of the historical and mythical landmarks visible from nearby hills. The blending of geography, history and myth is particularly pronounced in the Gaelic and so-called peasant memoirs of the twentieth century. In *Mo Scéal Féin* an tAthair Peadar O'Laoghaire, in recounting the experiences of his youth, provides a long litany of placenames and their associations. The fact that three other classics of this genre — Muiris Ó Súilleabháin's *Fiche Blian ag Fas*, Tomas Ó Criomhthain's *An tOileanach*, and Peig Sayers's *Peig* — deal with the Vanishing life on the Blasket Islands is symbolic of much of what these works set out to accomplish; they were written as records of a society at a given time and place, its customs, traditions, language and values. Titles of subsequent works in this tradition, for example, *Man of Aran, In a Quiet Land* and *The Man From Cape Clear*, draw attention to the strong identification of the individual with location.[19] It is also possible, of course, to trace this tendency of naming and describing setting, and one's relationship to it, to the dinn-senchas tradition of Gaelic poetry, in which the poet gives long lists of places, indeed establishes his authority and poetic identity to the extent that he is familiar with the historical and mythical associations of local places.

Perhaps the single most notable characteristic of Irish autobiographical style is the anecdotal approach to the narrative. This is a logical mode for an autobiographer who, in an attempt to describe and provide a context for the self, recounts relationships and perceptions of others. Of necessity, all autobiographers are, to some degree, mini-biographers of their friends and acquaintances, searching out those incidents which capture and reveal character at its most typical and essential. Thomas Kilroy, in a discussion of modern Irish fiction, has identified the anecdotal mode of narration as being crucial. He traces this influence to the oral tradition of the storyteller whose implicit assumptions about his world and his role in it reveal, in Kilroy's words, 'an unshakable belief in the value of human action, a belief that life may be adequately encapsulated into stories that require no reference, no qualification beyond their own selves'.[20] It is precisely this certainty in their own self-worth and this unquestioning confidence in absolute communication that produce the characteristics which Kilroy identifies when this oral tradition manifests itself in the Irish novel. When this same tradition finds expression in autobiography, a genre inviting an episodic and anecdotal approach, the danger is that the narrative mode is no longer obviously reflexive but almost self-sufficiently propelled by its own momentum, and thus becomes, in Kilroy's word, 'anonymous'. This tendency is evident in Kavanagh's *The Green Fool* and O'Connor's *My Father's Son*, in both of which accounts of incidents and characters frequently float free of all but the flimsiest relationship with the governing consciousness of the work.

On the other hand, George Moore exploits the anecdotal style in as daring, subtle and revealing a fashion for autobiography as Joyce, Flann O'Brien and Beckett do for fiction. In *Hail and Farewell* Moore imagines an elaborate conversation he and Edward Dujardin will have when they next meet in Paris. It consists of a series of wickedly unsympathetic anecdotes about Edward Martyn, after each of which Moore inquires of Dujardin if he now understands Martyn's character. When Dujardin acknowledges that he is getting a sense of the man, Moore replies, ' "But you haven't told me, Dujardin, which anecdote do you prefer? Stay, there is another, Perhaps this will help you to a still better understanding." ' This final anecdote has to do with the crisis of conscience Martyn faced in deciding if he should allow his play, *The Heather Field*, to be staged with Yeats's *The Countess Cathleen*, since Cardinal Logue had described the latter as being unfit for Catholic ears. Having related this story, and believing that he has successfully captured the essence of Martyn's character, Moore then reveals the autobiographical relevance of this string of spiteful anecdotes:

He wishes to act rightly, but has little faith in himself; and what makes him so amusing is that he needs advice in aesthetics as well as in morals. We are, I said, Dujardin, at the roots of conscience. And I began to ponder the question what would happen to Edward if we lived in a world in which aesthetics ruled: I should be where Bishop Healy is, and he would be a thin, small voice crying in the wilderness — an amusing subject of meditation, from which I awoke suddenly.[21]

By establishing and clarifying Moore's own aesthetic and moral predilections, the reflexivity of the narrative is reinforced; style is simultaneously an instrument of, and subservient to, the larger process of self-revelation.

The anecdotal tendency, along with other pronounced features of modern Irish autobiographical narrative might be traced to several sources, the first of which is the extraordinary amount of information available on this period of Irish history. In addition to the many literary autobiographies, there are social and cultural memoirs such as those by Oliver St. John Gogarty and Katharine Tynan, as well as the many accounts of political and military events of the time, such as Darrell Figgis's *A Chronicle of Jails* (1917), Peadar O'Donnell's *The Gates Flew Open* (1932), and Ernie O'Malley's *Army Without Banners* (1937). The effect on the literary autobiographer of this plethora of material concentrating on a few decades of Irish life was to accentuate the claim of personal truth. Thus, the revealing anecdote, the biographical sketch, the telling vignette, the accounts of shared beliefs and strong disagreements over cultural ideals, social goals or national aspirations all became a prominent feature of autobiographical writing. If one's own version of reality, the account of one's actions, was to achieve the desired effect, one had to appeal to one's audience through all the devices available, including the development of an assertive voice to dispute or negate the accounts of others. In addition, because an autobiographer was likely to find himself a secondary character in someone else's self-portrait, each author, as all autobiographers do, tries to win over, ingratiate, convince and elicit sympathy if not approval for behaviour and point of view. Thus, in Irish autobiography we find a sophisticated use of innuendo, caricature, gossip, the wisecrack, and the *bon mot*, all of which contribute to a highly personalised manner of writing.

Irish autobiographical style is also greatly influenced, of course, by the twin traditions of Gaelic and Anglo-Irish literature, by the Irishman's much-vaunted ability to take English language and, by stretching and exploring it in new ways, make it very much his own, so that it reflects the creative energies of a suppressed and often displaced people finding imaginative release in both oral and literary expression. The distinct cultural ethos and linguistic features of Gaelic society are reflected in the poetry of the bards and the fili, and in the longstanding tradition of storytelling. Many of the components of this world view — its attitude towards place, history and time, its perception of the real and the surreal — manifested themselves in Irish writing in English, lending it a unique vitality and imaginative energy. Thus, the Irish literary tradition, with its marked propensity for hyperbole, the fantastic, the episodic narrative, for invective and vituperation and linguistic self-indulgence, for all manner of wordplay and verbal high jinks, is a distinct inheritance of Irish autobiographical writing, profoundly influencing the way the self is defined and presented. No matter that this intoxication with words, this sheer exuberance of language, may distort or run away with the facts, as it sometimes does in Moore, O'Casey or Behan: the identity of the writer comes through in the language itself. On such occasions, in its very ability to suggest personal energy and passion, to reveal identity as well as convey meaning, style becomes the individual.

From this general consideration of Irish literary autobiographies it is perhaps evident that, to an extraordinary degree, they evince an unconstrained approach to selection and contents, constantly seek innovative structural principles and formal patterns, and employ a mode of writing often blatantly at odds with conventional descriptive and expository procedures. On the one hand, all such inventive features provide a more accurate, because a more diverse, means of understanding identity; through them the self is suggested and embodied rather than merely described, is revealed from several vantage points rather than portrayed from a single angle, is rendered as well as analysed. However, formal and representational innovations also reinforce how illusory and arbitrary is the autobiographical construct; they are vivid reminders that what is being read is a written life, a literary work which employs a wide range of narrative possibilities and stylistic devices. Consequently, experimental approaches are also indicative of the essential suspicion on the author's part of the whole epistemology associated with the autobiographical undertaking, an awareness of the distortions inherent in painting a self-portrait with words, of attempting to transform one's life into a literary artefact. Thus, they reflect a deep-seated mistrust of surrendering the details of one's personal history to the requirements of narrative and form, and are, in fact, repeated efforts to preserve the inviolability of the self from the distortive exigencies of plot and story. To the degree that the autobiographer resists such pressures, refuses to submit life to the demands of literary construction, a certain authenticity and integrity of the self — its amorphous, flexible, spontaneous and contradictory nature — is maintained.

Those autobiographies negotiating back and forth between these conflicting impulses not only readily engage our interest but achieve the most vital and genuine approximations of selfhood. Thus, in *Hail and Farewell* George Moore's elaborate strategies of weaving his narrative around and through personal experiences, his creation of a web of fact and fancy, his blending of historical and imaginative truth are, on the one hand, efforts to project and encompass aspects of character through those means he deems most appropriate. But they are also simultaneous attempts not to relinquish the integrity of identity to the inevitabilities of self-representation. Ultimately, this work of deliberate obfuscation reveals an individual who had a sensitive understanding of Ireland and its people, who was enthusiastic in his desire to enhance its cultural life, but who, above all, had the integrity, even at the cost of loyalty to family, friends and country, to remain true to his aesthetic beliefs and artistic principles. Yeats's episodic narrative, his inclusion of diary entries and dream fragments, his presentation of half-recollected events, and his creation of isolated scenes and imaginary conversations, are all evasions of more direct processes of self-revelation. Yet, in the masks created, the poses struck, and the conclusions drawn, the self-portrait goes beyond the presentation of its explicit objectives by offering fleeting glimpses into the working of consciousness. Behind many of Yeats's manoeuvres of avoidance, we sense feelings of unease, compromise, even failure, that are but precariously compensated for by his awareness of successes and accomplishments. In addition, intimations emerge that the restless search for truth, for a metaphysical framework that would allay the fear of time, change and death, has only yielded tentative and tenuous results. O'Casey too, not content with traditional approaches to autobiographical expression, continually experiments with aspects of representation, repeating and varying his assault on the citadel of the self in his determination both to reveal and assert the validity of identity. Thus, we are provided with a sense of his deep-rooted anger and humiliation at the forces in life that seemed constantly to thwart and deny an uninhibited expression of individuality. His feelings of constriction are, however, shot through with, and finally over-ridden by, a persistent optimism in the joy of life, its glories and rewards, its many colours and forms, all of which far outweigh moments of anguish and pain, setbacks and defeats. And O'Faolain, motivated by serious reservations about the autobiographical mode, and made uneasy by the quicksands confronting those attempting to salvage and assess personal history, involves himself in an ongoing dialogue on the difficulties and implications of his undertaking. Revealed by that dialogue is the anger — now fully expressed — at what was forever lost in childhood years as a result of his mother's constant ploys to deny their economic status. Her obsessive attempts to project a gentility which her actual circumstances could never sustain, inhibited any spontaneous feelings of joy, pleasure, even love. Coupled with this is an acute awareness of his own failure to relate in an other than prescribed and therefore perfunctory manner with his father. What emerge are O'Faolain's feelings of sadness and emptiness at the acknowledgement that while his father was kind and provident, he was unable, on a vital and fundamental level, to be simply human. It is in literary portraits such as these that the Irish autobiographical imagination finds its fullest and most remarkable expression; such texts provide not simply an impressive contribution to the literature of self-portrayal, but forcefully indicate some of the problems, procedures and possibilities of this challenging literary genre.

# ENGLISH POLITICAL WRITERS ON IRELAND: ROBERT SOUTHEY TO DOUGLAS HURD

TOM PAULIN

Robert Southey landed at Balbriggan in mid-October 1801. The Act of Union had come into force on January 1st and Southey had secured an appointment as secretary to Isaac Corry, a politician who was widely regarded as a renegade — he had played a distinguished part in the Volunteer movement, but had been bought over from the popular side by the Marquis of Buckingham and appointed surveyor-general of the ordnance of 1788. After the suppression of the 1798 rebellion, Corry was made chancellor of the Irish exchequer and in the Union debates he was the chief government spokesman against Grattan with whom he fought a duel. Corry was not wealthy and was a purely professional politician whose career, paradoxically, would be destroyed by the Union.

Southey had secured his appointment through the influence of his friend John Rickman, who had been employed by Charles Abbot as secretary in preparing the first census act (introduced in Great Britain in December 1800). When Abbot was appointed chief secretary for Ireland in 1801, Rickman accompanied him and was made deputy keeper of the privy seal. Rickman had held 'very seditious'[1] opinions in his youth and been an opponent of Pitt. He became a distinguished statistician, was friendly with the engineer Thomas Telford, and like Southey developed into a convinced Tory.

Landing in Ireland that autumn, a young English protestant with waning republican principles, Southey was disconcerted by the treeless landscape:

The country that I passed is destitute of trees as if there existed an instinctive dread of the gallows in the people. Indeed most of the young trees in the kingdom had been cut down to make pikes.[2]

Half of Southey's salary of £400 Irish was for travelling expenses and he regarded his position as a promising one — like Bunyan's

Christian he saw himself 'in the road to a future, a *clear* road . . . and not a very long way'.[3] That road lay through a country whose people, he reflected, 'will be difficult to civilize':

An Irishman builds him a turf stye, gets his fuel from the bogs, digs his patch of potatoes, and then lives upon them in idleness: like a true savage, he does not think it worthwhile to work that he may better himself. Potatoes and butter-milk — on this they are born and bred; and whiskey sends them to the third heaven at once. If Davy had one of them in his laboratory, he could analyze his flesh, blood, bones into nothing but potatoes, and butter-milk, and whiskey; they are the primary elements of an Irishman. Their love of 'fun' eternally engages them in mischievous combinations, which are eternally baffled by their own blessed instinct of blundering. The United Irishmen must have obtained possession of Dublin but for a bull. On the night appointed, the mail-coach was to be stopped and burnt, about a mile from town, and that was the signal, the lamplighters were in the plot; and oh! to be sure! the honeys would not light a lamp in Dublin that evening, for fear the people should see what was going on. Of course alarm was taken, and all the mischief prevented.[4]

The reference to Humphry Davy suggests that Southey viewed the Irish not simply as comic savages, but as the subjects of a great experiment in social science or engineering. Meeting his and Thomas Telford's friend, Rickman, in Dublin that October, Southey took his place in a mission designed to civilize a people who were, he told his friend Charles Danvers, 'filthy — beastly filthy. I cannot like them, and yet they are a people of genius'. And he adds characteristically, 'I have room for a Bull which Rickman heard'.[5]

Writing to Coleridge and other friends, he recounts examples of 'Paddyism' and in a letter to Grosvenor Bedford mentions: 'It is the opinion of Coleridge that the Irish are descended from certain aboriginals who escaped the deluge in a cock-boat that rested upon Mount Taurus. My own idea is that they are of Cretan race — the descendents of Pasiphae'.[6] Southey's view of the Irish as part 'bull', part human, issues from a type of English tribalism which has been little analysed by cultural historians, though it was briefly discussed after the Brussels soccer riot.

Southey revised his long poem, *Madoc*, in Dublin and left after a fortnight. He never returned to Ireland, though throughout his life he maintained an interest in the country's history and politics. His commonplace books contain a great deal of Irish material (volume three has approximately fifty pages devoted to Irish subjects), and in his essays Southey draws heavily on these entries. His attitude to Ireland evidences a strong sense of racial superiority[7] combined with a paternalist concern which sometimes reveals

fundamental feelings of guilt — a guilt that can give way to an
angry desire to completely reshape Ireland. Thus in 1805 he
remarks: 'England *was* free from the reproach of national cruelty
till the accursed proceedings in Ireland'.[8] Two years later he states
that nothing can redeem Ireland but such measures as 'none of our
statesmen — except perhaps Marquis Wellesley — would be hardy
enough to adopt — nothing but a system of Roman conquest and
colonization — and shipping off the refractory savages to the col-
onies'.[9] And in 1828 he remarks menacingly that Spenser 'was not
less highly endued with political sagacity than with poetical
genius'.[10]

During his brief stay in Dublin, Southey became friendly with
someone who was a close friend of Robert Emmet. Leon Ó Broin
suggests that this friend was either Tom Moore or 'young Curran'
and Southey appears to have felt that his conversations with Emmet's intimate friend were a kind of privileged knowledge which
virtually amounted to a personal friendship or tie with Emmet
himself. Like Coleridge, he felt a strange kinship with Emmet — the
Irish revolutionary was everything the two radical poets might
have been had they been born in Ireland.

Southey's sense of radical superiority shows in his reactions to
the Catholic Irish, but he appears to have been challenged and
disconcerted by the United Irishmen. Writing from Portugal in
1800, a year before his Irish visit, Southey comments on the
Portuguese refusal to accept the United Irish leaders whom the
British government had banished there:

some of the Leaders would soon have found their way to France, the only
place which is profligate enough for them; — there are others to whom any
country might gladly open her arms; virtuous and enlightened men; who
have indeed erred grievously in their contracted spirit of patriotism, but
who have acted however erringly, from the purest of motives. For such
sedition as theirs change of climate is an effectual cure, and any where
except in Ireland they would be among the best and most valuable
members of society. The alarm here was occasioned by the arrival of one
of the Secret Directory, Counsellor Sampson.[12]

This attitude of mingled admiration, criticism and something that
looks like an embarrassed guilt is expressed again in 1809:

England, indeed, may contemplate the sister-country with sorrow, and
painfullest shame, and deep humiliation, but not with fear. The time of
danger is gone by. A French army, with the lying invitation of liberty upon
its banners, would once have been joined by men, formidable for their
talents, and virtues, and enthusiasm. Some of these have expiated their
errors by death, others are living peaceably in America . . . men to be

blamed for these errors only, and fit to be the ornaments of any country, except their own. It was in these men that the strength of the united Irish lay; in Fitzgerald, and McNevin, and Emmett, and the republicans; men no otherwise connected with France than as they, most erroneously and unhappily for themselves, considered France to be the upholder of all free and enlightened principles.[13]

Elsewhere in this essay, Southey cries 'Peace to the spirit of Robert Emmett!' and it would seem that both he and Coleridge were haunted by Emmet's spirit.

Emmet was executed on 20th September, 1803. Eight days later, in a letter to John King from Keswick, Southey wrote:

Poor young Emmet! I knew much of him from many conversations with his most intimate friend at Dublin. He was an admirable man. God Almighty seldom mixes up so much virtue and so much genius in one, or talents as ennobled. In the last rebellion he escaped by excavating a hiding-place under the study in his father's house. There he lived six weeks, having food, books, and a light, by night going out into the park for exercise. And thus he continued till he found means for escaping. And now, — the stony hearts and the leaden heads that manage this poor world! as if the fear of death ever deterred any man from treason who could make treason dangerous! I would send Wm. Taylor this story of his hiding-place, for he, I know, will write his Eulogium in the 'Iris'; but it must not be published lest some other poor fellow may now be in the same asylum. To have spared that young man's life would have indeed strengthened the government. Had they said to him, 'Promise to plot no more and you shall be free', such a man would have been as safe under such a promise as in the grave. But so it is; the king has no heart for pardon: he wants goodness, and his counsellors want understanding. If they mean to extirpate disaffection in Ireland by the gallows, they must sow the whole island with hemp.[14]

It is clear that Southey was profoundly affected by Emmet's life and execution, and his impassioned letter was followed rapidly by a poem whose public rhetoric aims ultimately to formalize and dispel the volatile emotion of the private letter.

Southey's poem is entitled 'Written Immediately After Reading the Speech of Robert Emmet, on his Trial & Conviction for High Treason, Sept. 1803',[15] and he begins by verifying the conclusion to the speech which Emmet gave from the dock and which is cited in a footnote to the poem (this conclusion is not the romantic 'nations of the earth' version which is referred to, for example, in *Ulysses*). Having established his credentials as a sensitive and sympathetic onlooker, Southey then attempts a balanced assessment of Emmet's actions. The impression of balance is superficial because Southey's reaction is on one level apparently immediate and sincere, but on a deeper level is concerned to vindicate England of guilt: 'Here in free England shall an English hand / Build thy imperishable monument'. England, he insists, is a 'free isle' to which Emmet's 'erring zeal' was 'so perilous an enemy'.

Southey's 'mourning-song' expresses an uncertainty about the justice of Emmet's fate and imagines what might have happened if his 'lovely manhood' had been spared. He exclaims upon Emmet's future prospects had he been left to 'the slow and certain influences / Of silent feeling and maturing thought', and suggests how completely his heart might have 'clung to England'. It is the familiar argument for commonsense, for experience not theory, and it images a process by which Emmet might have aged into an Englishman. Instead of being simply bought by the government, as Southey's ex-employer, Isaac Corry, had been, Emmet might have been transformed into an upholder of the Union (by contrast, Shelley's poem of 1812 — 'On Robert Emmet's Tomb' — does not impose a ruling English style and instead draws on Moore's melodies in order to pay a republican tribute which is sincere and unpatronising). For Southey, Emmet's transformation into a sober middle-aged Englishman would have created a true union of hearts a bond of mutual kinship — and here there is an anticipation of the later Southey's paternalism, his feudal-conservative dislike of liberal economic individualism and his firm belief in state welfare. If the idea of 'clinging' to England seems merely demeaning, it should also be noted that Southey's essentially compassionate nature made him one of the early prophets of collectivism.

With a desperate sub-Wordsworthian eloquence, Southey insists that he must write Emmet's epitaph and he concludes by arguing that it was better for Emmet to have died than lived to witness the inevitable results of his 'disastrous triumph' — i.e. 'the ruffian slaves of France / In thy dear native country lording it'. It was 'happier' (i.e. both luckier and more pleasant) for Emmet to have died in 'that heroic mood / That takes away the sting of death':

> By all the good and all the wise forgiven,
> Yea, in all ages by the wise and good
> To be remember'd, mourn'd, and honour'd still.

Yet Southey's poem is less a tribute than a vulnerable and revealing piece of self-exculpation which serves finally to vindicate political necessity and colonial rule. The self-esteem of the English ruling class is a powerful and insidious force which cries out for that rational critical analysis it so often defies.

If Southey's poem descends to us as an item in his largely unread and forgotten collected works, it becomes significant when it is located historically, politically and biographically — i.e. when it is viewed not as a dusty 'transcendental' text which ought to be submitted to what are sometimes naively termed 'the exigencies of close reading'. Here, another letter of October, 1803 shows the complex historical forces which played upon and around Southey's attempt to get his poem published:

Have you seen or heard from King? Of some damnable articles in the *Morning Post* to advise us that we should give no quarter to the French? It really made Coleridge ill with vexation and anger. He is preparing an answer. You may whisper to King the secret history of this mystery of iniquity. The author is Irish — there is reason to believe a rebel in his heart, hence a cursed and devilish manifesto designed to please and irritate the people here and to be actually serviceable in France. I tell you this in confidence. The poem I wrote upon poor Emmet has not yet appeared and perhaps will not be in the *M. Post* for I do not suspect the new Editor of much interest or liberality. If it be delayed much longer I shall send it to William Taylor for the *Iris*.[16]

The publication history of a literary text, like the production history of a play, is an essential part of the text's 'meaning' and it is worth noting that since 1798 Southey had been contracted for a guinea a week to supply verses to the *Morning Post*. He was a professional writer, just as Corry was a professional politician.

Coleridge, who was then sharing Gretta Hall with his brother-in-law, appears to have reacted to contemporary political events both physiologically and intellectually, and the impact on him of Emmet's execution first shows in this notebook jotting:

Emmet = mad Raphael painting Ideals of Beauty on the walls of a cell with human Excrement.[17]

Coleridge's editor comments that this is a supposition as to what Raphael might have done had he been mad, 'an image for the extremes meeting in Emmet, eloquent idealism and fanatical violence'.[18] It is possible that this interpretation projects a typically Yeatsian and necessarily anachronistic tension into the note, and that the human excrement is Coleridge's symbol for the people whom he and Southey dismissed as 'savages'.[19] It may also be significant that Coleridge's protestant imagination transforms the Protestant Emmet into a Catholic, hypothetically insane, artist. As Seamus Deane has shown, the wisdom of Coleridge and other English commentators on Irish affairs 'has always been vitiated by the assumption that there is some undeniable relationship between civilization, the Common Law and Protestantism'. By breaking the law, Emmet ceased for Coleridge to be either Protestant or civilized.[20]

Two days after Southey's letter to John King, Coleridge addressed an extraordinary letter to his new aristocratic friends, Sir George and Lady Beaumont.[21] It is an hysterical and phantasmagoric reflection on Emmet's execution which begins with an expression of gratitude to the Beaumonts for their 'kind Letter' of that afternoon. Coleridge then gives an account of a severe toothache, analyses the effects of his new gout medicine (at this point he writes with the medicine instead of ink), and expresses a fear that a hot climate may be his only medicine, though 'it seems better to die than to live out of England'. Having established his gratitude, physical suffering and fundamental patriotism, Coleridge moves immediately from the idea of his being better off dead in England to this statement:

I have been extremely affected by the death of young Emmett — just 24! — at that age, dear Sir George! I was retiring from Politics, disgusted beyond measure by the manners & morals of the Democrats, & fully awake to the inconsistency of my practice with my speculative Principles.

Carefully, Coleridge mentions that his speculative principles were 'perfectly harmless — a compound of Philosophy and Christianity'. Then, in an apparently uncontrolled tone of hysteria and self-pity, he attacks those who attacked his youthful opinions and admits that he 'aided the Jacobins, by witty sarcasms & subtle reasonings & declamations'. But even as he makes this admission, he apologises for those declamations and adds that fortunately the government appears to have known that he and Southey 'were utterly unconnected with any party or club or society', and in an enormous parenthetical aria he adds:

(and this praise I must take to myself, that I disclaimed all these Societies, these Imperia in Imperio, these Ascarides in the Bowels of the State, subsisting on the weakness & diseasedness, & having for their final Object the Death of that State . . .

Then Coleridge imagines what might have happened if he had been imprisoned during his youthful and supposedly brief seditious phase:

my health & constitution were such as that it would have been almost as certain Death to me, as the Executioner has been to poor young Emmett. Like him, I was very young, very enthusiastic, distinguished by Talents & acquirements & a sort of turbid Eloquence; like him, I was a zealous Partisan of Christianity, a Despiser & Abhorrer of French Philosophy & French Morals; like him, I would have given my body to be burnt inch by inch,

rather than that a French Army should have insulted my native Shores /
& alas! alas! like him I was unconsciously yet actively aiding & abetting
the Plans, that I abhorred, and the men, who were more, far more unlike
me, in every respect, in education, habits, principles & feelings, than the
most anathematized Aristocrat among my opponents. Alas! alas! unlike
*me* he did not awake! the country, in which he lived, furnished far more
plausible arguments for his active Zeal than England could do; the vices
of the party, with whom he acted, were so palpably the effect of darkest
Ignorance & foulest oppression, that they could not disgust him / the
worse the vices & the more he abhorred them, the more he loved the men
themselves, abstracting the men from their vices, the vices from the men,
& transferring them, with tenfold Guilt, to the state of Society & to the
Orange Faction holding together that State of Society, which he believed
to be the cause of these Vices! Ah woe is me! & in this mood the poor young
Enthusiast sent forth that unjustifiable Proclamation, one sentence of which
clearly permitted unlimited assassination — the only sentence, beyond all
doubt, which Emmett would gladly have blotted out with his Heart's Blood,
& of which at the time he wrote it he could not have seen the Import — & the
only sentence, which was fully realized in action — ! This moment it was a
few unweighed words of an empassioned Visionary, in the next moment it
became the foul Murder of Lord Kilwarden! — O my heart give praise, give
praise! — not that I was preserved from Bonds, or Ignominy or Death! But
that I was preserved from Crimes that it is almost impossible not to call Guilt!
— And poor young Emmet [t!] O if our Ministers had saved him, had taken
his Oath & word of honor, to have remained in America or some of our Col-
onies for the next 10 years of his Life, we *might* have had in him a sublimely
great man, we assuredly sh [ould] have had in him a good man & heart &
soul an *Englishman!* — Think of Lord Mansfield — About the Age of poor
Emmett he drank the Pretender's Health on his Knees & was obnoxious to all
the pains & penalties of high Treason. And where lies the Difference between
the two? Murray's Plot had for it's object a foul Slave [ry] under the name of
Loyalty; Emmett's as foul a Slavery under the nam [e of] Liberty and
Independence. — But whatever the Ministers may have done, Heaven h [as]
dealt kindly with the young man. He has died, firm & in the height & heat
of his Spirit, beholding in his Partizans only the wickedly oppressed, in his
enemies the wicked oppressors. — O if his mad mad Enterprize had succeeded / ! — Thou most mistaken & bewildered young Man, if other
Punishment than the Death thou hast suffered, be needful for thy deadly
Error, what better Punishment, what fitter Purgatory can be imagined,
than a Vision presented to thee & conceived as real, a Vision of all the
Massacres, the furious Passions, the Blasphemies, Sensualities, Superstitions, the bloody Persecutions, and mutual Cannibalism of Atheist &
Papist, that would have rushed in, like a Torrent of Sulphur & burning
Chaos, at the Breach which thou thyself hadst made — till thou, yea, even
thou thyself hadst called out in agony to the merciless Gaul, & invoked an
army of Slave-fiends to crush the more enormous evil of a mob of Fiends
in Anarchy. — My honored Friends! as I live, I scarcely know what

I have been writing; but the very circumstance of writing to *you*, added to the recollection of the unwise & unchristian feelings, with which at poor Emmett's Age *I* contemplated all persons of *your* rank in Society, & *that* recollection confronted with my present Feelings towards you — it has agitated me, dear Friends! And I have written, my Heart at a full Gallop adown Hill. — And now, good night — I will finish this Letter tomorrow morning.

As he contemplates his radical youth, Coleridge seems to melt into the figure of Emmet, then to emerge as a courtier who addresses his aristocratic friends in order to put behind him both Emmet's views and his own early opinions. Intellectual autobiography becomes a mixture of flattery, self-pity, pathological bigotry and hypochondria, and the medicinal ink clears the way for the emergence of the mature conservative sage. Thus while Emmet becomes an influential figure in the martyrology of romantic nationalism in Ireland, in England he helped to inspire a conservative nationalism. Both readings distort him for their own purposes.

Kelvin Everest has persuasively traced the falsifications, inconsistencies, confusions and strategies which fill this letter.[22] In it we can sense both a deep personal anxiety and the public alarm at the prospect of a Napoleonic invasion. And behind Coleridge's professed pity and admiration for Emmet, there lies an ambitious strategy which was to take him from Jacobin heresy to the organic consolations of Anglican clerisy. Like Southey, he came to believe that the Church of England had to be preserved at all costs. Like Arnold's and Eliot's literary and social criticism, Coleridge's lavishly edited complete works may be regarded as influential propaganda for the state church, and it is necessary to determine how extensively committed to such a concept is English literary criticism.

It can be argued that some of the fundamental principles of English literary criticism derive from polemical, counter-revolutionary attitudes to French and Irish republicanism. Arnold, Eliot and Leavis share with the later Southey and the later Coleridge a conservative outlook which is often ethnically biased and which is profoundly influenced by Burke's *Reflections*. In Britain, now, many radical critics and scholars are engaged in a reassessment of traditional critical practice which often reveals its insidiously biased and reactionary nature. Chris Baldick's *The Social Mission of English Criticism*[23] exposes the essentially imperialistic and nationalistic attitudes which informed both English literary criticism and the establishment of English literature as an academic discipline between 1848 and 1932. Baldick's outlook is post-imperial — noting this, is it possible to contemplate in Ireland a critical attitude which is both open as to its political ideology and distinctively post-colonial? This cannot happen if we attempt to make a false separation between literature and politics. If we want to make such a separation, then we ought to be honest about our motives. Coleridge was, and in a letter to his publisher, Joseph Cottle, he discussed ways of increasing the sales of a new edition of his poems: 'by omitting every thing political, I widen the sphere of my readers'.[24] This strategic omission is similar to that gesture of 'wounded withdrawal'[25] from the public world which Matthew Arnold was later to perfect. The result is an idea of balance, disinterestedness and objectivity which can be seen, for example, in the myth of Shakespeare as, in David Nabrook's words, 'completely impartial and therefore necessarily a supporter of the Church of England'.[26]

Arnold's criticism shows a persistent interest in Irish politics. The day after the Clerkenwell bomb (13 December, 1867), he wrote to his mother from the Athenaeum:

Every one is full of the Clerkenwell blow-up; I was dining at the Garrick Club last night, when one of the guests came in saying that his hansom had been nearly knocked down by a string of cabs with policemen filling them inside and out . . . You know I have never wavered in saying that the Hyde Park business eighteen months ago was fatal, and that a Government which dared not deal with a mob, of any nation or with any design, simply opened the flood-gates to anarchy. You cannot have one measure for Fenian rioting and another for English rioting, merely because the design of Fenian rioting is more subversive and desperate; what the State has to do is to put down *all* rioting with a strong hand, or it is sure to drift into troubles. Who can wonder at these Irish, who have cause to hate us, making war on a State and society which has shown itself irresolute and feeble?[27]

And in *Culture and Anarchy* Arnold deploys the figure of an Irish Fenian strategically, even sympathetically, in order to ironize liberal individualism (the freedom to do as one likes) and to express his own distaste for British industrial society:

There are many things to be said on behalf of this exclusive attention of ours to liberty, and of the relaxed habits of government which it has engendered. It is very easy to mistake or to exaggerate the sort of anarchy from which we are in danger through them. We are not in danger from Fenianism, fierce and turbulent as it may show itself; for against this our conscience is free enough to let us act resolutely and put forth our overwhelming strength the moment there is any real need for it. In the first place, it never was any part of our creed that the great right and blessedness of an Irishman, or, indeed, of anybody on earth except an Englishman, is to do as he likes; and we can have no scruple at all about abridging, if necessary, a non-Englishman's assertion of personal liberty. The British Constitution, its checks, and its prime virtues, are for Englishmen. We may extend them to others out of love and kindness; but we find no real divine law written on our hearts constraining us so to extend them. And then the difference between an Irish Fenian and an English rough is so immense, and the case, in dealing with the Fenian, so much more clear! He is so evidently desperate and dangerous, a man of a conquered race, a Papist, with centuries of ill-usage to inflame him against us, with an alien religion established in his country by us at his expense, with no admiration of our institutions, no love of our virtues, no talents for our business, no turn for our comfort! Show him our symbolical Truss Manufactory on the finest site in Europe, and tell him that British industrialism and individualism can bring a man to that, and he remains cold! Evidently, if we deal tenderly with a sentimentalist like this, it is out of pure philanthropy.[28]

Rather like Coleridge, Arnold appears to briefly assume the identity of an Irish revolutionary and it is curious to observe a critic speaking for English high culture through the symbolic mask of an Irish terrorist. Arnold is here concealing himself behind a bomber in order to express his disgust at the British middle-class. This anticipates the subversive irony and radical disgust of Wilde, but with Arnold it is a temporary strategy rather than a consuming ideological commitment. Arnold is arguing the case both for his own good taste and for tough measures against English 'roughs'. He is in love with the idea of a classical discipline, while Wilde is an anarchist and Fenian sympathizer.

Arnold's strategy of using Irish politics as a lever for changing attitudes within England is evident in the preface to *Irish Essays* (1882):

English people keep asking themselves what we ought to do about Ireland. The great contention of these essays is, that in order to attach Ireland to us solidly, English people have not only to *do* something different from what they have done hitherto, they have also to *be* something different from what they have been hitherto. As a whole, as a community, they have to acquire a larger and sweeter temper, a larger and more lucid mind.[29]

For Arnold, Ireland ought somehow to produce a significant change in the British national character, but it is hard to credit what would be a cross between an imperialistic value system and an openminded, lucid, sweetly intelligent necessarily post-imperial outlook on the world. And Arnold's innate conservatism shows in his remarks on the Irish Land Act which he opposed because:

We shall have brought about a radical change . . . disturbed the accepted and ordinary and constitutive characters of property, − and we shall get little or no gratitude for it . . . To break down the landlords in Ireland, as we have already broken down the Protestant Church there, is merely to complete the destruction of the *modus vivendi* hitherto existing for society in that country; a most imperfect *modus vivendi* indeed, but the only one practically attained there up to this time as a substitute for anarchy.[30]

Southey, Coleridge and Arnold all see various facets of the British national character reflected in an Irish mirror and the contemplation of these self-images make them sometimes uncomfortable, sometimes impatient. Are the images cracked? or the mirror? or both? No critic is quite certain, but they are all haunted by a history that bumps around uneasily near the foundations of their world view.

Southey, Coleridge and Arnold share a common mission — to rescue their national self-esteem — and we may compare that mission with the more recent *écriture* of Douglas Hurd, the part-time writer of political thrillers who was until recently secretary of state for Northern Ireland. In *An End to Promises*, his sympathetic and patriotic account of the Heath administration, Hurd states that for the two months between Bloody Sunday and the imposition of direct rule:

Irish affairs were in the melting pot. Ministers went back to first principles on Ireland. A completely new policy had to be devised, and new people found to run it. I do not know enough of this effort to write about it, but watched from the sidelines it was one of the impressive things which the Government did.[31]

Eleven years after the imposition of direct rule, Douglas Hurd landed in the north of Ireland to administer the province. Like Southey he brought certain preconceptions with him and those attitudes can be discerned in the thriller, *Vote to Kill*, which he published in 1975.

One of the main themes of the novel is British withdrawal from Ireland: ' "We've had four hundred years of Ireland now. We've done them wrong, they've done us wrong. We're quits. It's time to go home." '[32] This statement is made by a Tory M.P., Jeremy Cornwall, who leads a populist Troops Out movement which threatens to unseat the aging Tory Prime Minister. And at the end of the novel there is an attempt to assassinate the Prime Minister with a crossbow concealed in a dispatch box. The crossbow is fired by Clarissa Strong, a young English civil servant who has had an undergraduate affair with Barry Barran, a republican who is now Professor of Poetry at Cork University. When her security clearance is re-examined, the affair is discovered and Clarissa is questioned about Barran:

'Was he very Irish then? Politically, I mean.'
'Yes. It went with the rest of the scenery. A strange and terrible beauty, that sort of thing. It meant nothing to me.'
'I could never stand Yeats.'
'I've never read him since.'[33]

Clarissa succeeds in convincing her colleagues that she is not a security risk and the plot moves to its finale with the Prime Minister delivering a speech in the general election campaign which swings the country in favour of keeping the British army in Northern Ireland:

'Bring the Troops home, so say I, so say we all. But bring them home when their job is done. To bring them home now would be a disgrace and a disaster . . . It is not for such an ending that I have spent thirty years in public life. It is not my purpose to preside over the disintegration of the United Kingdom. If that is the will of the British people, so be it. But the Conservative Party cannot sail with that wind, cannot be swept along with that current. We are not time-servers, we are the anchor. We must hold the ship steady till the storm has blown itself out. And so this evening we call to our aid against those who march and shout the stubbornness, the good sense, the steadiness of the British people.'[34]

The Prime Minister then quotes from Larkin's 'Homage to a Government':

> Next year we are to bring the soldiers home
> For lack of money, and it is all right.
> Places they guarded, or kept orderly,
> Must guard themselves, and keep themselves orderly.
> We want the money for ourselves at home
> Instead of working. And this is all right.[35]

In quoting Larkin's lugubrious, deliberately drab elegy for empire — an elegy prompted by the Labour government's withdrawal from Aden — the Prime Minister touches a theme which the British people 'desperately wished to believe. For if the British people were not at heart sensible and steady, of what use were all those tense hours of uncomfortable effort, that work which most of them found embarrassing?'[36]

The idea of national character can be felt strongly here — it is a character composed of stubbornness, good sense, steadiness, and is expressed in the maritime image of an anchor. Holding firmly to a belief in its civilizing mission, to a principle that is superior to mere economics, it underlies the Prime Minister's explanation that Clarissa 'caught a fire':

'Like a fever. The Irish fever, the worst variety known to man. It destroys all gentleness, truth, sensible calculation. When Englishmen catch it they get it worst of all. And Englishwomen.'

There is nearly a century and a half between treeless Balbriggan and the tree-muffled squares of Larkin's almost post-imperial Britain, but the attitudes of Southey, Coleridge and Hurd show a remarkable continuity (Arnold's case is more complex, because he is more slippery and sophisticated). On the one side we see a feverish, mad and bloody island, on the other a sober, decent world which combines self-esteem and realpolitik in a plainsong cadence — 'all gentleness, truth, sensible calculation'.

In my view, such values are an essential part of the self-image of the English protestant imagination and they have had a powerful influence on the practice of literary and social criticism. That self-image — with its false and facile ideas of literary transcendence — is now impossible of recovery in a polarized British society and in a cultural climate which demands that literature be related closely to history, rather than separated or transcended out of that more exacting discipline. It would be ironic if an essentially reactionary, ahistorical and ostensibly apolitical literary criticism survived in Ireland, when in Britain it had been replaced by a fully post-imperial, pluralistic criticism.

# JAMES JOYCE'S 'THE DEAD': THE SYMBOLIST INSPIRATION AND ITS NARRATIVE REFLECTION

WALTER T. RIX

'The Dead' holds a special position in *Dubliners* and has, conse-quently, received the most extensive attention from critics. It seems to me, however, that the highly detailed discussion has not yet touched upon a source which is apt to provide helpful insight into the intricate organization of the story. My intention, therefore, is to discuss 'The Dead' against the background of symbolist tenden-cies in contemporary art. Thus, making palpable the affinity bet-ween the Joycean text and these tendencies, I hope to uncover clues for interpretation which would otherwise be passed over. In fac:, putting 'The Dead' into the context of Symbolist thinking may help to get beyond the hermetic barriers of Joycean writing.

The parallels to be pointed out occur on several levels. Also, the projection of Symbolist elements into Joyce is bound to work two ways: it makes us aware of the artistic procedure Joyce chose to adopt as a writer, and it contributes to an understanding of the calculated intention of the narrative material so skilfully arranged. It will not be my concern to enter into a discussion of the more subtle questions of defining Symbolism. I will, rather, rely on what are generally accepted to be Symbolist touches in poetry, drama, painting, and music.

Even before Joyce paid his first visit to Paris, Symbolism was not totally unheard of in Dublin. But it was in Paris where Joyce moved into an intellectual climate with Symbolism in full bloom. On 2 December 1902, the day he set off from London to Paris, he made the acquaintance of Arthur Symons with the help of Yeats. As Richard Ellmann puts it, Symons had been for about ten years 'the principal middleman between Paris and London'.[1] Through this association, Joyce not only plunged into the flux of French literature which was to reach England but, for a certain period, his understanding of French literature was also directed into Symbolist channels.

Three years before Joyce had met him, Symons had published

the first major English work on Symbolism: *The Symbolist Movement in Literature*.[2] In addition, his literary work virtually nourishes itself on the spirit of the French Symbolists. As he proved highly instrumental in the publication of Joyce's early works, Symons's Symbolist orientation was bound to have a bearing also on these works. This is all the more likely as Joyce had read *The Symbolist Movement in Literature* the very year it had appeared.[3] obviously this incited him to continue the same year with Huysmans' *A Rebours*, to be followed in 1901 by *Là-Bas*. The next year he went on with Mallarmé's *Divagations*, and what was left of Mallarmé he consumed between 1904 and 1914, while staying in Trieste, a period highly relevant for 'The Dead'.[4] M. E. Kronegger in his article 'Joyce's Debt to Poe and the French Symbolists' has outlined some of the contacts Joyce had with French Symbolism. He holds: 'Joyce had learned to use the symbolist technique of expression in the short interval between the first and last drafts of *Dubliners*.'[5] However this remains an abstract statement and no textual evidence is given.

One idea, or to be more precise, a state of being, which the Symbolists were particularly attracted by, was the notion of night. This idea was handed down to them by the Romantics, but while keeping the shape of the night, Symbolists were to give it a totally new essence. For the Romantics, night was a metaphor to signal remoteness from profane reality, a state in which inspiration set the poetic mind to work. The frequent appellation of the stars by the poetic mind is indicative of this attitude.

As the theorists of Symbolism saw it, night is not just a poetic separation from the familiar world, but, going much further, it in essence amounts to an anti-world, an absolute inversion of reality which runs counter to all traditional forms of being. In the night a new cosmos unfolds which lies beyond any old order. And here there is no need for the artist to invoke the stars any longer. Neither does he rely on divine inspiration any more. He much rather creates the new world through his own imaginative mind. 'Night, a more perfect day', Arthur Symons terms it in his poem 'Venetian Nights' (1894), and Oscar Wilde, in his 'The Critic as Artist' (1890), classifies the outcome of the artistic process as 'a world more real than reality itself'.[6] What used to be divine and outside man has now passed over to man. In fact, the artist contends for the divine principle of creation: he has become Lucifer creative. The Jesuit warning against the Luciferian *'non serviam: I will not serve'*,[7] so prominent in *A Portrait of the Artist as a Young Man*, and Stephen's 'batlike soul waking to the consciousness of itself in darkness' (pp. 166, 200) are direct echoes of this position.

In his poem 'Obsession' (1860) Baudelaire describes the new notion as follows:

> Comme tu me plairais, ô Nuit! sans ces étoiles
> Dont la lumière parle un langage connu!
> Car je cherche le vide, et le noir, et le nu!
>
> Mais les ténèbres sont elles-mêmes des toiles
> Où vivent, jaillissant de mon oeil par milliers,
> Des êtres disparus aux regards familiers.

The poet now wishes to give himself up to a kind of night which is absolutely black. As opposed to the Romantics, he wants to do without the stars. Being the rival of God he renounces divine inspiration and aims at creation through his own mind. But since the night as such is still an entity outside his personal sphere of creation, he will only pass through it. Darkness is nothing more than an intermediary stage leading on to a more desirable sphere which proves to be an entire projection of the human mind. Therefore paintings, being man-made objects, surpass even the darkest night. They are, in fact, only variations of Baudelaire's famous *paradis artificiels*, artistic counterparts of the biblical paradise. Divine creation has given way to artistic creation. This is also Stephen's intellectual journey in *Portrait* when he travels from '*ad majorem Dei gloriam*' (p. 100) to a position where 'He would create proudly out of the freedom and power of his soul, as the great artificer whose name he bore . . .' (p. 154). Significantly enough, the vision of creation enters Stephen when the 'Evening would deepen above the sea, night fall upon the plains, dawn glimmer before the wanderer and show him strange fields and hills and faces' (p. 155).

And this is precisely Nietzsche's formula when, at the end of *Thus Spake Zarathustra*, after having renounced any kind of transcendentalism, the possibility of a totally new form of immanent creation assumes contours:

But Zarathustra for a third time laid his hand on his lip and spake: *Come! come! come! Let us be going! It is the hour*: *let us go into the night!* . . . Hearest thou not, how eerily, how terribly, how intimately she speaketh unto *thee* — old Midnight, deep, so deep?[8]

It is from this understanding that, as a recurrent motif, the night springs into the art of the late nineteenth century. *The Savoy* and *The Yellow Book* are teeming with poems and stories conjuring up dawn, dusk, twilight, night, or just darkness in general. It makes itself felt in works like Arthur Symons's *Days and Night* (1889), *Silhouettes* (1892) or *London Nights* (1895). It is inherent in an astonishing number of paintings, such as Whistler's famous nocturnes, and it appears in numerous musical nocturnes.

The tendency towards the use of darkness, inherent in the other stories of *Dubliners*, arrives at its most systematic realization in 'The Dead'. Night, as a complex metaphor, binds the various episodes together. The story opens with a party sometime in the evening 'in the dark gaunt house on Usher's Island'[9] and, set in various locations, moves through the night until dawn the next morning. From the start the darkness outside seems to correspond with the darkness inside. Gabriel and his wife Gretta entering the house 'from the dark' (p. 161) are met by the two sisters, Kate and Julia, 'toddling down the dark stairs' (p. 161). And Gabriel's comment shortly after his arrival, 'I think we're in for a night of it' (p. 162) bears a ring which obviously stretches beyond the reality of the situation. Similarly, when the guests bid each other 'Goodnight' so excessively after the party — of 48 words no less than 13 are made up of 'Good-night' — this appears to be more a magic evocation than an actual scene of leave-taking. Obviously the night does not seem prepared to retire so early because when the guests set off 'The morning was still dark' (p. 191). Although Gabriel felt highly uneasy and even nervous throughout the night, darkness seems to him more congenial than light. There are several hints that he rejects light. In the hotel he rather harshly tells the porter: 'We don't want any light' (p. 193). Even from his body language it becomes obvious that he wants to rule light out: immediately before he enters the dialogue with Gretta, which takes such an unexpected turn, 'he turned and leaned against a chest of drawers with his back to the light' (p. 193). When the dialogue becomes more uneasy, he still preserves his bearing: 'instinctively he turned his back more to the light lest she might see the shame that burned upon his forehead' (p. 198).

The hotel room again turns out to be a sphere in which the complexity of the night is further enriched as its meaning is transposed into a series of continually widening spheres. The night moves into the past to encompass the episode of Michael Furey wooing Gretta and accepting death for her sake. There seems even to be a subtle link between Michael and the night since his eyes reflect the night and its meaning. In the words of Gretta: 'Such eyes as he had: big dark eyes! And such an expression in them — an expression!' (p. 197). After Gretta's story, Gabriel in turn now adopts the night as an element of his psyche: 'The tears gathered more quickly in his eyes and in the partial darkness he imagined he saw the form of a young man standing under a dripping tree' (p. 200). In this psychic

state, all living beings become 'shades' (p. 200) to him and night set-
tles down all over Ireland as reflected in the 'dark central plain' (p.
200) and 'the dark mutinous Shannon waves' (p. 201). But Gabriel's
visionary journey goes much further, his own identity dissolves
and, within his personal psychic night, his consciousness unfolds
into the 'universe' (p. 201).

It can be shown that the fabric, the psychology, and the
cosmology of the night as depicted in 'The Dead' are obviously inspired by the Symbolist concept. Night in Symbolist imagery serves
a twofold purpose: it is to evoke the condition of man, and it is to
suggest the metamorphosis of man. Night, therefore, is just as
horrible as it is attractive. In 'Recueillement' (1861) Baudelaire
offers us a paradigm of this mood:

> Le Soleil moribond s'endormir sous une arche,
> Et, comme un long linceul traînant à l'Orient,
> Entends, ma chère, entends la douce Nuit qui marche.

Unlike the Romantics, the Symbolists frequently associate the
night with the urban sphere. Just as Baudelaire sees the night as surpassed by paintings, the Symbolists' idea is to enhance the night by
blending it with the sphere of absolute artificiality, for which the
city becomes a hallmark. French poetry after 1880 abounds with
references to a nocturnal Paris. And finally, the night was to be
fused with the idea of dance. In the Symbolist fashion all these images were calculated to influence each other. Thus the special
understanding of the night with its traits of urbanity worked upon
the image of the dance and gave it a turn in the direction of the
dance of death.

All this is, to quite a surprising extent, inherent in 'The Dead'.
Here night carries just as ambiguous a character as it has in Symbolist art. It winds up all the negative aspects of the preceding
stories and brings the 'Night after night . . . night after night . . .
Every night' (p. 7) of the first story, 'The Sisters', to its logical conclusion. Night in 'The Dead' becomes a continuum and reaches its
negative climax through the reference to the Trappist monks sleeping in their coffins (p. 181). But at the same time it is not only
welcomed by Gabriel, but is also linked with images of a new
beginning or even resurrection. Significantly enough, the party
takes place shortly before New Year's Eve when the old year is to
die and the new year to make its appearance.

The reflections of a night-time Paris in French poetry find their
counterpart in Joyce displaying a night-time caricature of Dublin
social life. In a way, the characters in 'The Dead' can be said to be

Félicien Rops: 'La mort au bal masqué', 1870 (courtesy of the State Museum Kröller-Müller, Otterlo, Netherlands).

Odilon Redon: 'Death, my Irony Surpasses all the Others', 1889
(Stickney Collection, courtesy of the Art Institute of Chicago).

Xavier Mellery: 'Rêve du soir', 1898 (courtesy of the Musées Royaux des Beaux-Arts de Belgique, Bruxelles).

Edvard Munch: 'In the Man's Brain', 1897 (courtesy of the Olso Kommunes Kunstsamlinger, Munch-Museet).

Edvard Munch: 'Lovers in Waves', 1896 (courtesy of the Olso Kommunes Kunstamlinger, Munch-Museet).

Xavier Mellery: 'Escalier', 1896 (courtesy of the Koninklijk Museum voor Schone Kunsten, Antwerpen).

Edvard Munch: 'The Kiss', 1895 (courtesy of the Olso Kommunes
Kunstamlinger, Munch-Museet).

Carlos Schwabe: poster for the first exhibition of the 'Rose Croix'
Group, 1892 (courtesy of the Bibliothèque Nationale, Paris).

abstractions of the dark side of Dublin life as it is depicted in all the other stories: a telescoped show of the Dublin cosmos. And finally, all those attending the dinner and the dance with such 'a great deal of confusion and laughter and noise' (p. 178) basically perform nothing more than a dance of death. One of the indications is the strong presence of the Joycean colour of death, brown, even directly embodied in the shape of Mr. Browne: 'Well, I hope, Miss Morkan, said Mr Browne, that I'm brown enough for you because, you know, I'm all brown' (p. 180). This, sometime later, challenges Aunt Kate to comment meaningfully: 'Browne is everywhere . . .' (p. 185). In his *The Literary Symbol* William York Tindall therefore concludes: 'their party is an embodiment of death and all the people there are living dead'.[10]

The close alliance of night and death lends itself to a further elaboration from the Symbolist point of view. According to Symbolist understanding, death is not the final stage. In a view of the special construction of the Symbolist anti-world, death means pushing open the door to the new cosmos. Just as night is considered as the passage between the old life and the new, so death can be defined as a new beginning. In his cycle of drawings called 'A Life' (1883), Max Klinger subtitles the first drawing with a contracted and slightly altered quotation for 1 Moses, III, 4/5: 'Ye shall not surely die, but your eyes shall be opened.' This is part of the artful insinuation of the snake causing man's fall. But in the cycle it is never entirely renounced, and it remains throughout strangely ambiguous. At the end of the cycle, when life draws towards its end, it has not wholly lost its promising ring and it still opens vistas of a new existence. The general time concept is more cyclic than linear and terminal. However, it is not the New Jerusalem of Christianity the Symbolists have in mind. Nietzsche, in his *Thus Spake Zarathustra*, aims at a revaluation of death. In the chapter 'Of the Preachers of Death' he fiercely rejects the traditional idea of death as embedded in transcendentalism. What he preaches in the chapter 'Of Free Death' is an image which lends itself to a vision of immanent creation. On the basis of 'Self-Surmounting', a new, higher form of reality will be created which springs exclusively from the human mind: 'Die at the right time: thus teacheth Zarathustra', Nietzsche proclaims, '. . . pour out a mighty soul [. . .] He that hath a goal and an heir willeth death to come at the right time for goal and heir'.[11] In principle this can be linked directly to Baudelaire's *paradis artificiels* or Yeats's *A Vision*. When Edvard Munch showed some of his paintings at the Paris Art Nouveau exhibition of 1896, August Strindberg gave an interesting analysis in *La Revue Blanche*.[12] With reference to the cosmology of Munch's painting 'Dusk', he points out that the on-coming night seems to change all mortals into corpses. But just as night will dissolve when the day breaks, so even the corpses will win a new existence.

Comparing these ideas to 'The Dead', one can once again see a close affinity. For Joyce death has finality only in one way. The night of the party suggests this finality. Out of this night, however, Gabriel's night of introspection grows. The night in 'The Dead' therefore bears both the terror and the challenge of the Symbolist night. It is the sphere of de-personalization and dissolution, but simultaneously a sphere of a new beginning, a new artistic cosmology. Within this context death acquires an inverted quality. Nietzsche's advice in his chapter 'Of Free Death' 'to pour out a mighty soul' is actually practised by Gabriel: 'His soul had ap-proached that region where dwell the vast host of the dead' (p. 201). What makes this fit so congenially into the Symbolist pattern is the fact that Gabriel's soul travels on, beyond the traditional realm of death. The Christ iconography at the very end — 'the crooked crosses and headstones . . . the spears of the little gate . . . the barren thorns' (p. 201) — together with the images of snow and water, signifying both death *and* life, suggest resurrection after death. As with the Symbolists, Gabriel's resurrection is a highly personal and subjective one irreconcilable with Christian doctrine. When he, with the overacuteness of the senses so typical of French poetry, actually *hears* the snow fall faintly 'upon all the living and the dead' (p. 201), one is almost tempted to use Zarathustra's words: 'thus he is at home with death and with life'.[13] Melting into the universe, Gabriel, in the true Symbolist sense, has created for himself a new cosmic reality through his mind.

As for the texture of the night emerging from 'The Dead', again Symbolist ingredients can be traced. With the night hovering over the borderline of existence, or being a medium of transience, twilight was the Symbolist way of expressing this condition. In other cases the effects of artificial lightning were made use of to convey the polarity of the night. By confronting or even mingling light with darkness the otherwise static sphere of the night was filled with metaphysical dynamics. Thus in terms of painting, night, and with it death, are brought to life through the polarity of white and black. Félicien Rops's paintings serve adequately to illustrate this. It is in particular his 'La Mort au Bal Masqué' (1870) which should be referred to in this connection. In the centre a skeleton, posing as a lady, is dancing in exquisite attire. While the precious dress shows various hues of red and white, even to the degree of glaring whiteness, the surroundings consist of different shades of black which threaten to swallow even the partner who is dancing in line with it. Examples in painting could be extended deliberately. Some of them work solely on the aesthetic principle excluding death altogether as Henry Le Sidaner's 'Ames blanches ou nuit douce' (1897). This painting sets a group of two ladies in hazy white against the darkness of the street. Others, like Aubrey Beardsley's drawings which thrive on the tension between black and white, reveal a more psychological orientation. If certain fashions reflect the dominant taste in a certain period then the collecting of Oriental porcelain in white and darkish blue, which suddenly became a craze in advanced art circles, is certainly a case in point.

Examples in literature are no less frequent. Valéry in his 'Vierge incertaine' (1891) addresses the imaginative beloved with:

> Toi qui verses, les nuits tendres, sur tes pieds blancs
> Des larmes de statue oubliée et brisée . . .

As in painting 'whiteness' and 'night' became almost a collocation and the idea of a 'white night' is by no means uncommon. In the 'White Nights' chapter of his *Marius the Epicurean* (1885) Walter Pater offers a striking example. To increase the effect of whiteness in the night even further, the image of the night was repeatedly merged with the idea of snow. In his unfinished but highly influential play in verse *Hérodiade* (1866) Mallarmé speaks of: 'Nuit blanche de glaçons et de neige cruelle!" Similarly, following the French example, Arthur Symons in his poem 'A White Night' (1892) makes snow the prevalent image of the night:

> Whiter, along the frozen earth,
> The miracle of snow;
> Close covered as for sleep, the earth
> Lies, mutely slumbering below
> Its shroud of snow.

With these examples as a perspective for Joyce, it becomes obvious that in his mixing the night frequently with snow imagery he proceeds fully in accordance with the general Symbolist trend.

Although green and yellow are traditionally associated with the period, white as a characteristic expression of a prevalent mood kindled the imagination no less. The versions which Whistler produced of 'The White Girl', 'Symphony in White' or 'Arrangement in Black and White' with their growing sophistication in treating white show clearly the trend towards Symbolism.[14]

When writing on the Renaissance painter Moretto of Brescia in his 'Art Notes in North Italy', published 1890 in the *New Review*, Walter Pater is significantly enough fascinated by the fact 'that Moretto had attained full intelligence of all the pictorial powers of *white*'.[15] Everything, in fact, points to Holbrook Jackson being right when concluding: 'But an examination of the *belles lettres* of the period proves that neither yellow nor green predominated, but that the average taste seemed to lead towards the sum-total and climax of all colours — white'.[16] Finally, Symbolism even reached the stage of 'infernal white'. The virtuous white ladies of Victorianism thus developed into ladies of a kind of white with their smiles showing taints of malignity — if they did not turn into devouring moon goddesses altogether. Again we find Joyce in tune with the Symbolist spirit, evoking white through snow imagery and presenting Gretta simultaneously as a highly complex character.

The colour collocations which develop around white reveal further affinities. In the Symbolist world certain fixed colours were linked with white to signify definite character value. Richard Le Gallienne's famous statement in *Prose Fancies* (1896), 'Innocence has but two colours, white or green',[17] is reflected in the corresponding tonal values Joyce attributes to the two colours, beginning with 'An Encounter' and ending with a special kind of white in 'The Dead'.

In other cases the opposition of white and black was varied by contrasting white with another colour, in most cases red. Pierre Louÿs in his poem 'La Femme aux Paons' confronts white peacocks with the red flesh of a nude:

> Les paons sont blancs, les plumes sont blanches:
> Elle est rouge et nue.

Apart from direct opposition, polarity is also expressed by patches of red, green, yellow or even gold protruding from or even peeling out of a background of grey or black. It is again Whistler who paves the way for the many twilight poems after 1880 which avail themselves of this technique.

All the aspects discussed are present in Joyce's image of Dublin after the party had come to an end:

The morning was still *dark*. A dull *yellow light* brooded over the houses and the *river*; and the *sky* seemed to be descending. It was slushy underfoot; and only streaks and patches of *snow* lay on the roofs, on the parapets of the quay and on the area railings. The *lamps* were still burning *redly* in the murky air and, across the *river*, the palace of the Four Courts stood out menacingly against the heavy *sky*. (p. 191, my italics)

In mood, perspective, and imagery these lines follow closely the French pattern. It is not only the general situation of night wrestling with day, of whiteness showing up in darkness; the Joycean indebtedness can be pinpointed even on the level of specific aspects. Dealing with the urban subject, French poetry frequently makes the colour red shine out in the night. In his 'La Chanson du mal-aimé' (1903) Apollinaire renders an impression of London which is just as semi-dark and half-misty as Joyce's Dublin. This he blends with the colour red which, in turn, is linked with water imagery thus paralleling the red lamps and the river of Joyce:

> Un soir de demi-brume à Londres
> [. . .]
> Nous semblions entre les maisons
> Onde ouverte de la mer Rouge

Similarly, Baudelaire in 'La Crépuscule du Matin' (1851/52) describing Paris gradually awakening, comes very close to the Joycean picture:

> La lampe sur le jour fait une tache rouge;
> Où l'âme, sous le poids du corps revêche et lourd,
> Imite les combats de la lampe et du jour.
> [. . .]
> Une mer de brouillards baignait les édifices,
> [. . .]
> S'avançait lentement sur la Seine déserte,
> Et le sombre Paris, en se frottant les yeux,
> Empoignait ses outils, vieillard laborieux.

The red speck of lamp light against the dawn, the new day reluctantly trying to overcome the night, the mist encompassing the whole scene, and the perspective across the river towards the Palaces of State (paralleling the palace of the Four Courts): all these elements find their way also into Joyce.

How strongly this collocation of images influenced English poetry as well may again be illustrated by Arthur Symons. In his 'On the Bridge' (1890) he speaks of the nocturnal Paris:

> Lights on bank and bridge glitter gold and red,
> Lights upon the stream glitter red and white;
> Under us the night, and the night o'erhead,
> We together, we alone together in the night.

Again the conjunction of night and white, the image of red lights shining through the night, the water imagery, and the merging of sky and river, together with a situation like that of Gretta and

Gabriel 'alone together in the night', all correspond with Joyce.

In his 'The Decay of Lying' (1889) Oscar Wilde has theorized upon introducing mist into art as a highly functional element. Several of his poems actually follow this theory. The impression of the River Thames in his 'On the Embankment' (1893) includes

> A mist on the darkened river
> Falls; on the rippled stream
> The yellow lights shake and quiver
> The red lights quiver and gleam.

The parallels discovered so far extend even to the effects of artificial lighting. For French poetry 'gaslight' became almost a stock device for playing on the antagonism of night and light. In 'Un Soir' (1904?) Apollinaire presents a prostitute under a gaslight, red like poisonous mushrooms. And in 'Les Fiançailles' (1908) he develops the image of gas jets sending their flames into the moon; in fact, the French is more drastic: 'Les becs de gaz pissaient leur flamme au clair de lune'.

English poetry was quick to adopt the gaslight image. Again Arthur Symons offers numerous examples. His poem 'In Bohemia' (1892) works on the image of 'Drawn blinds and flaring gas within'. Even in his 'A Winter Night' (1886) darkness is irregularly lit 'With shimmering streaks of gaslight'. And Oscar Wilde in turn, referring to a lonely woman on 'Old Battersea Bridge', also draws on the gaslight image:

> But one pale woman all alone
> [. . .]
> Loitered beneath the gas lamps flare.

All these examples point towards the prevalent atmosphere in 'The Dead'. Connecting the first word of the story, 'Lily' (160), with Gabriel's entry, Joyce describes the girl as 'pale in complexion' (p. 161). To increase this effect, he even presents her in gas light, thus calling to mind all the associations which go together with this image: 'The gas in the pantry made her look still paler' (p. 161f.). For the most part, the story moves through this climate of murky twilight caused by artificial lighting. Only occasionally, particularly at the banquet scene, do bright colours such as red, yellow and green protrude from the semi-darkness, indicating that Joyce is working along the structural principles of the nocturnes in poetry or painting. The image of the gaslight is sustained until the end of the party when, through the eyes of Gabriel, Gretta too is visualized in gaslight: 'Gabriel watched his wife who did not join in the conversation. She was standing right under the dusty fan-light and the

flame of the gas lit up the rich bronze of her hair . . .' (p. 190).
Later, in the hotel room, Joyce continues to apply the effects of
artificial lighting by making a street lamp shine into the room: 'A
ghostly light from the street lamp lay in a long shaft from one window to the door' (p. 193). The choreography of the characters as
linked with the effects of light reveals the obvious Joycean tendency
to go beyond the traditional narrative means by incorporating pictorial techniques. Consequently, he associates Gretta principally
with light: 'She turned away from the mirror slowly and walked
along the shaft of light towards him' (p. 195). And even later, when
she is close together with Gabriel, she is again linked with the light
from the window: 'She looked away from him along the shaft of
light towards the window in silence' (p. 197). This interplay of light
and Gretta, while Gabriel remains in the semi-dark, makes her just
one representative of the many ladies in white to be met so frequently in poetry and painting. In fact, poetry in many cases aimed
at using techniques otherwise characteristic of painting, either by
casting a strong light on a female character or by setting this
character against a source of bright light. Arthur Symons's poem
'Colour Studies' (1892/93), presenting a woman against a twilight
window while playing simultaneously on white and light, works in
a very similar way to Joyce's portrait of Gretta against the window
of the hotel room:

> White-robed against the threefold white
> Of shutter, glass, and curtains' lace,
> She flashed into the evening light.
> [. . .]
> So, in the window's threefold white,
> [. . .]
> She seemed, against the evening light,
> Among the flowers herself a flower,
> A tiger-lily sheathed in white.

Joyce goes even so far as to introduce the parallel with painting
into Gabriel's consciousness. Being 'in a dark part of the hall gazing
up the staircase' (p. 189) he makes out a female figure in the shadow
who he comes to identify as his wife. As in the paintings of Félicien
Rops, for example, the tonal qualities of the intermediary colours
are reduced to the characteristic opposition of black and white:
'. . . he could see the terracotta and salmonpink panels of her skirt
which the shadow made appear black and white' (p. 188). It is the
special arrangement of this situation which causes Gabriel to realize
the tableau-like character of the event, a composition which bears
all the traits of a painting:

There was grace and mystery in her attitude as if she were a symbol of something. He asked himself what is a woman standing on the stairs in the shadow, listening to distant music, a symbol of. If he were a painter he would paint her in that attitude. Her blue felt hat would show off the bronze of her hair against the darkness and the dark panels of her skirt would show off the light ones. *Distant Music* he would call the picture if he were a painter. (p. 188)

This is a striking passage which, internally, i.e. on the story's own reflective level, confirms of what has been pointed out so far in this analysis. What Gabriel deliberates in *style indirect libre* is the basic starting point of the Symbolist theory: ideas and emotions are not to be described directly, neither are they to be defined by overt comparisons with concrete images. Instead, their essence is to be reached by evoking these ideas and emotions, which, in artistic practice, means that that they are re-created in the mind of the spectator or listener by means of unexplained symbols. This is precisely what Gretta does for Gabriel. Absolute art, according to the Symbolists, is not limited by the traditional divisions of poetry, music and painting. It is to avail itself of the musical quality of the language and likewise of the visual effects of painting. Synaesthesia, therefore, is one of the most favourite Symbolist devices. Joyce's passage, then, is the typical *audition colorée*, breathing the spirit of the many nocturnes of that time. How heavily Joyce is leaning on Symbolist examples can be proved even by minor ingredients like Gretta's 'blue felt hat'. After Paul Gauguin's 'scandalous' statement of the special value of blue in the *Echo de Paris* of May 13, 1895, the devoted Symbolist simply had to make use of this colour in some way or other — if only a touch of it.

Later, on the way to the hotel, Gretta again is the source of Gabriel's synaesthetic perception: 'But now, after the kindling again of so many memories, the first touch of her body, musical and strange and perfumed, sent through him a keen pang of lust' (p. 193). With this Joyce virtually presents a textbook realization of what Baudelaire states in his famous 'Correspondances' (1857):

> Vaste comme la nuit et comme la clarté,
> Les parfums, les couleurs et les sons se répondent.

Apart from the light and colour imagery there are other devices in 'The Dead' to imply polarity. Quite obviously, throughout the story, movements upwards and downwards occur. There is always somebody rushing up or down the stairs, leaning over the banisters or looking from the landing. Staircase, landing and banisters combine to form an image connected with movement and circulation between two different spheres. In this case too contemporary art offers interesting parallels. In 1899 Freud's *Interpretation of Dreams* appeared, to lay the foundation of what was to be called psychoanalysis. In this work he devotes considerable space to discussing the image of the staircase. For him the staircase is, in the broadest sense, the link between the conscious and the subconscious, a kind of hidden path towards the concealed realm of the soul. The validity of this claim is totally irrelevant; the fascinating side of Freud's idea is that the image of the staircase is so abundantly represented in contemporary art, above all in painting. Odilon Redon's highly symbolic 'Je vis une lueur large et pâle' (1896) fills a deserted corridor and staircase with life through a dynamic interplay of light and darkness. Xavier Mellery's 'Escalier' (1889), also contrasting vividly light with darkness, depicts a woman who is about to disappear on the top of the stairs. His 'Rêve du soir' (1898), showing a seated figure who is apparently dreaming beside the staircase, demonstrates an even more psychological direction: the staircase grows into a direct path to the subconscious. Carlos Schwabe's poster for the first exhibition of the 'Rose Croix' group 1892 again presents a staircase, overgrown with lilies, leading out of water into the sky. On the staircase a lady in black and a lady in white, representing this life and the life to come, touch each other's hands.

This leads us back to Joyce. The movements on the staircase reach their symbolic climax through the final movements in the closing paragraph. Whereas the snow conveys the downward movement — 'falling' is mentioned seven times — Gabriel's soul with its 'journey westward' (p. 200) has begun the upward movement. It is a journey from water ('rain', 'waves', 'snow') into the infinite of ethereal spheres, a transfiguration from this life to a new form of life. Even here the polarity of two different spheres as well as the transient character of the situation are expressed by 'the flakes, *silver* and *dark*, falling obliquely against the *lamp-light*' (p. 200, my italics).

The general idea which underlies this situation called for another prevailing image in contemporary art: the image of the window was to picture the orientation from this reality towards a spiritually created reality. In Edward Munch's 'The Kiss' (last version 1898), for instance, the window acts largely as an intermediary between these spheres. The drawing portrays a nude couple embracing, the woman resting her hands on the man's shoulders. The two are seen in a twilight atmosphere from inside the dark room against a window through which falls the light of the gas lamps in the street.

Generally the atmosphere is one of extreme ecstasy. This pictorial rendering of a kiss does not seem to be far away from the parallel situation in Joyce's hotel room: 'He was in such a fever of rage and desire that he did not hear her come from the window. She stood before him for an instant, looking at him strangely. Then, suddenly raising herself on tiptoe and resting her hands on his shoulders, she kissed him' (p. 195f). With both Munch and Joyce, the scenes are anything but idylls. Since 1891, Munch had been working on this motif, and thus, through a series of paintings and drawings, he continually elaborated his philosophy.[18] Originally inspired by Rodin's famous 'Le baiser' (1889), he was soon to drop all the poetical implications. Instead, in his series of pictures, he moved the couple more and more to the centre of the window and stressed the tension between light and darkness. He further incorporated his own painting 'The Girl and Death' (1893) into the scene of 'The Kiss'. 'The Girl and Death' shows a young nude woman with an extremely voluptuous body dancing with a skeleton. Obviously this is a motif taken from the traditional dance of death. However, Munch turns the established relationship of life and death upside down: it is the young and blossoming woman who inflicts death. Thus, in the final version of 'The Kiss', the kiss is not far removed from a fatal bite into the man's neck. With this, the kiss goes beyond ecstasy, it is the transfiguration from one life to another through woman, with the symbolical reference of a window.

Thus it is Gretta who is the one who kisses Gabriel, resting her hands on his shoulders. And shortly after that, in a twofold move, she is associated with death and the dissolving of identity. The window imagery as it has appeared so far is now fused with the window which connects Gretta with Michael Furey: 'I heard gravel thrown up against the window. The window was so wet I couldn't see so I ran downstairs as I was and slipped out the back into the garden' (p. 199). It is highly significant that she does not just look out of the window but that she actually goes out into the rainy night. The outcome is: ' "I think he died for me", she answered' (p. 198).

Just as several of Munch's paintings show his interest in the symbolic value of the window, so Joyce in *Dubliners* repeatedly works on the window motif. It appears that in 'The Dead' he brings the point of 'Every night as I gazed up at the window I said softly to myself the word *paralysis*' (p. 7) in 'The Sisters' to its most systematic and symbolic conclusion. Whereas in the other stories the window had always remained an enigma, it now provides the answer of the other world. After Gretta's story, Gabriel is magically attracted by the window 'and walked quietly to the window' (p. 199). The window of Michael and Gretta now assumes the character of a window leading to the infinite since Michael's profane gravel turns into cosmic snowflakes: 'A few light taps upon the pane made him turn to the window. It had begun to snow again' (p. 200). It is the window through which his soul can set out on its journey westward. Leaving the world on this side of the window is equivalent to dissolving his identity, but a new world on the other side is to be won. That woman is associated with death in this context is just another of the many typically Symbolist notions.

One of the intriguing traits of Gretta seems to be her hair. Several times when Gabriel looks at her, his glance culminates in its sight. For example at the beginning of the party his 'happy eyes had been wandering from her dress to her face and hair' (p. 164). And after the night he 'looked for a few moments unresentfully on her tangled hair' (p. 199) which is reinforced only a few lines later by 'His curious eyes rested long upon her face and on her hair'. Within the nocturnal picture of leave-taking, it is for him again her hair which shines out of the darkness: 'the flame of the gas lit up the rich bronze of her hair which he had seen her drying at the fire a few days before' (p. 190). In the light of his reaction to the kiss, his caressing her hair seems to be a gesture of particular intimacy:

Gabriel, trembling with delight at her sudden kiss [. . .], put his hands on her hair and began smoothing it back, scarcely touching it with his fingers. *The washing had made it fine and brilliant.* His heart was brimming over with happiness. (p. 196, my italics).

This emphasis on Gretta's hair recalls the Symbolist preoccupation with female hair. Beardsley's drawings demonstrate this to the extent of obsession. In many of Munch's pictures, such as 'Separation II' (1896) or 'Man's Head in Woman's Hair' (1896), the man gets entangled in the woman's hair. In his 'Vampire' (1893/94) the woman is even fatally ensnaring the man with her hair. Examples in literature are equally frequent. Maurice Maeterlinck's *Pelléas et Mélisande* (1892) offers an unrestrained apotheosis of hair:

Oh! oh! qu'est-ce que c'est? . . . Tes cheveux, tes cheveux descendent vers moi! . . . Toute ta chevelure, Mélisande, toute ta chevelure est tombée de la tour! . . . Je les tiens dans les mains, je les tiens dans ma bouche . . . Je les tiens dans les bras, je les mets autour de mon cou . . . Je n'ouvrirai plus les mains cette nuit.[19]

The morbid air inherent in Munch and Maeterlinck can be generalised. Arthur Symons, too, celebrating the 'white' girl in his

'Bianca' (1894/95) links the description of the girl's hair with the fear of death:

> I drink the odours of her hair
> With lips that linger in her neck,
> [. . .]
> The whiteness of her bosom bare
> Beneath the fragant veil of hair.
> Death in her lilied whiteness lives,
> The shadow of Death's eternal lust.

Death in turn is associated with the idea of transformation. Transformation again evokes the idea of night and water. This explains why the imagery of hair includes within its associative field images of night and water — in Joyce's case, the washing of hair. In 'La Chevelure' (1859) Baudelaire praises blue hair which flows into darkness. The image of hair is thus synthesized with water imagery, 'ocean' and 'waves' being prominent references. Various portraits of women's heads in contemporary art tend to arrange the hair in a highly aesthetic and floating manner. The pattern resembles either the artful display of waterflowers or the rhythmical arrangement of waves. It is particularly the idea of the wave which connects hair with water imagery. Again Munch's pictures are fine examples of the psychological deep structure of iconography. His woodcut 'On Man's Mind' (1897) shows a nude whose hair, like whirling waves, swirls round the male's head. 'Couple in Waves' (1896) goes even further; as there is virtually no difference between the female hair and the waves, the woman appears to swim whereas her male counterpart is unidentifiable, totally submerged. Odilon Redon's 'La mort: Mon ironie dépasse toutes les autres!' (1889) combines a number of images: the white, voluptuous body of a woman contrasts with her black garment. While the hair is seen as a white wave in darkness, there is a maelstrom behind the female embodiment of death which threatens to absorb the spectator. Water as another image of transfiguration in fact complements the transformational rôle of night. As Maeterlinck's 'La dernière chanson de Mélisande' in *Treize chansons de l'âge mur* words it:

> L'eau qui pleure et l'eau qui rit,
> L'eau qui parle et l'eau qui fuit,
> L'eau qui tremble dans la nuit . . .[20]

All this carries the argument to the iconographic system of associative references at the end of 'The Dead'. It is here that the emerging net of images reaches its highest density, here that the various images coalesce in the true sense of the word. Night reaches its actual transfigurative quality. Just as 'Lily' is the flower of death *and*, being an Easter Flower, a symbol of resurrection, so snow is equally an image of death *and*, being frozen water, an element of resurrection. In the last lines the snow flakes falling into the Shannon waves signify this. The image of the night fully adopts the snow imagery and merges organically with water imagery — even Gretta's hair links up with the Shannon waves, night and rain combine in their tranfigurative function. In the beginning Gabriel shuns water and snow. He tries to protect himself through his extraordinary 'goloshes', and Gretta has the impression: 'The next thing he'll buy me will be a diving suit' (p. 164). But by the end, Gabriel comes to think of 'the pleasure of the walk along the river in the snow' (p. 200). Within the context of rivers, waves, rain, and falling snow, in the twilight of the morning and 'in the partial darkness he imagined' (p. 200), he experiences his own transfiguration, basically initiated through a woman and directed towards a window, through which 'His own identity was fading out into a grey impalpable world' (p. 200). When a tree, dripping in the rain, is referred to twice (p. 199, 200), then, yet again, an accord of images occurs which is typical of the time. Stefan George's 'Voices in the Stream' (1894) develops the image of submarine bodies which resemble shells with lips like corals, whose hair is entangled in branchlike cliffs. Giovanni Segantini's 'The Evil Mothers' (1891) depicts a woman whose hair is caught in a barren tree, surrounded by what appears to be the troubled surface of water. Similarly, Arthur Symons, in his 'The Dance of the Daughters of Herodias' (1897), fuses Salome with images of tree, hair, and water:

> Here is Salome. She is a young tree
> Swaying in the wind; her arms are slender branches
> And the heavy summer leafage of her hair
> [. . .]
>        her wide eyes
> Swim open, her lips seek;

With all the images working on one another, their complex texture at the end is woven into the image of the Symbolist garden. Oscar Wilde's 'The Garden of Eros' (1881) contains the elements of whiteness, snow, night, water, and tree. In painting too, the tendency to combine snow, water, and trees into a picture of the Symbolist garden is not uncommon, as can be seen in Constand Montald's 'Jardin sous la neige' (1910) or Léon Spilliaert's 'Hiver' (1915). Carlos Schwabe's 'La Vierge aux lys' (1899) makes the waves flow into the snow and exchanges the trees for highstemmed lilies. That rain was by no means an exceptional phenomenon in the Symbolist garden can be seen in the poems of Francis Vielé-Griffin, Henry Bataille, or André Gide.

That, finally, the Symbolist garden, as in Joyce, conjures up Christological references is well in accord with the Symbolist train of thought. References to Christ are introduced when Gretta explains Michael's death in terms of a sacrifice for her: 'I think he died for me' (p. 198). Obviously she is using an anthropocentric inversion of the Christian notion that Jesus dies for man. This inversion continually grows in meaning. Just as Jesus voluntarily took upon Himself the death of the Cross (John X, 18), so Michael purposely encompasses death through love. And his standing in the 'garden' (p. 199) suggests an immanent parallel to Jesus in the Garden of Gethsemane. (1 Cor. XV), speaking of Christ's Resurrection, carries much of what is inherent at the end of 'The Dead': 'For since by man came death, by man came also the resurrection of the dead. For as in Adam all die, even so in Christ shall all be made alive.' With Gabriel and Michael, however, these words are no longer centred on Jesus Christ. Although alive and, as her husband, closest to Gretta, Gabriel remains a peripheral figure in her feelings and thus virtually succumbs to death. On the other hand, Michael, being dead and having merely worshipped Gretta from afar, occupies her emotions and in this way becomes palpably alive. The idea of resurrection from death is reinforced when the image of snow-clad Ireland blends with the description of the lonely churchyard where Michael is buried. Here 'the crooked crosses', 'the spears', and 'the barren thorns' (p. 201) suggest crucifixion and resurrection. But in Joyce the resurrection of the Christian doctrine undergoes a fundamental change: on an immanent plane man becomes his own source of redemption and, with this, his own agent for resurrection.

In the chapter 'Death, Renewal, and Redemption in Apollinaire, Montale, Lorca, Yeats, and Rilke' of his *French Symbolism and the Modernist Movement*[21] J. P. Houston has shown that man's claim to create something absolutely new does not allow the creator to bypass Christianity. Even several of Munch's paintings bear Christological references by making a background moon or sun and their reflections in water look like Christ on the cross. Antagonism to Christian doctrine raises the most crucial problem, and, accordingly, Gabriel's soul is confronted with it in the most extreme situation when it begins its journey.

The question of the conclusion of 'The Dead' which has troubled critics so much,[22] is not the question of whether Gabriel is destined for life or death and the puzzling ambiguity of this, but it is the question of transfiguration, of re-defining life and reality. That this, in the last sentence, occurs through blending sight and sound: 'he heard the snow falling faintly', is Joyce's ultimate synaesthesia in 'The Dead'.

# 'WORDSWORTH AT THE FLAX-DAM': AN EARLY POEM BY SEAMUS HEANEY

NICHOLAS ROE

All year the flax-dam festered in the heart
Of the townland; green and heavy headed
Flax had rotted there, weighted down by huge sods.
Daily it sweltered in the punishing sun.
Bubbles gargled delicately, bluebottles
Wove a strong gauze of sound around the smell.
There were dragon-flies, spotted butterflies,
But best of all was the warm thick slobber
Of frogspawn that grew like clotted water
In the shade of the banks. Here, every spring
I would fill jampotfuls of the jellied
Specks to range on window-sills at home,
On shelves at school, and wait and watch until
The fattening dots burst into nimble-
Swimming tadpoles. Miss Walls would tell us how
The daddy frog was called a bullfrog
And how he croaked and how the mammy frog
Laid hundreds of little eggs and this was
Frogspawn. You could tell the weather by frogs too
For they were yellow in the sun and brown
In rain.

Then one hot day when fields were rank
With cowdung in the grass the angry frogs
Invaded the flax-dam; I ducked through hedges
To a coarse croaking that I had not heard
Before. The air was thick with a bass chorus.
Right down the dam gross-bellied frogs were cocked
On sods; their loose necks pulsed like sails. Some hopped:
The slap and plop were obscene threats. Some sat
Poised like mud grenades, their blunt heads farting.
I sickened, turned, and ran. The great slime kings

Were gathered there for vengeance and I knew
That if I dipped my hand the spawn would clutch it.
                                          'Death of a Naturalist.'

When introducing 'Death of a Naturalist' on his recent Faber
poetry cassette, Seamus Heaney draws attention to the poem's
'grunting, consonantal music' which he says may have derived
from his reading of Anglo-Saxon poetry and the work of Gerard
Manley Hopkins as a student at Queen's University, Belfast. But
the poem has another literary background that Heaney doesn't
mention, in the 'spots of time' in Wordsworth's *Prelude*: those
moments where the past resurfaces with a power to quicken the
poet's imaginative life.

For Wordsworth the formative experience in a spot of time was
usually associated with fear or guilt, as for example in the passage
which recalls how he would trap woodcocks to sell in the market:

And afterwards ('twas in a later day,
Though early), when upon the mountain slope
The frost and breath of frosty wind had snapped
The last autumnal crocus, 'twas my joy
To wander half the night among the cliffs
And the smooth hollows where the woodcocks ran
Along the moonlight turf. In thought and wish
That time, my shoulder all with springes hung,
I was a fell destroyer. Gentle powers,
Who give us happiness and call it peace,
When scudding on from snare to snare I plied
My anxious visitation, hurrying on,
Still hurrying, hurrying onward, how my heart
Panted; among the scattered yew-trees and the crags
That looked upon me, how my bosom beat
With expectation! Sometimes strong desire
Resistless overpowered me, and the bird
Which was the captive of another's toils
Became my prey; and when the deed was done
I heard among the solitary hills
Low breathings coming after me, and sounds
Of undistinguishable motion, steps
Almost as silent as the turf they trod.
                          *The Prelude* (1799 text), I, ll. 27–49.

Wordsworth recreates the child's anxious, expectant retrieval of his
snares, and the temptation to steal 'the captive of another's toils'.
His concern, though, was less with the theft itself than the reflex
of guilt projected in the 'Low breathings' and 'sounds / Of undistinguishable motion' that seemed to pursue the boy.

A comparable movement appears in 'Death of a Naturalist', which concludes with 'the angry frogs' gathered as if for vengeance. But where Wordsworth's spot of time is thoroughly assured, Heaney seems somewhat uneasy. Wordsworth intimates the transformation of 'anxious visitation' to stealthy retribution, whereas Heaney is comparatively explicit: 'I sickened, turned and ran', he writes:

> The great slime kings
> Were gathered there for vengeance and I knew
> That if I dipped my hand the spawn would clutch it.

The child's queasy retreat is at odds with the poet's evident relish for the 'slap and plop' of frogs and the rank stink of the dam itself. Heaney admits a Wordsworthian preoccupation with childish experience, but the imaginative heart of his poem lies elsewhere. It finds its true register in a vivid externality, in his description of the dam itself, 'green and heavy headed / . . . weighted down by huge sods'.

This tension between Heaney's 'grunting, consonantal music', and the Wordsworthian ancestry of his poem may offer one explanation for Heaney's failure to articulate the child's fear convincingly. Where Wordsworth's moment gathers towards unity, 'Death of a Naturalist' seems curiously divided against itself. It wants inner life as, I think, do a number of related early poems such as 'The Barn', 'An Advancement of Learning', and 'The Early Purges'. What follows is an attempt to explain why this might be so.

To make a very rough distinction, Wordsworth's imagination inhabits the child's feelings, whereas in 'Death of a Naturalist' Heaney dwells fruitfully upon contingent nature. Wordsworth recreates the child's nervous onward hurry, with a cumulative momentum to that final manifestation of his own conscience, 'steps / Almost as silent as the turf they trod'. The 'deed' itself is in fact tangential to the poet's deeper engagement with the child's mind. Rather than explore a comparable inner territory, though, Heaney's poem conveys the texture of landscape itself and in doing so his language acquires an emphatic life of its own. The child's memorial experience is correspondingly enervated, and Heaney's explicit interpolation 'I sickened, turned, and ran' appears as an attempt to steer the poem back into the child's world. The imaginative life of Wordsworth's spot of time is internal, in 'Death of a Naturalist' it is disengaged and external to the child. The implications of this for Heaney's subsequent development are, perhaps, worth looking at more closely.

Wordsworth's *Prelude* has linguistic and mythical roots in

*Paradise Lost*, and Milton's idiom is often a master key for Wordsworth's blank verse — here, for example, in the rotund sonority of 'strong desire / Resistless'. This is Wordsworth's recreation of the boy's overpowering temptation to steal, but its Miltonic ring also serves as a reminder that these recollected moments in *The Prelude* internalise the redemptive structure of Milton's Christian epic as a prerogative of the poet's imagination. Wordsworth is in effect his own Satan but he is also his own redeemer, for each spot of time enacts a fall that contains the promise of future restoration. It is therefore possible to see *The Prelude* as in some degree dependent upon the inner light and private intercession of protestant theology, and closely related to the spiritual journal and autobiography of puritan tradition.

'Death of a Naturalist' suggests that Heaney is drawn to the Wordsworthian spot of time, but unable to admit its redemptive adequacy. Wordsworth's 'spot' discovers its shape from within, but Heaney significantly imposes a mythic framework upon his experience in which 'Miss Walls' appears as external author of guilt — perhaps a sexual awakening — which infects the child's subsequent visit to the flax-dam. 'Miss Walls' is, therefore, an external symbol of the child's quickening conscience, a sort of primary school Eve who bears responsibility for the 'Death of a naturalist', the child's lost innocence.

Perhaps it isn't too much to claim, then, that 'Death of a Naturalist' offers a first glimpse of Heaney's mythic wish, his need to substantiate the 'verbal icon' within a larger symbolic correlative for his own experience. As such, the uneasy voice in 'Death of a Naturalist' offers an early adumbration of the 'Bog People' poems, where the victims of 'archaic barbarous rites' are appropriated as 'images and symbols' adequate to contemporary violence in Northern Ireland. In that identification, to paraphrase Heaney's essay 'Feeling into Words', present strife is subsumed within an enduring myth, or 'archetypal pattern' of sacrificial death, renewal, fertility. But in that pattern, Heaney significantly recognises the same elements of his own formative experience recalled in 'Death of Naturalist' — corruption and decay that feeds a fecund vitality. This, perhaps, was what Heaney meant by 'discovering a field of force' that remained true to 'the processes and experience of his poetry' up to that moment in 1969. The larger claims of these later poems to deal with 'present predicaments' can therefore be seen to return upon Heaney's earliest work and specifically upon the unreconciled promptings of a Wordsworthian, Protestant imagination.

Heaney's exploitation of myth was accelerated by the present war in Northern Ireland, and finds its deepest root in the primary tensions of that conflict: his catholic unwillingness to admit the efficacy of a protestant redemption. That division first emerges as a characteristic of Heaney's imagination in 'Death of a Naturalist'. From that poem one can trace some of Heaney's most distinctive later poetry and, in *Preoccupations*, some of the finest recent criticism of Wordsworth's *Prelude*.

# NOTES

MOBILIZING BYZANTIUM. Catherine Belsey

1  All W. B. Yeats's verse quotations are from *The Poems, A New Edition,* ed. Richard J. Finneran (Macmillan, New York, 1983, London, 1984).
2  All quotations from John Keats are from *The Complete Poems,* ed. Miriam Allott (Longman, London, 1970).
3  W. B. Yeats, *Explorations* (Macmillan, London, 1962), pp. 305–6.
4  W. G. Holmes, *The Age of Justinian and Theodora* (George Bell, London, 1905–7), p. 83.
5  W. B. Yeats, *A Critical Edition of Yeats's A Vision (1925),* eds. George Mills Harper and Walter Kelly Hood (Macmillan, London and Basingstoke, 1978), p. 191.
6  *The Age of Justinian and Theodora,* p. 47.
7  *Ibid.,* pp. 55, 227, 536.
8  Ernest Schanzer, ' "Sailing to Byzantium", Keats and Andersen', *English Studies,* 41, pp. 376–80.
9  Quoted in A. Norman Jeffares, *A New Commentary on the Poems of W. B. Yeats* (Macmillan, London, 1984), p. 294.
10  Jacques Lacan, *The Four Fundamental Concepts of Psycho-Analysis* (Penguin, Harmondsworth, 1979), p. 113.
11  Richard Ellmann, *Yeats, the Man and the Masks* (Faber, London, 1961), p. 275.
12  *A New Commentary on the Poems of W. B. Yeats,* p. 215.
13  W. B. Yeats, *Selected Criticism,* ed. A. Norman Jeffares (Macmillan, London, 1964), p. 259. I owe this reference to Michael Allen.

DOUBLES, SHADOWS, SEDAN-CHAIRS AND THE PAST: THE 'GHOST STORIES' OF J. S. LE FANU. Patricia Coughlan

1  See Patrick O'Neill, 'The Reception of German Literature in Ireland: 1750–1850, Pt. 2', *Studia Hibernica* 17–18 (1978), pp. 91–106; and 'German Literature and the *Dublin University Magazine,* 1833–50', *Long Room* 14–15, Autumn 1976–Spring 1977, pp. 20–31.
2  See J. C. Mangan's 'Chapters on Ghostcraft' (1842, XIX, pp. 1–17), and Ferris's 'German Ghosts and Ghost-Seers' (XXVII, 1845, pp. 33–50, 217–32) and 'Miscellanea Mystica' (XXVII, 1846, pp. 155–70). See O'Neill, *loc. cit.,* note 1 above.
3  See for example the vision ascribed to Maud by the Swedenborgian

sage, Dr Bryerly, near the beginning; it is never clear whether she sees it, or takes it on faith.

4   Ralph Tymms, in his study *Doubles in Literary Psychology* (Cambridge, 1949), pp. 37–8, describes the German Romantics' 'penchant for merging fantasy with an awareness of the existence of problems in abnormal psychology', and remarks that 'with Hoffmann the identification of the fairy-tale with the psychological case-book was to be deliberate, so as to invest the *Marchen* with a specifically symbolic meaning'.

5   See V. Erlich, *Russian Formalism* (2nd ed., The Hague, 1965), pp. 240–1.

6   The most accessible collections of the stories are E. F. Bleiler, ed., *Best Ghost Stories of J. S. Le Fanu* (N.Y., 1964) and *J. S. Le Fanu: Ghost Stories and Mysteries* (N.Y., 1975). All subsequent page-references are to these editions, which I abbreviate as *BGS* and *GSM* respectively.

7   Punter, *op. cit.*, p. 422.

8   Quoted in Ludwig Binswanger, 'The Case of Lola Voss', tr. E. Angel, in *Being-In-The-World* (N.Y., 1963), p. 306.

9   *Op. cit.*, pp. 306–7.

10  *New Introductory Lectures on Psychoanalysis*, tr. J. Strachey (Penguin, Harmondsworth, 1973), p. 105.

11  'Paris — the Capital of the Nineteenth Century', tr. Q. Hoare, in Harry Zohn (ed.), *Charles Baudelaire: A Lyric Poet in the Era of High Capitalism* (London, 1976), pp. 166–7.

12  See J. Rosenberg, ed. *Pelican History of Art: Dutch Art and Architecture* (Penguin, Harmondsworth, 1972), pp. 145–7, and A. Czober, *Rembrandt and His Circle* (Budapest, 1969), commentary on Pl. 18 — a Douw portrait which, however, treats the person as merely decorative and stresses a collection of gleaming objects in the foreground.

13  The cleaning of the portrait typically releases these catastrophic energies, as in 'Carmilla' and 'The Haunted Baronet'.

14  See Otto Rank, *The Double: A Psychoanalytic Study*, tr. and ed. H. Tucker, Jr. (Chapel Hill, North Carolina, 1971).

15  *Essay Concerning Human Understanding* (1690) II. 1, 10–11 (quoted in Tymms, *op. cit.*, pp. 21–2).

16  A. E. Crawley, 'Doubles', in J. Hastings, ed., *Encyclopaedia of Religion and Ethics* (London, 1908–26).

17  Tymms, *op. cit.*, p. 38.

18  *Loc. cit.*, p. 39 (the work referred to is *Reiseschatten* (1811)).

19  'Epilogue' to *Madam Crowl's Ghost and Others Tales* (London, 1923), p. 274.

20  See the discussion in D. Ó hÓgain, 'An É an t-Am Fós É?' *Bealoideas* 42–44 (1974–6), pp. 213–309, and 'Gearoid Iarla agus an Draíocht', *Scriobh* 4 (1979), pp. 234–59. I am grateful for these references to Diarmuid O Giolláin.

21  *Sybil* (London, 1845), p. 54.

22  Here in 'The Haunted Baronet', in 'The Last Heir of Castle Connor', and in 'A Chapter in the History of a Tyrone Family'.

23  As in 'The Murdered Cousin' (1838), its later version *Uncle Silas* (1863), and 'The Fortunes of Sir Robert Ardagh' (1838). The only crime which can be pinned on Silas during most of that novel is that of 'waste', cutting down and selling timber from Maud's land.

24  Le Fanu often uses gipsies as figures standing at the threshold of the Other and possessing a knowledge denied ordinary characters: in *Uncle Silas* Maud encounters the gipsy camp on the journey from her father's house — secure and familiar — to Bartram-Haugh where they will plan to murder her; and in 'Carmilla' only the gipsy pedlar notices Carmilla's long pointed vampire teeth (*BGS*, p. 296).

## NATIONAL CHARACTER AND NATIONAL AUDIENCE: RACES, CROWDS AND READERS. Seamus Deane

1   Lawrence Lipking, *The Ordering of the Arts in Eighteenth Century England* (Princeton, 1970), p. 329.

2   *History of English Poetry*, II, p. 462.

3   *A Literary History of Ireland*, 2nd impression (London, 1901), pp. x–xi. The Dedication reads: 'To the members of the Gaelic League, The only body in Ireland which appears to Realise the fact that Ireland has a past, has a History, has a literature, and the only body in Ireland which seeks to render the present a rational continuation of the past, I dedicate This attempt at a review of that literature Which despite its present neglected position they feel and know to be a true possession of national importance.'

4   See my forthcoming article on 'Irish National Character, 1790–1900' in *Irish Historical Studies*.

5   Warton, II, p. 463.

6   *The Collected Letters of W. B. Yeats*, ed. John Kelly and Eric Domville (Oxford, 1986), I, p. 229.

7   Lipking, pp. 328–30.

8   True also of Warton's *Essay on Pope*; see Lipking, p. 362ff.

9   Although he indicated its outlines in *Biographia Literaria* and in the *Miscellaneous Criticism*, ed. T. Raysor (London, 1936).

10  See L. P. Curtis, Jnr., *Apes and Angels: The Irishman in Victorian Caricature* (Newton Abbot, 1971); L. C. B. Seaman, *Victorian England* (London, 1973), pp. 232–61.

11  On the *exemplum virtutis*, see Robert Rosenblum, *Transformations in Late Eighteenth Century Art* (Princeton, 1967), pp. 50–106.

12  *Collected Letters*, I, p. 296.

13  See Harold Perkins, *The Origins of Modern English Society, 1780–1880* (London & Toronto, 1969), pp. 218–339.

14  *Ibid.*, pp. 237–51; Mark Girouard, *The Return to Camelot: Chivalry and the English Gentleman* (New Haven and London, 1981).

15  See Tom Gibbons, *Rooms in the Darwin Hotel: Studies in English Literary Criticism and Ideas 1880–1920* (University of Western Australia Press, Redlands, 1973).

16   Cf. Michael Steinman, *Yeats's Heroic Figures: Wilde, Parnell, Swift, Casement* (London, 1983).
17   *Yeats and the Occult*, ed. G. Mills Harper (London, 1976), p. 219.
18   See Gibbons, *Rooms in the Darwin Hotel*, pp. 1–38.
19   Elizabeth Cullingford, *Yeats, Ireland and Fascism* (London, 1981), esp. pp. 144–232; Conor Cruise O'Brien, 'Passion and Cunning. An Essay on the Politics of W. B. Yeats' in *In Excited Reverie*, eds. A. N. Jeffares and K. W. G. Cross (London, 1965), pp. 207–78.
20   *Explorations*, p. 414.
21   Cf. Frederic Jameson, *The Political Unconscious: Narrative as a Socially Symbolic Act* (London, 1981), pp. 123–9.
22   See John Kelly, 'Choosing and Inventing: Yeats and Ireland' in *Across a Roaring Hill: the Protestant Imagination in Modern Ireland*, eds. G. Dawe and E. Longley (Belfast and Dover, 1985), pp. 1–24.
23   Quoted by Cullingford (from *Letters*, ed. Wade), pp. 197–8.
24   Cullingford, pp. 197–214.
25   *Ibid.*, quoted on p. 203.
26   Quoted in Ian Jack, *The Poet and his Audience* (Cambridge, 1984), p. 168.
27   *The Variorum Edition of the Poems of W. B. Yeats*, eds. P. Allt and R. K. Alspach (New York, 1977), p. 836.
28   *Letters of W. B. Yeats*, ed. A. Wade (London, 1954), pp. 250–1.

## GARNERING THE FACTS: UNRELIABLE NARRATORS IN SOME PLAYS OF BRIAN FRIEL. Gerald FitzGibbon

1   Seamus Deane, Introduction to *Selected Plays of Brian Friel* (Faber, London, 1984), p. 17. All page references to Seamus Deane's introduction and to the plays, apart from *Lovers*, are taken from this edition.
2   In *A Critical History of Modern Irish Drama 1891–1980*, (Cambridge University Press, Cambridge 1984), D. E. S. Maxwell refers to this as being 'remembered differently by father and son' (p. 201), which rather misses the point.
3   See Elizabeth H. Winkler's article, 'Brian Friel's *The Freedom of the City*: Historical Actuality and Dramatic Imagination', *Canadian Journal of Irish Studies*, Vol. 7, No. 1, pp. 12–31.
4   Fintan O'Toole, 'Friel's Lost Tribe', *The Sunday Tribune*, 24 March, 1985.
5   *Lovers* (Faber, London, 1969), p. 11.
6   Robert Hogan, *'Since O'Casey' and Other Essays on Irish Drama* (Colin Smythe, Gerrards Cross, 1984).
7   D. E. S. Maxwell avoids this dimension of the play, seeing it as representing 'prismatic individuality of character' in opposition to 'the simplicities of dogma' (*op. cit.*, p. 206).

FATHERS VANQUISHED AND VICTORIOUS. A HISTORICAL
READING OF SYNGE'S *PLAYBOY*. Ruth Fleischmann

1  Michael MacLiammóir, Preface to the Everyman edition of Synge's
   *Plays* (London, 1961).
2  The edition used of *The Playboy of the Western World* is that edited
   by Robin Skelton, *Four Plays and the Aran Islands* (London, 1962).
   The numerals in brackets after quotations refer to the pages of this
   edition.
3  J. C. Beckett, *The Making of Modern Ireland 1603–1927* (London and
   Boston, 1981), p. 408.
4  R. N. Salaman, *The History and Social Influence of the Potato* (Cambridge, 1949), pp. 330–31, and Maud Gonne MacBride, *A Servant of
   the Queen* (Dublin, 1950), p. 220.
5  Patrick F. Sheeran, *The Novels of Liam O'Flaherty* (Dublin, 1976), p.
   27.
6  George Russell (AE), *Co-operation and Nationality* (Dublin, 1982),
   pp. 13–14.
7  See K. H. Connell, 'Illicit Distilling' in *Irish Peasant Society* (London,
   1968), pp. 1–50.
8  Michael D. Higgins and John P. Gibbon, 'Shopkeeper-Graziers and
   Land Agitation in Ireland 1895–1900' in P. J. Drudy (ed), *Ireland:
   Land, Politics and People* (Cambridge, 1982); and Patrick Bolger, *The
   Irish Co-operative Movement* (Dublin, 1977), p. 45.
9  Peig Sayers in *An Old Woman's Reflections*, by Seamus Ennis (London, 1962, originally published 1939) tells us that when mainland
   women were no longer willing to marry into the Blaskets, the fate of
   the community was sealed. See too Hugh Brody, *Inishkillane: Change
   and Decline in the West of Ireland* (Penguin, Harmondsworth, 1974),
   pp. 126–30.
10  The politicians of the United Irish League are obviously not considered as being a substitute. Though William O'Brien's movement,
   founded in Mayo in 1898, spread quickly all over the country, and
   was a decisive factor in bringing about the final land settlement of
   1903, it was nevertheless primarily a political rather than a social
   organisation, and never became anything like as powerful as the Land
   League. It succeeded in re-uniting the divided Irish Party. See F. S. L.
   Lyons, *Ireland since the Famine* (London, 1971), pp. 211–13 and
   256–9, Charles Townshend, *Political Violence in Ireland* (Cambridge,
   1983), pp. 226–34, and E. Strauss, *Irish Nationalism and British
   Democracy* (London, 1951), pp. 206–15.
11  See Mary Hayden and G. A. Moonan, *A Short History of Ireland*,
   (Dublin and Cork, n.d.), Vol. I, pp. 72–5.
12  See Una Ellis-Fermor, *The Irish Dramatic Movement* (London, 1964),
   pp. 163–74 and Seán O Tuama, 'Synge and the Idea of a National
   Literature', pp. 6–7 in *J. M. Synge Centenary Papers*, ed. Maurice
   Harmon (Dublin, 1972), pp. 6–7.

13   The word 'gallous' is the Middle English adjective 'gallows', which can
     be pronounced 'gallous'. This originally meant 'fit for the gallows',
     'villainous', 'wicked'; then came to mean 'very great', 'fine!' See *The
     Shorter Oxford English Dictionary* (Oxford, 1980) vol. 1, p. 828.

14   Seán O Tuama and Thomas Kinsella, *An Duanaire 1600–1900: Poems
     of the Dispossessed* (Dolmen, Dublin, 1981), p. 139 introducing
     Aogán O Rathaille's 'Is Fada Liom Oiche Fhirfhliuch'. See too the ac-
     count in Thomas Flanagan's *Irish Novelists 1800–1850* (New York and
     London, 1963), pp. 181–2, of pathetic nineteenth century attempts to
     salvage heroic images out of disaster: how Thackeray was mystified
     during his visit to Ireland by the popularity among the poor of ballads
     and chapbooks written by rabid anti-Papists exulting over the
     downfall of the Irish, and who, the better to celebrate their victory,
     'had painted Sarsfield and the other Irish officers in bold and mock-
     heroic colours'.

15   Quoted in Ruth Dudley Edwards, *Patrick Pearse: The Triumph of
     Failure* (London and Boston, 1979), pp. 102–3.

16   Padraic Pearse, *Collected Works: Political Writings and Speeches*
     (Dublin, n.d.), pp. 145–6.

17   James Connolly, quoted in C. Desmond Greaves, *The Life and Times
     of James Connolly* (London, 1972), p. 395.


'IT IS MYSELF THAT I REMAKE': THE SHAPING OF SELF IN YEATS'S
AUTOBIOGRAPHIES. Margaret E. Fogarty

1    Shirley Hazzard, 'We Need Silence to Find Out What We Think', *The
     New York Times Book Review*, 14 Nov. (1982), p. 28.

2    *Ibid.*, p. 11.

3    W. B. Yeats, 'Ego Dominus Tuus', *The Poems. A New Edition*, ed.
     Richard Finneran (Gill and Macmillan, Dublin, 1984), p. 162.

4    As quoted by Sarah Kofman in: 'No Longer Full-Fledged *Autobiogrif-
     fies*', *Sub-Stance*, 29 (1981), p. 6. Freud's actual viewpoint is expressed
     in two letters. To E. Bernays, Freud wrote: 'What deprives all
     autobiographies of their value is that they are untruthful' (Aug. 10,
     1929); and to A. Zweig he declared: 'Whoever becomes a biographer
     is obliged to lie, dissimulate, embellish and even hide his own lack of
     comprehension, for one cannot possess the biographical truth' (May
     31, 1936). See Sigmund Freud, *Letters 1873–1939*, ed. E. L. Freud, tr.
     T. and J. Stern (New York: 1960).

5    *Cf.* Robert Elbaz, 'Autobiography, Ideology, and Genre Theory', *Or-
     bis Literarum*, 38 (1983), pp. 187–204. The argument being, in the
     main, that generic classification is historically and aesthetically
     untenable: 'For what is genre if not an ideological grid forced upon
     consciousness?' (p. 199).

6    Daniel T. O'Hara has written a book-length study of the topic
     in *Tragic Knowledge: Yeats's 'Autobiography' and Hermeneutics*

(Columbia University Press, New York, 1981). But the text is quite the
'. . . tissue . . . of simple mistakes, bad readings, false descriptions,
and tendentious paraphrases', that James Olney calls it in his review
of O'Hara's book. See Richard J. Finneran (ed.), *Yeats Annual No. 2*
(Macmillan, London, 1983), pp. 112–25.

7   As mentioned by James Olney, in the review cited in the previous
    footnote, O'Hara's misreadings of Yeats's *Autobiographies* stem at
    least in part from the American publishers' insistence on the singular
    title, *'Autobiographs'*.

8   In *Yeats At Work* (Southern Illinois University Press, Carbondale,
    1965), Curtis B. Bradford supplies much useful material on
    manuscript dating and extrapolation, particularly pp. 337–85, in a
    chapter on *'Xutobiographies* and *On the Boiler'*.

9   Paul L. Jay, 'Being in the Text: Autobiography and the Problem of the
    Subject', *MLN*, 97 (1982), p. 1058.

10  Kathryn Riley, 'Autobiography and Fiction: Francis Stuart's *Black
    List, Section H'*, *Critique: Studies in Modern Fiction*, XXV:2 (Winter
    1984), p. 122.

11  All quotations from Yeats's *Autobiographies* are drawn from the Mac-
    millan Papermac edition (London, 1980). It should be noted that Yeats
    annotates his use of the word 'Image' in this quotation, as follows:
    'There is a form of Mask or Image that comes from life and is fated,
    but there is a form that is chosen' (p. 274).

12  Marc Eli Blanchard, 'The Critique of Autobiography', *Comparative
    Literature*, 34: 2 (Spring 1982), pp. 100–8.

13  Paul de Man, 'Autobiography as De-facement', *MLN*, 94–5 (1979), p.
    920.

14  *Ibid.*

15  Paul L. Jay, *op. cit.*, p. 1052.

16  Marshall Grossmann, 'The Subject of Narrative and the Rhetoric of
    the Self', *Papers in Language and Literature*, 18 (1982), p. 399.

17  *Ibid.*, pp. 401–2.

18  Cyrus Hamlin, 'The Conscience of Narrative: Toward a Hermeneutics
    of Transcendence', *New Literary History*, 13 (1982), p. 228.

19  *Cf.* Charles Altieri, 'Ecce Homo: Narcissism, Power, Pathos, and the
    Status of Autobiographical Representations', *Boundary 2*, 9/10
    (1981), pp. 394ff.

20  *Cf.* Charles Altieri, *op. cit.* and Robert Elbaz, *op. cit.*

21  James Olney, *Autobiography: Essays Theoretical and Critical*
    (Princeton: Princeton University Press, 1980), pp. 22–3. As quoted in:
    Candace Lang, 'Autobiography in the Aftermath of Romanticism',
    *Diacritics* (Winter 1982), p. 4.

22  Bernard Levine, *The Dissolving Image. The Spiritual-Esthetic Develop-
    ment of W. B. Yeats* (Wayne State University Press, Detroit, 1970),
    p. 13. Levine notes (p. 157) that Yeats used the phrase 'impersonal
    poetry', something Levine has preferred to call the 'transpersonalizing
    voice' — that is, '. . . that manner of expression which evolves

from a feeling deeper than personal emotion: the ordering power of language or "song", as Yeats puts it, that is capable of "getting rid of the bitterness, irritation and hatred my work in Ireland has brought into my soul" '.

23  *Ibid.*, p. 15.
24  W. B. Yeats, 'The Return of Ulysses', *Essays and Introductions* (Macmillan, London, 1961; rpt. 1980), pp. 201–2.
25  F. A. C. Wilson, *Yeats's Iconography* (London, 1960), pp. 20–1. As quoted in Bernard Levine, *op. cit.*, p. 157.
26  W. B. Yeats, *The Poems, op. cit.*, p. 548.
27  Richard Ellmann, *The Man and the Masks* (O. U. P., Oxford, 1979), p. 218. For Yeats's own explanation, see: W. B. Yeats, 'Introduction to The Cat and the Moon', *Explorations* (Collier, New York, 1973), p. 403.
28  See Shirley Hazzard, *op. cit.* In his 1983 Reith Lectures, Denis Donoghue passes salient comment, too, on the need to restore to its rightful place the impenetrable mystery of the arts.
29  Bernard Levine, *op. cit.*, p. 24.
30  W. B. Yeats, 'The Coming of Wisdom With Time', *The Poems, op. cit.*, p. 94.
31  W. B. Yeats, 'Ego Dominus Tuus', *The Poems, op. cit.*, p. 162.

## THE POLITICAL UNCONSCIOUS IN THE AUTOBIOGRAPHICAL WRITINGS OF PATRICK KAVANAGH. Eamonn Hughes

1  Daniel Corkery, *The Hidden Ireland: A Study of Gaelic Munster in the Eighteenth Century* (1925, Gill and Macmillan, Dublin, 1970); *Synge and Anglo-Irish Literature* (1931, Russell and Russell, New York, 1965).
2  In this discussion of nationalism I am indebted to the following books: Sean Cronin, *Irish Nationalism: A History of its Roots and Ideology* (1980, Pluto Press, London, 1983); Clifford Geertz, *The Interpretation of Cultures* (Hutchinson, London, 1975); Tom Nairn, *The Break-up of Britain,* (2nd edn Verso, London, 1981); E. Rumpf and A. C. Hepburn, *Nationalism and Socialism in Twentieth Century Ireland* (Liverpool University Press, Liverpool, 1977).
3  More information on unionism can be found in J. C. Beckett, *The Anglo-Irish Tradition* (Faber and Faber, London, 1976); Geoffrey Bell, *The Protestants of Ulster* (Pluto Press, London, 1976); F. S. L. Lyons, *Ireland Since the Famine,* (rev. edn) (Fontana, London, 1973); and *Culture and Anarchy in Ireland, 1890–1939* (Oxford University Press, Oxford, 1982).
4  See for example, E. Stuart Bates, *Inside Out: An Introduction to Autobiography* (Sheridan House, New York, 1937); Anna Robeson Burr, *The Autobiography: A Critical and Comparative Study* (Houghton Mifflin, Boston, 1909); A. M. Clark, *Autobiography: Its*

*Genesis and Phases* (Oliver and Boyd, Edinburgh, 1935); André Maurois *Aspects of Biography*, trans. Sydney Castle Roberts (Appleton and Co., New York, 1929).

5   Roy Pascal, *Design and Truth in Autobiography* (Routledge and Kegan Paul, London, 1960); Wayne Shumaker, *English Autobiography: Its Emergence, Materials and Form* (University of California Press, Berkeley and Los Angeles, 1954). Mention should also be made of Georges Gusdorf, 'Conditions et limites de l'autobiographie', (1956) which is translated in James Olney (ed.), *Autobiography: Essays Theoretical and Critical* (Princeton University Press, Princeton, New Jersey, 1980), pp. 28–48. This collection also contains a useful bibliography, pp. 343–52.

6   Avrom Fleishman, *Figures of Autobiography: The Language of Self-Writing in Victorian and Modern England* (University of California Press, Berkeley, Los Angeles and London, 1983).

7   Jeffrey Mehlman, *A Structural Study of Autobiography: Proust, Leiris, Sartre, Levi-Strauss* (Cornell University Press, Ithaca and London, 1974).

8   Karl J. Weintraub, 'Autobiography and Historical Consciousness', *Critical Inquiry*, 1 (1975), pp. 821–48, 847.

9   Frederic Jameson, *The Political Unconscious: Narrative as a Socially Symbolic Act* (Methuen, London, 1983), p. 180.

10  Terence Brown, *Northern Voices: Poets from Ulster* (Gill and Macmillan, Dublin, 1975), p. 215.

11  Seamus Heaney, *Preoccupations: Selected Prose 1968–1978* (Faber and Faber, London, 1984), pp. 115–30.

12  *Ibid.*, p. 127.

13  Patrick Kavanagh, *The Green Fool*, (1938) (Penguin, Harmondsworth, 1975), p. 8. References hereafter in the text as *TGF*.

14  Patrick Kavanagh, *Tarry Flynn*, (1948) (Penguin, Harmondsworth, 1978), p. 44.

15  Patrick Kavanagh, *By Night Unstarred*, (ed.) Peter Kavanagh (The Goldsmith Press, The Curragh, 1977). It should be noted that this work is unusual for Kavanagh in that it covers a wider period than is usual, from the 1870s to the 1930s. (For some historical background to my remarks on this work see: Liam Kennedy, 'Farmers, Traders, and Agricultural Politics in Pre-Independence Ireland' in Samuel Clark and James S. Donnelly, Jr. (eds), *Irish Peasants: Violence and Political Unrest 1780–1914* (Manchester University Press, Manchester, 1983), pp. 339–73.) References hereafter are in the text as *BNU*.

16  Patrick Kavanagh, *Collected Poems*, (Martin Brian and O'Keeffe, London, 1964), p. 3.

THE AUTOBIOGRAPHICAL IMAGINATION AND IRISH LITERARY
AUTOBIOGRAPHIES. Michael Kenneally

1  *Self-Portrait* (Dolmen Press, Dublin, 1975), p. 6.
2  'Some Versions of Memory/Some Versions of Bios: The Ontology of
   Autobiography', in *Autobiography: Essays Theoretical and Critical*,
   (ed.) James Olney (Princeton University Press, Princeton, New Jersey,
   1980), p. 239.
3  'A Portrait of the Artist as an Old Man', *Irish University Review*, (ed.)
   Maurice Harmon, 6 (Spring 1976), p. 10.
4  *Vive Moi!* (Little, Brown, Boston, 1964), pp. 65–6.
5  Mandel, Barrett J., 'Full of Life Now', in *Autobiography: Essays
   Theoretical and Critical*, (ed.) James Olney, p. 63.
6  *Self-Portrait*, p. 7.
7  *Shame the Devil* (Wolfhound Press, Dublin, 1981), p. 9.
8  *The Autobiography of James Clarence Mangan*, (ed.) James Kilroy
   (Dolmen Press, Dublin, 1968), p. 11.
9  *Seventy Years*, edited with a foreword by Colin Smythe (Colin
   Smythe, Gerrards Cross, Buckinghamshire, 1974), p. 152.
10  *The Autobiography of William Carleton* (MacGibbon and Kee, Lon-
    don, 1968), p. 15.
11  *Autobiographies* (Macmillan, London, 1973), p. 3.
12  In particular, see Georges Gusdorf's 'Conditions and Limits of
    Autobiography', in *Autobiography: Essays Theoretical and Critical*,
    (ed.) James Olney, pp. 41 ff.
13  *Irish University Review*, 6 (Spring 1976), pp. 10–11.
14  *Vive Moi!*, p. 164.
15  *Ibid.*, p. 148.
16  *Autobiographies*, pp. 193–94.
17  *An Only Child* (Pan Books Ltd., London, 1970), p. 199.
18  *Ibid.*, p. 218.
19  Written by Patrick Mullen, John O'Donoghue and Riobárd P. Breat-
    nach, respectively.
20  'Tellers of Tales', *Times Literary Supplement* (17 March, 1972), pp.
    301–2.
21  *Hail and Farewell*, (ed.) Richard Cave (Macmillan of Canada, Toron-
    to, 1976), pp. 593–94.


ENGLISH POLITICAL WRITERS OF IRELAND: ROBERT SOUTHEY
TO DOUGLAS HURD. Tom Paulin

1  Jack Simmons, *Southey* (London, 1945), p. 67.
2  Letter to Charles Danvers, Dublin, 15th October, 1801. In *New
   Letters of Robert Southey*, (ed). Kenneth Curry (New York and
   London, 1965), I. p. 252.
3  Letter to Grosvenor C. Bedford, Dublin, 20th October, 1801. In *Selec-*

*tions from the Letters of Robert Southey*, ed. by his son-in-law John Wood Warter (London, 1856), I, p. 174.

4   Letter to Mrs. Southey, Dublin, 14th October, 1801. *Ibid.*, I, pp. 169–70.

5   *New Letters*, I, p. 252.

6   Dublin, 20th October, 1801.

7   'A journey in Ireland has, also, the great advantage of enabling us to study savage life.' Letter to Samuel Taylor Coleridge, Dublin, 16th October, 1801, *Life and Correspondence*, (ed). Charles Cuthbert Southey (London, 1849), p. 171.

8   Quoted in Geoffrey Carnall, *Robert Southey and his Age: the Development of a Conservative Mind* (Oxford, 1960), p. 62.

9   Carnall, p. 80.

10  'On the Catholic Question', in Robert Southey, *Essays, Moral and Political* (London, 1832), II, p. 331.

11  Letter to John King, Keswick, 28th September, 1803, in *Letters*, (ed.) Warter, I, p. 236.

12  Robert Southey, *Journal of a Residence in Portugal 1800–1801 and a Visit to France 1838, supplemented by Extracts from his Correspondence*, (ed.) Adolfo Cabral (Oxford, 1960), pp. 78–9.

13  'On the Catholic Question', Southey, *Essays, Moral and Political*, II, pp. 286–7.

14  *Letters*, (ed.) Warter, I, pp. 236–7.

15  *The Poetical Works of Robert Southey*, collected by himself, II, pp. 245–7.

16  Letter to Charles Danvers, Wednesday, ? October, 1803, *New Letters*, I, p. 331. The new editor of the *Morning Post* was Dennis O'Bryen, a dramatist, political pamphleteer and partisan of Fox, who earlier in his career had been a radical friend of Sheridan. O'Bryen was probably the author of the offending article. Southey's poem was eventually published in the *Morning Post* after the ownership of the paper had changed.

17  *The Notebooks of Samuel Taylor Coleridge, 1794–1804*, (ed.) Kathleen Coburn (London, 1957), I, *Text*, entry no. 1522.

18  *Ibid.*, *Notes*, 1522.

19  Cp. Southey's remark, 'the very dregs and faeces of the most corrupt Catholicism', in 'On the Catholic Question' (1809), *Essays, Moral and Political*, II, p. 300.

20  Seamus Deane, *Civilians and Barbarians*, Field Day Pamphlet No. 3 (Derry, 1983), p. 7.

21  Letter to Sir George and Lady Beaumont, 1st October, 1803. In *Collected Letters of Samuel Taylor Coleridge, 1801–6*, (ed.) Earl Leslie Griggs (Oxford, 1956), pp. 998–1005.

22  Kelvin Everest, *Coleridge's Secret Ministry: the Context of the Conversation Poems, 1795–1798* (Sussex and New York, 1979), pp. 105–11.

23  (Oxford and New York, 1983). Baldick quotes (p. 71) from

Macaulay's speech 'The Literature of Britain' where the Whig historian looks forward to the conscious propagation of 'that literature before the light of which impious and cruel superstitions are fast taking flight on the banks of the Ganges . . . And, wherever British literature spreads, may it be attended by British virtue and British freedom!'

24  *Collected Letters*, I, p. 241. Quoted by Everest, p. 106.

25  Baldick, p. 27.

26  'Shakespeares', *London Review of Books*, volume 7, no. 13, 18 July 1985.

27  *Letters of Matthew Arnold 1848–1888*, completed and arranged by George W. E. Russell (London, 1895), p. 376–7.

28  Matthew Arnold, *Culture and Anarchy, with Friendship's Garland and some Literary Essays*, (ed.) R. H. Super (Ann Arbor, 1965), pp. 121–2.

29  Matthew Arnold, Preface to *Irish Essays* in *English Literature and Irish Politics*, (ed.) R. H. Super (Ann Arbor, 1973), pp. 312–3.

30  *Ibid.*, pp. 312–4.

31  Douglas Hurd, *An End to Promises* (London, 1979), p. 102.

32  Douglas Hurd, *Vote to Kill* (London, 1975), p. 134.

33  *Ibid.*, p. 148.

34  *Ibid.*, pp. 207–8.

35  *High Windows* (London, 1974), p. 29. The poem is referred to indirectly in the text and the first and last stanzas are printed as an epigraph to the novel. Hurd omits the middle stanza which says 'The places are a long way off, not here, / Which is all right, and from what we hear / The soldiers there only made trouble happen'.

36  *Vote to Kill*, p. 208.


JAMES JOYCE'S 'THE DEAD': THE SYMBOLIST INSPIRATION AND ITS NARRATIVE REFLECTION. Walter T. Rix

1  Richard Ellmann, *James Joyce* (Oxford Univ. Press, New York, 1959), p. 115.

2  Arthur Symons, *The Symbolist Movement in Literature* (Heinemann, London, 1899).

3  David Hayman, *James Joyce et Mallarmé* (Lettres modernes, Paris, 1956), Vol. 1, p. 32.

4  *Ibid.*

5  M. E. Kronegger, 'Joyce's Debt to Poe and the French Symbolists', *Revue de littérature comparée*, 39 (1965), p. 120.

6  *The Portable Oscar Wilde*. Selected and Edited by Richard Aldington (Penguin, Harmondsworth, repr. 1980), p. 120.

7  James Joyce, *A Portrait of the Artist as a Young Man* (Granada, London, repr, 1979), p. 108. All quotations are from this edition, pages will be given in the text in parenthesis. − As for the develop-

ment of the Lucifer-motif in literature cf. Ernst Osterkamp, *Lucifer. Stationen eines Motives* (de Gruyter, Berlin, New York, 1979). (Komparatistishe Studien/Beihefte zur *arcadia*, Vol. 9).

8  Friedrich W. Nietzsche, *Thus Spake Zarathustra*. Translated by A. Tille. Revised by M. M. Bozman (Dent, London; Dutton, New York, repr. 1960), pp. 280ff. (Everyman's Library no. 892).

9  James Joyce, *Dubliners* (Granada, London, repr. 1977), p. 160. All quotations are from this edition, pages will be given in the text in parenthesis.

10  William York Tindall, *The Literary Symbol* (Indiana Univ. Press, Bloomington, 4th printing 1965), p. 224. Further examples of fin de siècle literature dealing with the motif of the city of death can be found in Hans Hinterhäuser, 'Tote Städte in der Literatur des Fin de Siècle', *Archiv*, 206 (1970), pp. 321–344.

11  F. W. Nietzsche, *Zarathustra*, p. 63.

12  August Strindberg, 'L'Exposition d'Edvard Munch', *La Revue Blanche*, 72 (1 June 1896).

13  F. W. Nietzsche, *Zarathustra*, p. 64.

14  Denys Sutton in his *Nocturne: The Art of James McNeill Whistler* (Country Life, London, 1963) provides a very helpful and beautifully illustrated insight into the growth of Whistler's art.

15  Walter Pater, *Miscellaneous Studies. A Series of Essays* (Macmillan, London, 2nd ed. repr. 1913), p. 103. (New Library Edition of the Works of Walter Pater, Vol. 8).

16  Holbrook Jackson, *The Eighteen Nineties*. New illustrated edition with an introduction by Christophe Campos (Harvester Press, Hassocks, Nr. Brighton, 1976), p. 140.

17  Quoted from H. Jackson, *The Eighteen Nineties*, pp. 139ff.

18  Goesta Svenaeus, *Edvard Munch. Das Universum der Melancholie* (Vetenskaps-Societeten, Lund, 1968), pp. 102–28. (Skrifter utg. av Vetenskaps-Societeten i Lund, Vol. 58).

19  Maurice Maeterlinck, *Pelleás et Melisande*. Drama lyrique en cinq actes (Fasquelle Editeurs, Paris, n.d.), p. 34.

20  Joseph Hanse (ed.), *Maurice Maeterlinck. Poésie complètes* (La Renaissance du Livre, Bruxelles, 1965), p. 243.

21  John Porter Houston, *French Symbolism and the Modernist Movement. A Study of Poetic Structures* (Louisana Univ. Press, Baton Rouge and London, 1980), pp. 227–68.

22  Cf. Florence L. Walzl, 'Gabriel and Michael: The Conclusion of "The Dead"', *James Joyce Quarterly*, 4 (1966), pp. 17–31. Repr. in James Joyce, *Dubliners*. Text, Criticism, and Notes Edited by Robert Scholes and A. Walton Litz (Viking Press, New York, 1969), pp. 423–43. (The Viking Critical Library).

# NOTES ON CONTRIBUTORS

CATHERINE BELSEY teaches at University College, Cardiff and is the author of *Critical Practice* (1980) and *The Subject of Tragedy: Identity and Difference in Renaissance Drama* (1985).

PATRICIA COUGHLAN teaches at University College, Cork. She is currently editing a collection of essays on Spenser and Ireland.

SEAMUS DEANE is Professor of English and American Literature at University College, Dublin and has recently published *Celtic Revivals* (1985) and *A Short History of Irish Literature* (1986).

GERALD FITZGIBBON teaches at University College, Cork. His research and publications include work on Anglo-Irish drama.

RUTH FLEISCHMANN teaches in Bielefeld, West Germany, and is preparing a book on Catholic Nationalism and the Irish Literary Revival.

MARGARET FOGARTY teaches at University College, Galway; her research and publications chiefly concern Iris Murdoch and W. B. Yeats.

JOHN WILSON FOSTER teaches at the University of British Columbia, is the author of *Forces in Ulster Fiction* (1983) and will shortly publish a book on the fictions of the Irish Revival.

EAMONN HUGHES is completing a doctorate on the work of Patrick Kavanagh.

MICHAEL KENNEALLY teaches at Marianopolis College, Montreal. He published *Portraying the Self: Sean O'Casey and the Art of Autobiography* in 1987.

TOM PAULIN teaches at the University of Nottingham and is the author of several volumes of poetry as well as *Thomas Hardy: the Poetry of Perception* (1975) and *Ireland and the English Crisis* (1984).

WALTER RIX teaches at Kiel University in West Germany; his publications include books and articles on Shaw, Nietzsche, Charles James Lever and Brian Friel.

NICHOLAS ROE teaches at the University of St Andrews, was contributing editor of *Coleridge's Imagination* (1985) and has just published *Wordsworth and Coleridge: the Radical Years* (1987).

# INDEX